THE WARE-PAINE TESTIMONIES

*The Story of Arthur Ware and Frank Paine
Bible Chronologers*

Oliver Bayley

Copyright © 2019 Oliver Bayley

All rights reserved. This publication may not be reproduced or transmitted in any form or by any means, electronic or mechanical, including photocopying, recording or any information storage and retrieval system, without permission in writing from the Publisher.

Unless otherwise stated, all Scripture quotations are from the Authorized Version of the Holy Bible. Extracts from the Authorized Version of the Holy Bible, (also known as the King James Version), the rights in which are vested in the Crown, are reproduced by permission of the Crown's Patentee, Cambridge University Press.

ISBN: 9781076884213

Published by Faithful Sheep Ministries
info@fsmins.org

To honour the men, women and children
who were involved in these events,
and to give glory to Almighty God,
Father, Son and Holy Spirit

**

The author of THE WARE-PAINE TESTIMONIES is Oliver Bayley, a retired evangelical Minister of the Gospel now based in Southampton, England. He and his wife have served in churches and schools both in Britain and overseas.

Oliver continues a ministry of writing, preaching and teaching, and is the Director of Faithful Sheep Ministries.
(info@fsmins.org)

CONTENTS

Acknowledgements

Introduction 1

Part One: The Bible Chronologers' Story   11

   Beginnings to 1933 11
   The Bible Watchmen at Work 22
   Some Findings and Results of the Bible Chronologers 37
   Their Further Statements and Conclusions 49
   The Present Situation 58
   "So What?" for People like Us 63

Part Two: Extracts from the Personal Letters of Arthur Ware   72

   Introduction 72
   1930 -1934 79
   1935 -1936 96
   1937 -1938 112
   1939 134
   1940 -1941 150
   1942 -1945 168
   1946 – 1949 186
   1950 – 1957 200
   1958 – 1978 213

Part Three: Extracts from the Personal Letters of Frank Paine   234

   Introduction 234
   1969 – 1975 239
   1976 – 1983 250

Part Four: To Take You Further 263

Afterword 272

Index 273

ACKNOWLEDGEMENTS

A book such as this needed to be written, and, by an unlikely chain of events, the privilege of writing it fell to me.

I gratefully acknowledge with thanks the friendship and fellowship with surviving members of the Ware family in recent years, and for their permission and support in the writing of this book, including in particular the inclusion of extracts from the more than 1200 personal letters of the late Mr Arthur Ware.

Equally warm thanks are given to Grace, the daughter of Frank and Kathleen Paine, whose warm support during the writing of this book has also been so important. She too has allowed the inclusion in this book of extracts from the letters of her late father – many fewer than those of Mr Ware for these were written over a much shorter period of time, but nonetheless proving to be very helpful in filling out our understanding of the work and findings of these faithful Bible Chronologers.

My grateful thanks are also given to my wife and granddaughter and other friends for their help with timely suggestions, practical expertise, proof-reading and ongoing prayers during the long process of my researching and writing of this book.

May Arthur Ware and Frank Paine and their colleagues receive the honour to which they are due, and may Almighty God have all the glory.

Oliver Bayley
Southampton
Summer 2019.

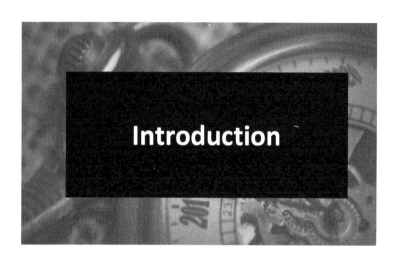

INTRODUCTION

GOD'S USE OF TIME IN THE BIBLE

The Bible is filled with dates and numbers. At first sight these may appear to have no great interest or relevance for us, but the more that we study HOW God has used Time in the Bible, and WHY, the more He grants us remarkable revelations and prophetic insights from His Word.

In particular, by our gaining an understanding of the great framework of Time undergirding the biblical text, we are able to place Bible verses into their particular "time-zones". This knowledge gives us a much clearer understanding of the context and significance of any particular passage in God's Word.

In this way, the faith of "those with ears to hear" is greatly strengthened, leading in turn to a deeper understanding of where the Lord has reached in His dealings with this fallen creation. Are there not many signs now around us suggesting that long-promised events in the Bible are now nearing their fulfilment? The great confidence that this understanding gives us in our witnessing to Jesus Christ as Lord, Redeemer and Saviour, can be easily imagined.

Surely the precious truths concerning God's use of Time in the Bible are needed more than ever these days, in a world that has clearly lost its way and is in greater need than ever of the Good News so freely given to us in our Lord Jesus Christ.

ARTHUR WARE AND FRANK PAINE

From the late 1920s Arthur Ware (AEW) and Frank Paine (FLP) were members of a small group of God-fearing men who spent many years prayerfully studying God's use of Time within the Holy Bible, the subject known as "Bible Chronology".

Their faith was remarkable, their perseverance amazing, their results jaw-dropping and their statements bold, as will become clear as their story is told in the following pages.

But Bible Chronology is a complex subject, so sometimes their predictions about the timing of future events were just plain wrong. After all, as they fully recognised themselves, they were not superheroes but ordinary, fallible Christians like the rest of us. Because of these timing mistakes, many within the Church and beyond angrily dismissed these men as dodgy "date-fixers" who were to be avoided at all costs, and that is still the reaction of some people today at the mere mention of Arthur Ware and Frank Paine.

But that reaction is seriously unjust, for it dismisses the work of these diligent men as 100% chaff, with not a grain of good spiritual wheat to be found. That is simply not the case, as any fair-minded inspection of their findings soon demonstrates.

Under the patient guidance of the Holy Spirit over the years, and despite some mistakes along the way, these faithful men were shown many precious truths deeply embedded in God's Word, which are as timely today as when they were revealed and publicised decades ago.

BUT WHY BOTHER WITH "BIBLE CHRONOLOGY" ANYWAY?

But why should we bother with any of this anyway? After all, Bible Chronology is not in itself a "salvation issue", and we are all busy people with "a Gospel to proclaim", in a world in desperate need of that Gospel.

Fair comment. This book, **THE WARE-PAINE TESTIMONIES**, is clearly a specialist book in a specialist subject, and nobody is arguing that an understanding of Bible Chronology is essential for all Christians today. Yet many find that knowing even the basics of God's use of Time in His Word does make a real "discipleship-difference", by helping those who so wish to know more of the Lord Himself, and His Word and His ways.

For a start, **Bible Chronology displays the glory of God, clearly, wonderfully and irrefutably.** Only God could arrange the extraordinary Time patterns that we find in God's Word from the beginning of Genesis to the end of Revelation, patterns which we now know, in the light of key events, continue today.

Arising from an understanding of God's control over Time, **God's people gain greater confidence in their Christian faith and discipleship.** Bible Chronology demonstrates beyond all doubt that God IS in control; that this world is not simply hurtling towards some awful man-made self-destruction; that God's judgment on sin and wickedness is sure; that Christ's long-promised and long-prayed-for kingdom shall be established on the earth; and that that great day shall surely come when "every knee shall bow and every tongue confess – that Jesus Christ is Lord" (from Philippians 2.10-11).

Such faith in these great Bible promises that are yet to be fulfilled has nothing to do with "fingers crossed and let's hope for the best". It has everything to do with being **solidly grounded in the Facts, Facts which in no small part draw their strength from the Time patterns divinely placed within God's Word and uncovered by the study of Bible Chronology.**

So, Bible Chronology in itself gives glory to God and confidence to His Christ-redeemed people.

But we are also wise to "bother" with this subject because of the two men who are at the heart of this book, Arthur Ware and Frank Paine, even though, as previously mentioned, they remain criticised in some quarters today because of mistaken date predictions.

A browse through their books, letters, papers and talks clearly shows that Arthur Ware, Frank Paine and their colleagues come over as being **remarkable men of God.** These men were devout, patient, prayerful and meticulously thorough. They strove to set aside preconceived ideas and simply to study what Scripture actually says concerning time, dates, events and prophecies.

A second reason for giving them our attention concerns **the years they spent on this work**. This was no evening hobby for a few men for a few months. They spent many years of their lives on these tasks, often at considerable personal cost in terms of their families, careers and incomes. None of their critics came or comes anywhere close to matching the years these men gave to the task! Do all those years of study really make it likely that the whole thing is nonsense?

The third reason has to do with **their repeated requests that their results be fully checked**. Time and again in the pages of their books the authors urge their readers to check out the facts and figures in the Bible for themselves. They assert repeatedly that every statement they make can be verified from Scripture, either directly or by inference, and is consonant with the various secular astronomical calendars that are available to us. Would they really keep urging us to do that if they were not utterly sure of their ground?

A final reason involves **the significance of their work and results**. If their Bible Chronology results are true, and the weight of evidence strongly suggests that they are, then these results serve as a major, urgent and challenging wake-up call to both the Church and the wider world.

So the answer to that question, "Why bother with Bible Chronology anyway?" is two-fold and quite simple: the subject itself holds a pivotal place within the underlying framework of Scripture, with far-reaching consequences; and the two Bible Chronologers with whom this book is primarily concerned, Arthur Ware and Frank Paine, have shown themselves to be "giants" in the subject in their own right, whose work, perhaps more than ever in these dangerous times, merits our serious attention.

A WINDOW PANE

It is helpful to remember throughout that Bible Chronology is not an end in itself, and we must never let it become so. For example, we look THROUGH a window pane to what lies beyond it, far more than our looking AT a window pane for its own sake.

Just so with Bible Chronology: we look THROUGH the findings of this fascinating subject to understand more of what – or rather Who - lies beyond them, namely, Almighty God Himself, Self-revealed to us in the Holy Bible as Father, Son and Holy Spirit.

Looking AT Bible Chronology only as an end in itself can get us on to a wrong track – wrong because, ironically, that approach will take our attention away from the Lord God Himself to an example, (admittedly a very wonderful example), of His handiwork.

So we aim to keep a balanced approach, neither writing Bible Chronology off as freaky nonsense nor becoming over-obsessed with it. We show prayerful respect to the findings of Bible Chronologers, taking care as we do so to "quench not the Spirit" (I Thessalonians 5.19). Equally we tread with caution and apply prayerful spiritual discernment.

Our reactions will vary. For most, gaining a basic understanding of Bible Chronology will suffice to strengthen everyday discipleship and witnessing. For others who may feel led to explore the subject more deeply, please see Part 4, "To Take You Further".

Over their many years of study, Arthur Ware, Frank Paine and their colleagues proved themselves to be both faithful "Bible Watchmen", (a term they often used of themselves) and remarkable "Bible Chronologers". It is no exaggeration to state that their Chronology findings show beyond doubt that God has always been in control over His creation – and He still is.

THE WARE-PAINE TESTIMONIES

To conclude this Introduction it is helpful to clarify at this point just what is meant by the "Ware-Paine Testimonies".

These "Testimonies" comprise four distinct strands.

The first two strands were, as far as the Watchmen were concerned, the "kernel" of all their work, and is what they themselves meant when speaking of their **"Testimony"**, in the singular. In the pages of this book **THE WARE-PAINE TESTIMONIES**, whenever the word "Testimony" is mentioned in the singular, this refers primarily to these first two strands which are now explained as follows.

Strand 1. The central Testimony of Arthur Ware, Frank Paine and their colleagues concerns **God's remarkable use of Time within His Word**. This involves the unveiling of the various **Calendars and Chronologies divinely placed within Scripture**; and arising from that unveiling, **a meticulous list of dates of biblical events, accurate to the day, from Creation to June 1933.**

These dates are 100% interdependent, meaning that they stand, or fall, together. As Mr Ware (AEW) often points out in his letters and books, if there is one error anywhere in those figures, the whole edifice is thrown out.

These Bible-derived figures are extraordinary, and are listed in meticulous detail in Part 4 of **World in Liquidation**, with some examples included in this book in Part 1 / Chapter 3. The fact that they do stand, as being demonstrably accurate scripturally, astronomically and mathematically, gives them a place of supreme importance within both the Church and the nations.

It is important to note that it was NOT this strand of their Testimony – the Bible Chronologies and the figures themselves – that was rejected. Few people ever got to the stage of studying these matters seriously for themselves in their own Bibles (as the Company members repeatedly requested), because they were put off by the second strand which is mentioned next.

It is very hard to argue that this first, central strand of their Testimony does not show beyond all doubt the divine authorship of the Holy Bible, and the continuing sovereignty of Almighty God over all aspects of His creation, including Time.

Strand 2. The second strand of their Testimony involves **the interpretation, statements and conclusions drawn by the Company members** from the remarkable Bible Chronology figures that they had been shown (see in this book, Part 1 / Chapter 4).

Within these interpretations there were of course **the solemn date-predictions** they sometimes issued, based on their then-current understanding of the various divine calendars and chronologies in operation, and/or on their application of biblical types and antitypes in the light of current world events going on around them. It was these date predictions which, more than anything else, caused their whole Testimony to be widely rejected as being the work of self-deluded cranks.

As some of the letters-extracts demonstrate, (see Parts 2 and 3 of this book) we can now see with hindsight that much of the antagonism levelled against the Company by those they were trying to reach could have been avoided if there had been a greater willingness on both sides simply to engage with one another. This would have given time and space for the Holy Spirit to oversee a careful sifting of "wheat from chaff", for everyone's benefit.

The first strand of the Testimony, the Bible Chronology principles and figures, is firmly in the category of "wheat". It is in this second strand - the various conclusions the Company members drew from those figures - where there is the need for some sifting of the wheat, of which there is much, from any chaff.

Strands 1 and 2 thus comprise their "Testimony" as far as the Company members were concerned. However, in this book we now include two further strands - the books and letters-extracts of Arthur Ware and Frank Paine – which stand as two further "testimonies" in their own right. These four strands, when combined together, give us a broader picture of the various testimonies involved, which turn out to be much more than the single, "official" version of their Testimony as the Watchmen themselves regarded it.

Strand 3. The third strand of the Ware-Paine Testimonies concerns **the books that were written**, notably, by Arthur Ware, **WORLD IN LIQUIDATION** and **THE RESTORED VISION**; and by Frank Paine, **MIRACLE OF TIME**.

Between these two authors with their different characters, gifts and perspectives, these books cover the whole range of the work, results and conclusions of this Company of Bible Watchmen and Chronologers. (See Part 4 "To Take You Further" should you wish).

These books never achieved the widespread popularity that their authors longed for (not for the money, but that their Testimony might "get out there" and be widely accepted). This disappointment arose in part from the complex, and at times controversial, nature of their findings, and in part from the Company's reputation having been already damaged by date-predictions that turned out to have been mistaken.

Strand 4. As a fourth strand within these Testimonies are **the personal letters of Arthur Ware and Frank Paine,** detailed extracts of which are published for the first time in this book, by kind permission of the two families involved.

By their very nature these letters were never intended for publication, and hence they give us an extra, hitherto-unknown insight into these faithful Bible Chronologers going about their work. Full details of these letters-extracts are given in Parts 2 and 3 of this book.

The aim in producing **THE WARE-PAINE TESTIMONIES** is to present the important work of these men afresh to today's generation.

May these men and their work be given the respect they deserve. May Jews and Christians of today be informed, blessed and encouraged by their results. May the world be fairly warned of biblical prophecies now being fulfilled before our eyes.

And above all, may Almighty God, Father, Son and Holy Spirit, be given all the glory.

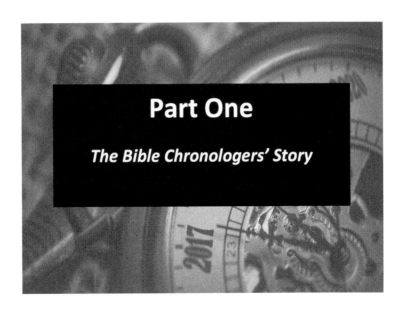

CHAPTER 1
Beginnings, to 1933

Sir Edward Denny (1796 – 1889) was an Irish Protestant living in London and involved with the Brethren movement in its early years.

Because he had a private income Sir Edward had the time, linked to a strong sense of calling, to study the Scriptures in great depth, giving particular attention to Bible Chronology.

SIR EDWARD DENNY, Bart.

Over the years he was shown how marvellously God has caused Time to be the underlying framework of His written Word – a framework that is ever-present though often concealed.

Two of Sir Edward's findings were of pivotal importance for those Bible Chronologers who came after him, notably Arthur Ware and Frank Paine:

1. The understanding of one of the main prophetic texts of the whole Bible - Daniel 9.24-27 - concerning **the "Seventy Weeks"**.

Sir Edward was able to establish that the original 70th week of the prophecy, (later established as AD 26 – AD 33), has been set aside by God in His "Redemption Chronology" because His covenant people rejected their Messiah, and this final week is to be re-run in the future.

2. The awareness of **the Jubilee Principle** underlying God's whole Plan of Redemption. This is revealed in Leviticus Chapter 25, with a further small but vital pointer found in the "seventy times seven" of Matthew 18.22.

This enabled Sir Edward to understand that God has timed great events affecting redemption within a meticulous Time framework. This framework is based on the Jubilee cycle of 49 years, or multiples of this at 490 years and 4900 years, and lies at the heart of God's Word and of His dealings with the Jews and with us all.

Sir Edward thus established the great truth that Time in Scripture, far from being random, is of critical importance. Quite simply, God links Events to Time and Time to Events – *as He is still doing.*

As a result of this pioneering Bible Chronologer, the scene was set for those coming after him to build on the foundations that Sir Edward Denny had been privileged first to be shown, and then to make known in his careful books and charts.

***

Dr Henry Grattan Guinness (1835 – 1910) was also an Irish Protestant, and a well-known astronomer of his day.

Dr Guinness's great contribution to Bible Chronology involved the key prophecy in Daniel Chapter 4 about **the "Seven Times"**.

It had long been known that a "time" in this context was a Chaldean year of 360 days, but Dr Guinness learned that this could also be applied to years – to "seven times" of 360 years totalling 2520 years, this period being the foretold length of Gentile domination of the earth. He then marked off 2520-year periods from the various dates of Nebuchadnezzar's progressive defeat of Judah and Jerusalem, and in his book "**Light for the Last Days**" (1886) for example, he predicted that in the following years (see below) Christians could expect to see God's gracious movements regarding the return of His covenant people the Jews to their land.

Here are some of Dr Guinness' main workings mentioned in brief, (published in 1886 remember), in each case involving his naming the end-date of a 2520-year period from various known start-dates under Nebuchadnezzar. (Allowing for there being no year 0 BC, the simplest sum in each case is 2520 minus (x minus 1), thus for example 2520 minus (60**6**)) -

1. **607 BC** (Daniel 1.1) to **1914**: the start of the Great War

2. **604 BC** (Daniel 2.1) to **1917**: the Balfour Declaration

3. **598 BC** (II Kings 24. 6-16) to **1923**: the Palestine Mandate

4. **588 BC** (Ezekiel 24.1 and others) to **1933**: the rise of Hitler and the meeting of the World Monetary & Economic Conference

5. **573 BC** to **1948**: the rebirth of the nation of Israel.

***

Arthur Ware (1885 – 1978), along with others, knew of the work of Denny and Guinness, and when the Balfour Declaration was published in November 1917 he came under conviction to give serious time and attention in his own life to the study of Bible Chronology. This he duly did over the next sixty years.

During the 1920s Arthur Ware (AEW) became a well-known Bible teacher, and by 1930 had become the leader of a small group of like-minded men (six in all), who devoted themselves to the study of God's Word, with particular reference to God's use of Time within the Scriptures. Like his colleague Frank Paine, Mr Ware was adept at working on the many sums involved with vast numbers of days or years within the Bible Chronology, a task he would casually describe as "simple mathematics".

Arthur Ware was the leader and public face of the group, the main speaker, the main author, and, when it came to it, the main "flak-taker".

***

A key member of this group was **Frank Paine (1906 – 1983)**, 20 years younger than Mr Ware, a very different character who brought different gifts to the group and to their work.

Mr Paine (FLP) was also a meticulous mathematician, and his notes contain hundreds of pages of handwritten sums, often involving literally millions of days, and all calculated in the pre-pocket calculator era. He was diligent, faithful, prayerful and supportive, more of a "behind-the-scenes" man, working steadily away in the engine room of Bible Chronology.

Other group members brought further gifts: deep prayer; spiritual insights into baffling scriptural passages; the faith to keep going in the frequent times of trial and testing; the cross-checking of the many facts and figures that were emerging; the exploration of new chronological possibilities in the scriptural texts; and last but not least, the numerous practical tasks of typing, proof-reading and preparing the various Papers, charts and books that were produced.

***

Throughout this book these men will be referred to as "the Company" (one of their own descriptions), or "the Bible Chronologers", or "the Bible Watchmen", or simply "the group". In keeping with the formal manner in which the members of the group addressed themselves, a normal feature of the times in which they were living, in this book Arthur Ware and Frank

Paine are not referred to by their Christian names alone, but either by their Christian name and surname, or by "Mr ....", or by their initials AEW or FLP.

This Company was based at that time in the Eastbourne area, gathering frequently for study, prayer and fellowship. In the years to come, while building on the work of "the Chronology giants" who had gone before, God's remarkable patterns of Time embedded in Scripture gradually began to be revealed to them. It was slow, patient work, but what they were being shown was extraordinary.

1932 - 1933

From the work of Grattan Guinness in particular, the group understood that 1933 was likely to be a significant year, but at that time they still knew little of the treasures of Biblical Chronology that were soon to be unfolded to them.

In mid-November 1932 they were drawn to study with great care the fishing episode recorded in John 21, with particular attention given to the apparently trivial details of the "200 cubits" of verse 8, and the 153 "great fishes" of verse 11. From their knowledge of "Bible numbers", based on the studies of men such as R T Naish and E W Bullinger, along with the work of Grattan Guinness previously mentioned and various other signs of confirmation, the group members came under conviction to give **a public 200-day warning in London** regarding an expected divine intervention in mid-June 1933. (Further details of how they came to this decision are given at the end of Chapter 2).

At some expense, the Friends' Meeting House, Euston Road, London, was booked for Friday evening 25th November 1932 and for the afternoon and evening of the next day, Saturday 26th November.

On the evening of 25th November 1932, Mr Ware addressed their first meeting. The essence of what he said was - "at or about Pentecost 1933, there would be 'an interposition of God, a breaking of His silence of 1900 years'".

At that time he and his colleagues believed that this divine intervention would involve:

a) **The completion of the "Seven Times" (2520 years) of Gentile world dominion** that had begun in 588 BC, with the Gentile nations now being "cut off" by God as part of the process towards establishing the millennial reign of Christ on earth (eg., Revelation 20).

b) **The return of the Lord Jesus Christ for His Bride, the Church**, (the event known as "the rapture", of I Thessalonians 4.13-18 and I Corinthians 15.51-52).

After this first meeting they learned that the number of people present had been 153, the same number as that of the "great fishes" caught in the net that is so carefully recorded in John 21.11. They took this as a small sign of confirmation from the Lord that they had acted in accord with His wishes in calling the meetings and giving the 200-day warning.

This message was repeated at the two further meetings on the following day. Many were keen to know more, but scarcely any Christian leaders showed interest and a wave of hostility came from parts of the Christian press with the advice, "Avoid this date-fixer like the plague", the "date-fixer" being Mr Ware.

Arthur Ware, Frank Paine and their colleagues, rather surprised at the negative reactions, returned to their studies, confident that they were "on the right track".

***

In April 1933 they felt called to utter **a 40-day warning**, giving much the same message as in November 1932. Accordingly, on Tuesday 25th April Mr Ware reserved the large Queen's Hall in central London, for him and his colleagues to hold a meeting there on the evening of Tuesday 2nd

May 1933, which was one week ahead.

In one of his Papers about this planned meeting (Reference BB44b/141, quoted by kind permission of his family), Mr Ware then writes –

"We spent the Tuesday night in a suburb of London. On the morrow (that is, Wednesday 26th April 1933), *we went up about midday to London to obtain quarters and await directions. At the station my eye caught the black headline of the London Evening Standard. The words forming the headline were: "WORLD CONFERENCE – JUNE 12". Knowing that on 12th June the 200 days ended* (from their warning of 25th November 1932)*, as well as the 40 days from 2nd May (that is, if we were to hold a meeting on that day, as it appeared increasingly likely that we should so do), we all felt certain that this date for the World Economic Conference had been chosen by God, and had definite relation to what we were about to do. This was the first occasion that the date of 12th June had been suggested for this World Conference".*

Spurred on by this encouragement, on Saturday 29th April they delivered full-page advertisements to major national and provincial newspapers announcing the meeting of Tuesday 2nd May and giving details of the meeting's content. These advertisements were to be published on Monday 1st May.

The large hall and the press advertisements were now booked, but on the Sunday afternoon, 30th April, the Watchmen were told that these advertisements could only be published on Tuesday 2nd May, just hours before their evening meeting, because of lack of space in the newspapers.

What was worse, apparently some editors were reluctant even to accept the advertisements because of their controversial nature, and were to meet on the Monday morning to decide their joint response.

The prospects for their public meeting now looked grim. With such short notice it was likely that few people would be able to attend on the Tuesday evening, and even that assumed that the newspaper editors would agree to publish the advertisements, an agreement which on that Sunday afternoon looked far from certain. Arthur Ware, Frank Paine and their colleagues were thus facing a humiliating and expensive public-relations disaster, and they fell on their knees in prayer.

On the Monday morning news came through that all the editors except one had decided to publish the advertisements, and these duly appeared in the evening papers of Monday 1st May and the morning papers of 2nd May.

The Watchmen had booked the large Queen's Hall in faith before they knew anything about the "World Monetary and Economic Conference" (WMEC) as it came to be called, an event which they soon discovered had been privately planned in November 1932, and was to open in London at 3 pm on Monday 12th June 1933, *40 days on from 2nd May*. At this Conference representatives of virtually all the world governments would gather, the first such gathering since the Tower of Babel (Genesis 11).

These finer details of the pre-2nd May meeting have been given to demonstrate the general approach of these Bible Watchmen as they proceeded "under the Lord" in their work: a steady blend of study, prayer, fellowship, discussion and decisions, followed by practical, step-by-step, "out-on-a-limb" faith when they felt called to act, backed up by earnest prayer.

In view of the twists and turns they encountered in setting up this 2nd May meeting, we can see why these Bible Watchmen had the confidence to act as they did, humbly believing throughout that they were indeed responding to the prompting of the Holy Spirit.

About 2000 people turned up on the evening of 2nd May 1933 despite the late publication of the advertisements. Mr Ware spoke thus in the light of their understanding of Bible Chronology at that time (an understanding which they were to learn later was still quite limited in 1933) –

"On or about the 12th June, our Lord Jesus Christ shall rise up from the right hand of God and descend to a point over this earth to gather to

Himself, in less than one second of time, every man, woman and child upon this earth who ... is 'born of water and of the Spirit' (John 3.5)".

Some subsequent meetings were held giving the same message and warning, and copies of Mr Ware's words were sold in their thousands. Despite strong opposition once again from some fellow Christians there was much public excitement, with some people selling their homes and possessions in anticipation of events expected in mid-June.

THE WORLD MONETARY AND ECONOMIC CONFERENCE, MONDAY 12TH JUNE 1933

Monday 12th June 1933 duly arrived, the date fixed for the opening of the World Conference. The Conference was held in the newly-built Geological Museum in Kensington, with 66 nations of the world officially represented.

At 3 pm King George V opened the Conference, *but was prevented by the British Government from saying a prayer for God's guidance and blessing upon the proceedings, for fear of giving offence to some representatives.*

This refusal to acknowledge Almighty God at the start of this crucial Conference was later understood by AEW and his colleagues to be God's final test of the Gentile nations. By completely ignoring God the nations starkly failed this divine test, despite the serious financial crisis they were all facing, so God proceeded with His judgments.

But as for the expected return of the Lord Jesus Christ for His Church - nothing visible happened.

The reactions towards AEW and his colleagues can thus be easily imagined, (still to be found today in some quarters) – anger, criticism, ridicule, rejection and ostracism, much of which, on the surface at least, seemed justified. Yet by now they knew enough to be sure that the work they were doing was indeed "of the Lord", so they kept going.

In their defence, we remember the following facts —

- Dr Grattan Guinness's date predictions, based on the 2520-year period of Gentile domination - "the Seven Times" (Daniel 4.25 and 32) - had proved completely correct.

- Concerning the mid-June date, the Watchmen's 200-day and 40-day warnings were proved completely correct.

- In faith that they were following the Lord's leading, the Queen's Hall was reserved for the evening of 2nd May 1933, *one day before the WMEC date was announced.*

- The 12th June date turned out to be "spot on".

- Their belief that Jesus would visibly return for His Church at that time was well-founded, in view of the limited chronological understanding they possessed in 1932-1933.

- In that aspect alone - Christ's return for His Church - they were mistaken at that time, but learned later on that in one crucial sense they were quite correct, as is explained in a later chapter in their story.

- Because the findings of Bible Chronology show such strong evidence of the divine authorship of the Holy Bible, we can presume that Satan was (and still is) keen to silence such findings if possible.

What was to happen next? Their story continues ...

CHAPTER 2
The Bible Watchmen at Work

When there was no visible intervention from the Lord at the opening of the World Monetary & Economic Conference in June 1933, not surprisingly Arthur Ware, Frank Paine and their colleagues attracted a great deal of criticism. They themselves were taken aback over how things had turned out, and it would have been understandable if the group had simply split up.

But they didn't split up. They realised that there was still much for them to learn about Bible Chronology, but of course at that stage they had no idea just how much there was to be revealed, and how much the Lord was going to reveal.

Yet they had had enough encouragements from the Lord that, despite their apparent public failure in June 1933, they were indeed doing the Lord's work and were not the fools or fraudsters that many accused them of being. So they carried on.

"THE COMPANY"

This carrying-on was no mere jaunt for a few single men, for four of them were married with typical family responsibilities.

Their commitment to one another as a "company", and to the task before them, was costly. It involved them giving up their secular employment, career prospects and assured income, for a life of isolation, ostracism and a great step of faith into the unknown.

They committed themselves in their dealings together to following as much as possible the practices of the Church in its earliest days, as described in Acts 2 and 4 and the Epistles - simplicity, based in homes, close, practical fellowship, and the pooling of their resources. This was to be no easy life.

On the plus side, they had the Lord, His Word, the Holy Spirit and prayer; they had their loved ones and each other; they had the work of the pioneers who had gone before; they had a range of gifts and abilities; they had time, peace and space; and in Arthur Ware they had a single-minded leader, one of whose mottoes, along with Churchill later on, was clearly "Never give up".

SOLITUDE AND EVACUATION

After June 1933 the group remained based in various rented properties in and around Eastbourne.

Arthur Ware himself needed space and solitude as he wrestled with the Lord on these matters, so was frequently separated from his wife, family and colleagues for long periods, his favourite spot being the Newlands Valley in the Lake District. Here he would live in rented accommodation, spend days in prayer on the hills, spend hours in his room working on the dates, and frequently write long letters to his wife and colleagues regarding progress or problems (extracts from which we include in Part 2 of this book, by kind permission of the Ware family). When the need arose or he felt so called, AEW would "go south" on the overnight train from Keswick for a few days or weeks, before returning north.

The work went steadily on, until by 1937 the company possessed nothing less than a full understanding of the "Chronology of the World" from Creation to 1933 – the dates and events, and the calendars and chronologies embedded within and throughout the Holy Bible. Here before them was as sure a proof, if any more was needed, of the divine authorship of the Bible from Genesis 1.1 to Revelation 22.21.

In June 1940, after the evacuation from Dunkirk and with the threat of imminent invasion, the order was given for all children to be evacuated from Eastbourne within three days. Mr Ware arranged a collection of vehicles and sufficient petrol to move the whole Company – men, women and children – to the Lake District. Within a few days he had sorted out accommodation for them all in the Newlands Valley, an area which he already knew very well.

THE APPROACH OF THE BIBLE WATCHMEN

We can now consider just what was involved in this remarkable journey of chronological discovery.

First it is emphasised at this point that this book provides a wide-ranging coverage of the work, findings and conclusions of these Bible Chronologers. This is done in the hope that those who may wish to study their work further will acquire for themselves copies of the books written by Arthur Ware and Frank Paine, notably **The Restored Vision** and **Miracle of Time** (details of which are provided in Part 4 "To Take You Further"). There is thus no attempt in this book to make redundant the original books written by the Chronologers themselves, by trying to give in these pages every last "jot and tittle" of all that went on; such an attempt would be impossible to achieve anyway.

At the heart of the Company's approach to the work was their holding **"a high view" of Scripture**, that is, the conventional Protestant view that the original Bible text was infallible and inerrant. They accepted that by God's grace the biblical text we have before us now has been divinely preserved, albeit with minor discrepancies, so the group members held to the assumption born in Reformation times that "What Scripture says, God says".

They accepted therefore the plain, literal meaning of the biblical text unless the passage was obviously symbolic or figurative. They assumed that nothing in the text is superfluous, and that everything, (notably for them every date or number that is mentioned), has been placed there by the Holy Spirit for a reason.

Building on their total confidence in the Bible as God's Word was **their equally-total confidence in the Lord's leading**. They were completely sure that God the Father and God the Son would indeed "lead (them) unto all truth" by God the Holy Spirit, "the Comforter" (John 14.16-17,26 / 15.26 / 16.7,13).

Linked to **this settled confidence in both the written Word and the living Word,** they ensured that **simple, earnest, patient prayer** undergirded all that they were, sought and did. A key verse was - "Be careful for nothing; but in everything by prayer and supplication with thanksgiving let your requests be made known unto God ..." (Philippians 4.6) – even when "the going got tough" as it certainly did at times.

Patience was vital. Over the years they encountered many apparently insurmountable "brick walls" in the Bible text concerning Chronology, and they had to learn to wait, wait and wait if necessary, for God's timing and not theirs, as to how these walls were to be overcome.

Diligence was also vital. The Watchmen were often dealing with arithmetical sums involving thousands or even millions of days, where one slip could throw the whole thing out. In this era of no pocket calculators, everything had to be carefully checked between the group members, and crucially every date calculation they arrived at had to match any biblical reference to the "age" of the moon, as measured in days from the start of the month, on any particular date. Having natural mathematicians among their number was a great help, who needed to be armed with an endless supply of rough paper and pencils.

Very quickly they learned, sometimes the hard way, the need for **humility, mutual respect and forbearance** among the group members. Among their number were strong characters with strong opinions, and sometimes stresses arose over family matters or finances. It soon became clear that of course each man had his faults, and each man was fully capable of getting things wrong. Yet equally each man also brought particular strengths to the work (e.gs., Romans 12.3 / Colossians 3. 12-17 / Philippians 2.1-5), and between them all they formed a good balance of character, gift and experience. How they rubbed along together is a fine example in itself of Christians learning to cope with one another in a difficult task and in conditions that could be far from easy.

But while they were no strangers to trials, difficulties and spiritual opposition, another aspect of their approach was that of **awe**. In and through the struggles they learned so much of the character and ways of God, and of the meticulous accuracy that God has implanted within His Word. This meant that when they encountered the next "insurmountable wall", they simply KNEW that there was a divine way through, which the Lord would reveal to one or other of them in His own way and time.

THEIR "RAW MATERIALS"

In their daily working lives, what did these Bible Chronologers actually *do?* The brief answer to that question is just this: they patiently studied the Scriptures with particular emphasis on references to dates and numbers. By using their growing knowledge of how everything was inter-related they were able to build up the Bible Chronology step by step until the full, final picture was before them.

In the chapters of this particular book an overview of the men, their work and their story is given. Some selected examples of their findings are thus included in this and in later chapters, while "the full works" are to be found of course in their own books and charts, details of which can be found in Part 4 "To Take You Further".

In terms of their chronological "raw materials", the Bible Watchmen worked with:

1. CALENDARS, CHRONOLOGIES and DATES

The Watchmen realised quite early on – a fresh discovery hitherto unknown - **that God has embedded several calendars and several chronologies within His Word.**

A **"calendar"** is simply a method of measuring which year, month, week or day it is, within a long, full sequence of time *in which no days are omitted.* A calendar has a definite starting date, and is probably related to the position of the Earth in relation to the Sun or Moon.

A well-known example is the Julian calendar, introduced by Julius Caesar in 45 BC, a straightforward solar calendar which we still use today. Because the Earth takes approximately 365 1/4 days to orbit the Sun, the calendar gives us 3 years of 365 days, and a fourth year of 366 days to compensate for the quarter-days of the previous years.

A **"chronology"** is different. For much of the time, a "Chronology" may run hand in hand with a calendar, but there is one crucial difference between the two: *a chronology may have omissions of time within it.*

Imagine two stop-watches, started at precisely the same moment. The **calendar stop-watch measures "real time"** and ticks on regardless. But the Watchmen were shown that **the chronology stop-watch is stopped and re-started by God according to His purposes** *with no apparent loss of time.*

The result may be that the calendar stop-watch shows, say, 700 years, which have really elapsed, while the chronology stop-watch shows only, say, 450 years; *in other words, 250 "real" years are unaccounted for on the chronology stop-watch.*

It is no exaggeration to say that this simple principle is the key to Bible Chronology.

Once the Watchmen understood that calendars run alongside chronologies within the Bible, and that all Bible years are lunar years of 354 days, many old chronological "brick walls", which had defied understanding for virtually nineteen hundred years, could be dismantled quite quickly. Little by little the whole glorious framework of Bible

Chronology began to emerge.

2. THE JUBILEE CYCLES (also sometimes spelt "Jubile")

The significance of these cycles had been revealed to Sir Edward Denny over a hundred years before, and now the Watchmen were able to explore the wonder of these cycles in great depth.

We learn of them in Leviticus Chapter 25. Briefly, each cycle consists of 49 years (these are "Bible", lunar, years of 354 days each), on top of which is placed the fiftieth, Jubilee year, which starts in the mid-49th year (Leviticus 25.9-10) and finishes in the mid-1st year of the next cycle. In other words, in each single cycle we count 49 years, but God counts 50 years. In multiple cycles the principle continues: in 40 Jubilee cycles for example, we count 40 x 49 years, or 1960 years, on to which God adds 40 Jubilee years, making in His sight 2000 years.

These Jubilee cycles lie at the heart of what the Watchmen termed **The Chronology of Redemption.** They learned that this chronology has a fixed limit of 6000 years, (that is, 120 Jubilee cycles of 49 years each, totalling 5880 years, plus the 120 Jubilee years seen in God's sight), which began on the day after the Fall and will terminate at the setting-up of Christ's Kingdom on earth (Revelation 20).

Now crucially this Chronology of Redemption era runs in parallel with the secular calendars, except that (and we quote) - "it omits various periods of years or days that are 'marked by circumstances incompatible with the Principles of Redemption and Forgiveness'" **(The Restored Vision (TRV)**, page xxii).

In other words, these Jubilee cycles of redemption are *chronological* not calendrical. So when a major cycle of 1960 years is reached in the Chronology of Redemption for example, that figure may well be less than the actual number of calendar years that have passed because of periods "incompatible with the Principles of Redemption and Forgiveness". This discrepancy between the number of actual Calendar Years and the lesser number of Redemption Years is explained by a simple sum of addition:

Redemption Years plus Unreckoned Years = Calendar Years.

This Chronology of Redemption, based on single or multiple Jubilee Cycles, lies at the heart of God's use of Time in Creation, for since Creation, God has marked critical events and dates according to this Chronology. We give examples in Chapter 3, "Some Findings and Results".

3. "DISPENSATIONS" or "AGES"

The Watchmen kept in mind the Lord's use of distinct periods of Time since Creation, known as "dispensations" or "ages", which act like the progression of chapters through a book. The following major biblical dispensations can be distinguished for example, stretching from the beginning of the Bible's timescale to its end: from Creation to the Flood, termed the "Age of Conscience"; from the Flood to the first coming of Christ, the "Age of Law"; then the Church period, the "Age of Grace"; then the "Age of the Kingdom" (Revelation 20), followed by the "Perfect Age" (Revelation 21.1-2).

The Bible Watchmen would expect any time of transition from one of these "chapters" to the next one to have particular spiritual significance, and hence was likely to be chronologically marked in some way. This was indeed found to be the case, as shown and explained in their books and charts.

4. KEY BIBLICAL PROPHECIES

The Holy Bible is unique in world literature in possessing hundreds and hundreds of specific, detailed prophecies. Many of these have been fulfilled to the letter, so we have every reason to assume that the still-future prophecies of our day will also be fulfilled to the letter.

Key prophecies which were particularly helpful for the Bible Watchmen include the following:

a) Daniel 2 - the image of gold, silver, bronze and iron, with feet of iron and clay, representing the empires of Babylon, Medo-Persia, Greece and

Rome.

b) Daniel 4 - the dream of the tree, and the prophecy, "till seven times pass by him" (verses 16, 23, 25, 32). A "time" is applicable to a 360-day year and also, as Grattan Guinness demonstrated, to 360 years. This is a key prophecy regarding the times of the Gentiles and the restoration of the Jews to their land.

c) Daniel 7 - the four beasts, similar to Daniel 2 with the four world empires.

d) Daniel 9 - the seventy 'sevens' or 'weeks', in which Sir Edward Denny's work was so helpful. The issuing of "the commandment to restore and rebuild Jerusalem until Messiah the Prince" is given as 69 weeks, with Messiah being "cut off" in the 70th week (Daniel 9.25-26).

The Church Age, unforeseen here as this prophecy is focussed on the Jews, comes in halfway through verse 26.

The prophecy continues with the seventieth week - the 7-year "week" of the ministry of John the Baptist and the Lord Jesus Christ. Because Christ was rejected in that week, God in His mercy has cancelled it, seeing it as "unreckoned" in the Chronology of Redemption.

But the seventieth week of 7 years is to be re-run after the removal of the Church, as a time of judgment on Jew and Gentile alike because of their rejection of Jesus Christ. It is the terrible time of the antichrist and the great tribulation (Revelation 4–19), at the end of which Christ will return in visible glory and His people will "look on Him whom they have pierced" (Zechariah 12.10 and Revelation 1.7).

All these things are prophesied, and there are many pointers today suggesting that they are not far ahead, but the world cares as little as ever and also much of the Church seems hardly concerned either. These pointers are another reason for taking the work of these Bible Chronologers seriously.

e) Isaiah, Jeremiah, Ezekiel, Zechariah – many prophecies speaking of God's future dealings with His covenant people the Jews, involving both judgments and blessings.

f) The Gospels – notably the Lord's "Olivet Discourse" of Matthew 24 and parallels concerning the Jews. As is often the case with scriptural prophecy, the content of these passages has a double-fulfilment: in the short-term and on a smaller scale, (though still horrific), in the years 66 – 73 AD; and then, yet in the future for us, the major fulfilment in the seven years of tribulation known as "Jacob's trouble" (Jeremiah 30.7), the re-run of Daniel's seventieth week.

g) I & II Thessalonians and I Corinthians 15 – prophecies concerning the Christian Church and its removal before the seventieth week, the event known as "the Rapture".

h) Revelation – the prophecies to the seven churches, Chapters 1-3; then the Tribulation, Chapters 4-19; then Christ's Kingdom and beyond, Chapters 20-22.

5. TYPES and ANTITYPES

A "type" in the Bible is the term used for an event which is a forerunner, a "pointer towards", something that is yet to come.

The "antitype" is the fulfilment of the type, when the something that was looked forward to is now actually on the scene.

For example, the Passover, with its shedding of the blood of a perfect lamb to cover the forgiveness of sins, is clearly a "type" of the Lord Jesus, the true Lamb of God. He later became the "antitype", shedding His own innocent blood for the forgiveness of sins.

The Bible Watchmen were always on the look-out for biblical "types", by assuming that any person or event might turn out to be a pointer towards something else to be revealed later on. They might look up the cross-references in the Concordance for any word they came across: where else does this word occur? and in what circumstances? and is it translated by different English words? In this way they could "fill out" the meaning and significance of every word, often thereby discovering links and truths which were not apparent on the surface of the text. Any such discoveries would be noted for possible assistance elsewhere in their studies.

For example, there is an extraordinary **Type and Antitype Chart on page 192 of Frank Paine's book Miracle of Time**, (one of many such charts in the book). This chart shows how the sequence of the days of the first Passover and Exodus is a perfect type of the sequence of the days of Christ's death and resurrection as the Passover Lamb of God, the antitype. The symmetry is perfect, and beyond any possibility of human contrivance. God alone could arrange such as this; we can only react, along with the Bible Watchmen themselves, with awe.

6. THE FEASTS

The Bible Watchmen soon learned that the annual "Feasts of Jehovah", recorded in Exodus 12.3-6 and Leviticus 23, lie at the heart of the Bible Calendar, and turned out to be critically important within the life and ministry of the Lord Jesus as recorded in the Gospels.

These Feasts appear in the following order through the year:

a) The **10th Day of the First Month** (Exodus 12.3) - the Passover Lamb is set aside.

b) The **14th Day of the First Month** (Leviticus 23.5 and Exodus 12.6) - the Passover Lamb is slaughtered in the evening.

The authors explain that these four days are a chronological type of the 4000 years which elapsed, to the day and hour, between the Fall of Adam and the Crucifixion of the Lord Jesus Christ - "the Lamb of God who takes away the sin of the world".

c) The **15th to the 21st Day of the First Month** (Leviticus 23.6) - "On the fifteenth day of the first month is the Feast of Unleavened Bread unto the

Lord: seven days you must eat unleavened bread...".

These seven days can be seen as a type of the "Christian Dispensation" (frequently marked by the number 7), when the Church, not the Jews, would partake exclusively of the Bread of God which came down from heaven - that is, the Lord Jesus Christ Himself.

d) **The Seven Weeks of Harvest** (Leviticus 23.9-22)

In Leviticus 23.9-22, we are told that the seven weeks of harvest, (another seven, so perhaps another sign of the Christian Dispensation), are to begin "from the morrow after the Sabbath" which follows after the Passover, by the presenting of "the sheaf of the first-fruits" to the Lord in heaven.

This sheaf, (made up of new grain from the new harvest which has sprung from old grain that has died in the earth), is a perfect type of Christ on the morning of His resurrection, when, as the "first-fruits of them that slept", He presented Himself to God the Father. Hence His words to Mary - "Do not touch me, I have not yet ascended to my Father" (John 20.17).

After the seven weeks comes Pentecost, when the two loaves termed the "bread of the first-fruits" were presented to God. These two loaves are seen as a type of the Church. They consist of both Jews and Gentiles whose members have died - (who are thus "sleeping in Christ") – and who are bodily raised at the end of the age.

e) The **10th Day of the 7th Month** (Leviticus 23.27) - the Day of Atonement.

f) The **15th to the 23rd Day of the 7th Month** (Leviticus 23.34-44).

In Leviticus 23.34-44 we learn of two Feasts which were "concurrent" - that is, running together side by side at the same time. These are the Feast of Tabernacles and the Feast of Ingathering.

Both of these feasts began at 8 am on the 15th of the 7th month, and lasted for 7 days, followed by an eighth day (see John 7.37) - "the last day, that great day of the feast".

All these Feasts play their part in God's precise, beautiful system of Time and Pattern He has set within His Word, and act as the basic Time framework underlying Jesus' earthly ministry, as is demonstrated so thoroughly in Mr Ware's book, **The Restored Vision**.

7. NUMBERS

The Bible often mentions numbers, and arising from the repeated use of these numbers throughout Scripture, many of them are found to have particular spiritual significance of their own.

Here is a brief list of examples:

Number One in Scripture signifies oneness and unity, especially in relation to God Himself

Number Two - either witness or division, depending on the context

Number Three - God in His divine perfection

Number Four - God's creation in its entirety

Number Five - Grace

Number Six - Man

Number Seven - Spiritual perfection

Number Eight - Resurrection

Number Nine - Finality, often in association with Ten

Number Ten - Completeness

Number Twelve - Governmental or administrative perfection

Number Forty - Trial and testing

Number Fifty – Liberty

By noting the various occurrences of such numbers, or multiples of two or more numbers and in what contexts they appear, the Watchmen could often detect a deeper truth that was being told, which was especially helpful with regard to types and antitypes.

For example, in Matthew 14.15-21 we hear of the five loaves, two fishes, twelve baskets of left-overs and five thousand men; then in Matthew 15.32-38, seven loaves, "a few little fishes", seven baskets of left-overs, and four thousand men. The Watchmen would get to work over such passages, seeking to discover why all these numerical details are given.

8. "GEMATRIA"

This is the technical term for the fact that every *letter* in both the Hebrew and Greek alphabets has a number, along the lines of "a = 1, b = 2", and so on.

This means in turn that every *word* in the Hebrew and Greek sections of the Bible has its own number, made up of the sum of each of its letters. So, by adding the numbers belonging to each letter of a Hebrew or Greek word a total figure for that word can be found.

For example, the Greek word for Jesus - Ἰησους - has a numerical value of 888. The number 8, scripturally, stands for RESURRECTION - and 3, scripturally, stands for TRINITY. So, the very name of Jesus proclaims Resurrection, Resurrection, Resurrection, within the Trinitarian Godhead.

9. AN EXAMPLE OF THEIR USE OF TYPES, ANTITYPES & NUMBERS – The Fishing Episode of John Chapter 21. (Fully Explained in **The Restored Vision** by Arthur Ware, page 465ff; in **Miracle of Time** by Frank Paine, pages 119-123; and in **Understanding the Sign Miracles of John** by Jonathan Hill, pages 152-166: see Part 4 "To Take You Further")

In the autumn of 1932, the Bible Watchmen were confident that the ending of the 2520 years of the "Seven Times" of Daniel 4 would be marked by God in mid-1933.

They were led to study the post-resurrection fishing episode of John 21, with particular reference to verses 8-11. Why the mention of 200 cubits and of 153 fishes, and that the net was not broken? They prayed, pondered and discussed, and were led to the following answers. The 200 cubits stood for the final 200 days of the Age; the fishes were all those to be gathered in the net of the Gospel out of the sea of the Gentiles; the net in not breaking showed that none of those fishes would be lost; and the figure 153 (9 x 17) is full of chronological significance concerning Christ and resurrection.

As the eighth "sign miracle" in John's Gospel, the whole incident covers the Age of the Church or "Christian dispensation", and carries the immense resurrection significance, that at the "end of the Age", Christ's Church will be complete and safe, joining Him in resurrection fellowship "on the heavenly beach".

These findings prompted the Watchmen to announce the 200-day warning in November 1932, as described in Chapter 1.

CHAPTER 3
Some Findings and Results of the Bible Chronologers

With the kind permission of the families of Arthur Ware and Frank Paine, in this Chapter we begin by giving some quotations from their two main books, **THE RESTORED VISION** (by Arthur Ware) and **MIRACLE OF TIME** (by Frank Paine).

These quotations are obviously only a sample of their work, and those who are keen to take things further are recommended to read the books for themselves, details of which are given in Part 4 "To Take You Further".

QUOTATIONS FROM **THE RESTORED VISION** (pp xvi ff) "A BRIEF SUMMARY OF FACTS ESSENTIAL TO THE UNDERSTANDING OF TIME IN THE LIFE OF JESUS CHRIST OUR LORD"

1. Time and all its divisions, except minutes and seconds, originated with Almighty God. The Holy Bible spans a plan of Time which covers Seven Thousand years of human history.

2. Time in the Bible is reckoned exclusively by the secular, civil, lunar calendar of 354 days, a period closely equivalent to 12 revolutions of the Moon around the Earth.

3. The Bible year of 354 days is divided into 12 months, the 6 odd-numbered months of the year having 30 days and the 6 even-numbered months having 29 days. This order never varies throughout the Bible.

After the Exodus in 1639 BC until the Lord's death in 33 AD, the first month in each Bible year began at the New Moon in the Spring season.

4. All that we need to know about the Bible Calendar, with one important

exception, is to be found in Leviticus XXIII, where the annual Feasts of Jehovah are recorded. (These have been listed in Chapter 2 of this book, under the "Raw Materials" heading).

5. A crucial difference came in, of one day, between the Divine Calendar of Jehovah and the Calendar of Israel. We are told that the Lord and His disciples ate the Passover Supper on the night before Jesus' crucifixion, but that the Jews ate the Passover on the following evening, after the crucifixion. Why the difference?

In Exodus 12.2, God gave Moses and Aaron a new calendar, which ensured that each first month would occur in the spring season, and that every month would begin with a New Moon.

But the "astronomical" New Moon, on which this new calendar was based, is not visible from the Earth. The New Moon is only visible from the Earth (what is termed the "phasis", the appearing, of the Moon), one day later, when the tiny sliver of the New Moon is visible from the Earth for the first time in that month. This discrepancy meant that the Calendar of Israel was always **one day behind** the Divine Calendar of Jehovah.

The dates of the Levitical Feasts each year were to be measured from the "real" New Moon - the astronomical New Moon. Not surprisingly, the Lord Jesus obeyed this correct system of dating the Feasts, and hence on the evening before His trial and crucifixion He observed the Passover with His disciples ("the Last Supper"), on the true date of the New Moon, which was **one day earlier** than the Passover held by the Jews.

6. God's Sabbath was **one day ahead** of the Jews' Sabbath.

In the wilderness the people of Israel were in the habit of forgetting, and hence desecrating, the Sabbath of the Lord (see for example Exodus 20.8). The Lord thus separated His true Sabbath from the Sabbath observed, or not as the case may be, by the people of Israel.

In Joshua 10.12-14, we read that He caused "the sun to stand still" - so there were still two normal days as far as the Lord and His calendar were concerned, but only one, albeit double-length, day, on the Earth. This meant that the Jews' day of the week was always one day after Jehovah's day of the week.

This helps to explain some of the apparent discrepancies between the Gospels concerning the actual day of the Lord's crucifixion.

THE VARIOUS CHRONOLOGIES OPERATING WITHIN THE BIBLE DURING THE EARTHLY LIFE OF OUR LORD JESUS CHRIST

1. THE SECULAR CHRONOLOGY (Anno Mundi) (TRV pp xxi)

This begins on the first day of the Bible (4th March 4075 BC), and runs an unbroken course of 354-day years to 12th October 33 AD.

It then takes one further stride of 1960 years up to 12th June 1933, with an overall total of 6198 years and 22 days.

This is the Bible's inspired and therefore faultlessly accurate record of time and it forms the basis of all Bible Chronology. It is the world's only such record. Its astronomical accuracy may be proved by anyone who will take the trouble to do it. It accounts for every year, month, week, day, hour, minute and second from the first day of the Bible to the end of the 6000 Years of Man on 12th June 1933.

At the opening of the day of our Lord's birth, this Secular Chronology had reached a total of 4204 Bible years and 21 days. This is the exact equivalent of 4074 Solar years and 239 days".

2. THE CHRONOLOGY OF REDEMPTION (TRV pp xxii)

This is an era with a fixed limit of 6000 years. It began on the day after the Fall and will terminate at the setting-up of the Kingdom.

This era is concurrent with the secular Chronology, except that it omits periods of years or days that are "marked by circumstances incompatible with the Principles of Redemption and Forgiveness", such as the 70-year period of exile in Babylon. Because of these omissions, this era has no relationship to the astronomical calendars.

The years of this era are 350 days in length, as it takes no account of the 4 days each year when the Passover lambs are set aside awaiting death.

This era is measured throughout the Bible in Jubilee cycles of 49 years, and major cycles of 490 years.

The 6000 Years of Redemption had exactly reached the middle of the 3888th year at our Lord's birth, a highly significant number. (see Chapter 2 of this book, under the Numbers heading).

3. THE CHRONOLOGY OF MAN (Anno Hominis) (TRV pp xxii)

This is an era of 6000 years reckoned in terms of the solar year of 365 1/4 days.

This era began on the 9th day of the Bible and terminated at the close of 12th June 1933, when exactly 6000 Julian years were completed. Thereafter "the consummation of the age" began, which by 2019 has lasted 86 solar years.

The Chronology of Man had reached a total of 4074 years and 231 days at our Lord's birth. This is 8 days less than the Secular Chronology which begins on the first day of the Bible.

4. THE YEARS OF THE MESSIAH (TRV pp xxiii)

"This is the most deeply concealed series of years in the Bible, and its existence we believe has never before been recorded".

It is measured in seven cycles of 888 years each. These began on the 8th day of the Bible, that is, on the day after the first Sabbath.

The number 888 is the numerical value of the Greek letters which form the name "Jesus".

The eighth days of the two concurrent Feasts, Tabernacles and

Ingathering, typify the ultimate "Messianic Kingdom", while the previous 7 days of these two Feasts are "types" of the 7 cycles of 888 years which lead up to that Messianic Kingdom.

These years of the Messiah are independent from all the other series of years within the Bible, and they relate "exclusively to Jesus the Messiah and to the seed through whom He was to come".

The Years of the Messiah had reached a total of 4204 years and 14 days at the time of our Lord's birth.

THE VARIOUS CALENDARS OPERATING WITHIN THE BIBLE DURING THE EARTHLY LIFE OF OUR LORD JESUS CHRIST (p xxv)

1. THE CALENDAR OF ISRAEL lies on the surface of Scripture.

2. THE CALENDAR OF JEHOVAH differs from the Calendar of Israel by being one day of the month, and one day of the week, ahead.

3. THE MESSIANIC CALENDAR is based on the years of the Messiah.

4. THE ROMAN, GENTILE, JULIAN CALENDAR was inaugurated by Julius Caesar in 45 BC.

5. THE CALENDAR OF THE LORD'S OWN EARTHLY LIFE runs from his birth to His ascension:

"The annual Feasts of Leviticus XXIII were viewed by God as also applying to this series of years". Thus, for example, Mary's anointing of the Lord at Bethany occurred on the Day of Atonement, the 10th day of the 7th month in His 33rd year".

(This completes the direct quotations from the Introduction within **THE RESTORED VISION**).

AN OVERVIEW OF KEY EVENTS AND THEIR SOLAR DATES: (i) CREATION TO JUNE 1933

There now follows one list of specific dates, being one list among the many others shown in their books, identified by Arthur Ware, Frank Paine and their colleagues as a result of their being shown the calendars and chronologies within Scripture.

These examples can only "whet the appetite". For the "full meal", you are advised to read the main books – see Part 4 "To Take you Further".

As we examine these findings, we remember the need on the one hand to remain cautious, and on the other hand to remain humbly open to what these godly, diligent men believed the Holy Spirit was showing them.

They repeatedly state - "You don't believe us? Then go and check these things out for yourself in your own Bible alongside the astronomical calendars". The nature of their work was such that every figure concerning specific dates had to be meticulously accurate, or else the whole system would be thrown out.

Here to start with is the Overview List of key events and their solar dates, (taken from **Miracle of Time** by Frank Paine, pages 189 and 182):

Creation and the Fall of Man - 4075 BC

The Flood - 2470 BC

The Birth of Abraham - 2129 BC

The Exodus from Egypt - 1639 BC

The Dedication of the Temple - 1019 BC

The Commandment to restore Jerusalem - 458 BC

***

John the Baptist heralds "the Prince" - 26 AD

The Messiah is "cut off" (Daniel 9.26) - 33 AD

Stephen is martyred - 33 AD

Conversion of Cornelius - 36 AD

Jewish Revolt - 66 AD

Jerusalem and the Temple are destroyed - 70 AD

Fall of Masada, the end of Jewish resistance - 73 AD

***

The Balfour Declaration and Liberation of Palestine - 1917 AD

The Palestinian Mandate - 1923 AD

The World Monetary & Economic Conference opens in London (12th June 1933), and the Nations of Christendom are "cut off" - 1933 AD

AN OVERVIEW OF KEY EVENTS AND THEIR SOLAR DATES: (ii) EXAMPLES FROM THE FOURTH PAPER OF WORLD IN LIQUIDATION

We now include some short extracts from Mr Ware's book **WORLD IN LIQUIDATION** which was first published in 1953.

In this book the author confidently predicted what he and his associates believed to be the imminent return of the Lord Jesus for His Church, the timing of which turned out to be mistaken, that is, premature. As a result, the book was dismissed by its reviewers, with copies of the book now being hard to obtain.

Yet once that date-prediction mistake is allowed for, and, crucially, the reasons for it being made at that time, it is clear that much of the contents of the book remain valid for today, in particular its remarkable Fourth Paper.

In this Fourth Paper, the whole 6,000-year history of Time, from Creation to June 1933, is recorded in meticulous detail across nine Divisions of Time. All the information given is drawn from Scripture itself, and is shown to be astronomically accurate to the day as measured by the age of the moon as given in Scripture at each critical date.

As the authors point out, this record has to be 100% accurate from start to finish or else the whole thing fails. They repeatedly urge their readers to check all that is being said by studying these matters in the Scriptures for themselves.

It is no exaggeration to say that the contents of this Fourth Paper, prayerfully gleaned over the years from Scripture itself, are not only unique in the world, but are astronomically established beyond doubt.

If these truths were made known today within and beyond the Church, how great would be, and should be, their effect.

Two examples from **the Fourth Paper of The World in Liquidation** are now included**.**

FIRST EXAMPLE:

Shown here is the duration of each of the nine "Divisions of Time", stretching from the Day of Creation in 4075 BC to June 1933. You will see that these nine Divisions of Time are accurate to the day.

(The crucial role played by the Jubilee Cycles throughout Biblical Chronology, the particular significance of both the unreckoned week in Division Eight and of 12th June 1933, and the working methods of these Bible Chronologers, are fully explained in their books - see Part 4, To Take You Further, at the end of this book).

FIRST EXAMPLE FROM 'WORLD IN LIQUIDATION', THE FOURTH PAPER: THE NINE DIVISIONS OF TIME:

Division One - Day of Creation to Fall of Adam = 47 days

Division Two - Fall of Adam to the Flood = 1656 Bible years and 46 days

Division Three - Flood to Birth of Abram = 352 Bible years and 101 days

Division Four - Birth of Abram to Exodus = 505 Bible years and 4 days

Division Five - Exodus to Dedication of the Temple = 621 luni-solar years and 1 day

Division Six - 15th Year of Solomon (1018 BC) to Nehemiah's Return (458 BC) = 560 luni-solar years

Division Seven - Return of Nehemiah to Jerusalem to John the Baptist in AD 26 = 483 luni-solar years

Division Eight - John the Baptist to Jesus' Ascension = the unreckoned week of 7 years

Division Nine - The Ascension to Day of Consummation, 12th June 1933.

SECOND EXAMPLE:

As a second example the full figures are now shown here for the ninth and final Division of Time only, which runs from the Ascension to 12th June 1933. This demonstrates the degree of detail involved, (and all these sums were worked out before the era of pocket calculators).

This is only one of the nine Divisions of Time. All nine Divisions are shown in this level of detail in a booklet which is an authorised reprint of **the Fourth Paper of World in Liquidation**, pages 249 - 322. (See Part 4, To Take You Further, at the end of this book).

SECOND EXAMPLE FROM 'WORLD IN LIQUIDATION', THE FOURTH PAPER:
DIVISION NINE –
THE ASCENSION TO THE "DAY OF CONSUMMATION", 12th June 1933:

From the Ascension, 8 am 13th June AD 33, to End of Bible Day, 6 pm 12th June 1933:

a) **8 am 13th June AD 33 to 8 am 11th June 1933** = 1,900 years, 0 days, 0 hours

b) **8 am 11th June 1933 to 8 am 12th June** = 1 day, 0 hours

c) **8 am 12th June to 6 pm 12th June** = 10 hours

Adding a) + b) + c) = 1,900 years, 1 day, 10 hours

This = 693961 days, 10 hours

These = 99,137 weeks, 2 days, 10 hours

The weeks began at 8 am on Saturday 13th June AD 33 (Sabbath), and therefore ended at 8 am, Saturday 10th June 1933.

The remaining 2 days and 10 hours therefore reach to 6 pm, Monday 12th June 1933 (the day on which the World Economic Conference opened in London at 3 pm London time, 6 pm Middle Eastern time).

AN OVERVIEW OF KEY EVENTS AND THEIR SOLAR DATES:

(iii) THE "CONSUMMATION OF THE AGE AND THEREAFTER"

The "Consummation of the Age" begins – 12th June 1933:

The Nation of Israel is restored – May 1948

The Jews regain control of Old Jerusalem – June 1967

At the time of writing, in 2019, we are currently here in the sequence of prophesied events, still within the "Consummation of the Age". The following scriptural prophecies are yet to be fulfilled. This list is followed by some brief explanatory notes.

The Rapture of the Church

The 7-Years of Tribulation ("the time of Jacob's trouble")

The Return of Christ to Reign on Earth ("Thy kingdom come...")

The Lord's Thousand-Year Reign

The Loosing of Satan at the End of Christ's Reign

The Final Judgment

The New Heavens and a New Earth

The next event to occur in this list of as-yet unfulfilled prophecies is therefore what is termed **"the Rapture"** - the removal of the true Church from this earth by the Lord Jesus Christ (I Thessalonians 4.13-18 / I Corinthians 15.51-52).

The Rapture is to be followed by **the final seventieth week of seven years of the Daniel 9 prophecy** (v.27). This is a re-running of the 7-year ministry to the Jews of John the Baptist and Jesus Christ their Messiah (26 – 33 AD), when the Jews rejected their Messiah. As a result, this re-run is to be a time of judgment on the Jews and on the Gentile nations.

The first half of this 7-year "week" will see the antichrist figure on the loose, leading in the second half of the week to what is termed "the great tribulation", as dreadful a time as the world has ever seen (e.g., Matthew 24.21 / Revelation Chapters 4-19). It will end when the Jews cry out to God for mercy, and Jesus Christ, their Messiah, will come visibly in power and glory to rescue His original covenant people.

After the division of the "sheep and goat nations" (e.g., Matthew 25.31-46), there will follow **the thousand-year reign of Christ on earth, the**

loosing of Satan for a final rebellion, **the final judgment**, and **the "new heavens and the new earth"** (e.g., Revelation Chapters 20-22).

A crucial point now needs to be emphasised: in the run-up to June 1933, and in view of their fairly limited knowledge of Bible Chronology at that time, the Bible Watchmen did not foresee this **"Consummation of the Age"** – that is, this current "unreckoned interval of time" through which the world has been passing since June 1933.

But they fully understood that June 1933 was so significant in Bible Chronology terms because it marked a final ending of the 2520 years of the "Seven Times" of Daniel 4 (concerning which they had found the work of Dr Grattan Guinness so helpful). So, based on their clear understanding of the ending of those 2520 years, we can see why they assumed that that ending would be followed straightaway, first by the return of Christ for His true Church (**"the Rapture"**), and second by the re-running of **the final seventieth week of the Daniel 9 prophecy**.

It was on these grounds that Mr Ware asserted so confidently in their public meetings in November 1932 and May 1933 that Christ was about to return for His Church – an assertion which turned out to be mistaken for that time. In this expectation they were mistaken, and in later years, often by over-interpreting types and antitypes, they made further date predictions concerning the Rapture which also turned out to be premature.

In making such predictions regarding the date of the Rapture, be that in 1933 and in later years too, the Watchmen were of course acting in good faith in the light of the extensive knowledge they came to possess concerning Bible Chronology. It is not surprising that these repeated forecasts about the predicted date of the Rapture, each one clearly seen to have been mistaken when nothing had happened, seriously damaged the reputation of both the men and their work.

As a result, their extraordinary understanding of the dates and figures of Bible Chronology has received far less attention than is surely deserved.

CHAPTER 4
Their Further Statements and Conclusions

A brief recap of "the story so far" is appropriate at this stage.

We have seen how, from November 1932 to June 1933, Arthur Ware, Frank Paine and their colleagues came to prominence due to their warnings that God was expected to make "a significant intervention" in the affairs of the nations in mid-June 1933.

In the light of their understanding of Bible Chronology at that time (which later on they found to have been quite limited), they assumed that Christ would return for His Bride, the Church, this to be followed straightaway by the final "seventieth week" of the great messianic prophecy of Daniel Chapter 9, then by the return of Christ in glory and the establishment of His Kingdom on earth.

Their warnings gained credence beforehand when it was announced that the World Monetary and Economic Conference (WMEC), involving representatives of virtually all the world's nations, was to open in London at 3 pm on Monday 12th June 1933; this was the first such global gathering since the Tower of Babel of Genesis Chapter 11.

The Conference was duly opened by King George V, accompanied by two very significant non-events: first, there was no opening prayer acknowledging the sovereignty of Almighty God and seeking His guidance and blessing on the proceedings, (the British Government apparently having refused the King's request for such a prayer, for fear of giving offence to some delegates); and second, there was no sign of any return of Christ.

The Conference ended after six weeks having achieved little. The Bible Watchmen faced a torrent of anger and criticism, and retreated quietly back to their bases around Eastbourne to try to make sense of it all.

Whatever had gone wrong? Were they mistaken? Putting it bluntly, what was God "playing at" in letting them go so far out in faith, only to make them look like self-appointed, time-wasting cranks in the eyes of the world? There followed much soul-searching and much prayer as they tried to understand why things had turned out as they had done - and apparently so catastrophically.

As they were given deeper insights into God's use of Chronology within the Bible over the following months, the whole situation around June 1933 gradually became clearer.

In their subsequent books they made known the following statements and conclusions. These argue that those two non-events in June 1933 - no prayer lifted to God and no visible intervention by God - were highly significant, were closely related, and were entirely "of the Lord" in view of what had happened. In other words, the Watchmen's warnings had been valid after all, and indeed they came to believe that Christ DID come, just as they felt they had been instructed to foretell.

For the many who believed that they had been badly misled by the "false prophets" and "date-fixers" of Arthur Ware, Frank Paine and their colleagues, these statements and conclusions about June 1933 were written off as feeble attempts at self-justification made years after the event.

But others, as Mary had done long ago in a very different context, "kept all these things and pondered them" in their hearts (Luke 2.19). We are bidden to make our own responses today as these statements and conclusions are held forth afresh in today's generation.

FIRST STATEMENT: "until the times of the Gentiles be fulfilled" (Luke 21.24)

The Watchmen had "gone public" in November 1932 because they understood that the "Seven Times" of God-granted Gentile domination over the earth, as typified by Nebuchadnezzar, were drawing to a close over a period of some years, just as these "Seven Times" had started over a similar period of years with Nebuchadnezzar's various visits to Jerusalem from 606 BC onwards.

They had seen that the dates mentioned in 1886 by Dr Grattan Guinness had indeed proved to be significant – 1914, 1917 and 1923 - and now 1933 was the next date on his list. They then considered the Lord's words that – "Jerusalem shall be trodden down of the Gentiles, until the times of the Gentiles be fulfilled" (Luke 21.24).

In 1917 the Moslem Turks had been driven from Jerusalem, with Great Britain, recognised in those days as a Christian power, granted the Palestine Mandate in 1923 on behalf of the League of Nations. This transfer of Jerusalem from Moslem to Christian control (though still a Gentile power) was clearly a significant "step in the right direction" as far as Jesus' words of Luke 21.24b-28 were concerned, especially as it came so soon after the Balfour Declaration of November 1917.

Here therefore were clear signs before their eyes that "the times of the Gentiles" were indeed drawing to a close, with the return of the Jews to their land now becoming a real possibility for the first time in nearly 1900 years.

The World Monetary and Economic Conference (WMEC) in June 1933 was thus a crucial test of the Gentiles as far as God was concerned. Would the Gentile nations, and more particularly, the religious and political powers of Christendom, still "bow the knee" and acknowledge the living God, as Nebuchadnezzar had done so memorably (Daniel 4.34-37)? Or not?

During the months of warning from November 1932 to June 1933, when the churches of Christendom were being urged to repent and to "watch for the coming of the Lord", basically these churches shrugged their proverbial shoulders.

The warnings of the Bible Watchmen among the Christian denominations were either completely ignored, or dismissed as the work of self-deluded nutcases. Such churches were in no state of watching and readiness for the return of Christ the Bridegroom to call away His Bride.

The attitude of the governments was equally dismissive, so the answer to that crucial question, "Would God be acknowledged at the opening of the WMEC in this time of global crisis or not?", was quick in coming: the churches were far from watching and ready, and the nations lifted no prayer - Almighty God was wilfully ignored.

The Watchmen thus concluded that the churches and nations had failed the divinely-set test, and that as a consequence God therefore made the following responses.

SECOND STATEMENT: Jesus DID come, "as a thief in the night"

(II Peter 3.10 & I Thessalonians 5.2-3)

These two scriptural references speak of "the day of the Lord" as coming "as a thief in the night". In the context of WMEC in June 1933 and the signs that "the times of the Gentiles" were indeed being fulfilled, to be followed by the period known as "the day of the Lord", the Watchmen concluded that Jesus really had come, but in an unseen, unknown way – just as a thief in the night.

Instead of Jesus coming joyfully for His Church, found ready and watching for Him, which could have been expected if the churches had paid heed to the Watchmen's warnings, this coming of Jesus was very different.

It was a coming in judgment, and the fact that it had happened at all was only apparent afterwards, again, just as the coming of a real thief is only clear after the thief has been and gone.

THIRD STATEMENT: Jesus DID remove "the candlestick of testimony" from the churches of religious Christendom …. (Revelation 2.5)

In the messages to the seven churches in Revelation Chapters 2 and 3, the candlestick in each case represents that church's God-given permission and authority to "hold forth the word of life" (as in Philippians 2.16a).

The Watchmen stated that the refusal of the churches of religious Christendom in 1932-1933 to heed the Watchmen's warnings and urgings to "watch" for the Bridegroom, led to Jesus' removal of those God-granted candlesticks in June 1933. As a result we come to their fourth statement.

FOURTH STATEMENT: The Government of the earth passed into Christ's hands

Both religious and political Christendom came under judgment after June 1933 because they had failed "the final test of faithfulness".

As a result, "On that day (12th June 1933) man's history under probation ended and the Government of the Earth passed into the hands of Christ ... The world then entered the current "chronological hiatus" or "parenthetical era", prior to the setting up of the Kingdom of the Messiah at the opening of the Seventh Thousand years" (**World in Liquidation (WIL)**, by Arthur Ware, Page 69 / and e.g., John 5.22,27).

FIFTH STATEMENT: "It suited God ..."

Mr Ware and his colleagues had to wrestle with the problem of their apparent failure over June 1933, for Jesus did not visibly come for His Church as they had confidently predicted. How was it that they had got things so wrong? And, more painfully, why had God let them make this apparent mistake?

They came to believe - "It suited God at that time (that is, in 1933) that we thought the Second Coming would be at the same time as His turning from religious and political Christendom ..." (e.g. WIL page 80).

In other words, God in His foreknowledge allowed their apparently mistaken prediction as to the Lord's coming for His Church. The Watchmen's understanding at that time was limited; the criticism that came their way as a result of their apparently-false predictions forced them on to their knees to "seek the Lord" in repentance, from which much blessing was to flow; and all the criticism was also a severe test of their own faith – would they continue to trust in the Lord "even though He slay me" – as in Job 13.15?

Perhaps most crucially, in later years they understood that in two vital senses their prediction about the Lord's coming in June 1933 was absolutely correct after all. First, they became sure that the Lord had indeed come, but as a "thief in the night" as previously mentioned.

And second, of equal importance, they understood something very significant about how the Lord runs the Years of Redemption. Whenever the Redemption "stop-watch" is re-started after a pause (and the world has been in such a pause since June 1933), the Years of Redemption are then resumed *with no apparent loss of time.* Critically therefore, when the Lord does finally come for His Church at "the Rapture", that coming, as reckoned in the Years of Redemption, will indeed be as if on 12th June 1933.

Each of us needs prayerfully to weigh up these statements under this fifth heading: are these statements either merely ingenious excuses in the Watchmen's defence for their apparent "false prophecies", or are they indeed "of the Lord"?

SIXTH STATEMENT: The Holy Spirit's Expectations

The Watchmen made the point that the Holy Spirit had chosen to make these things known at that time (the 1930s), via the Watchmen, to religious and political Christendom and to the wider world beyond, for one good reason: time was becoming critical, so God was "on the move".

The Watchmen's Testimony therefore served as "a wake-up call" for all concerned, to be humbly received and promptly acted upon.

In particular, to demonstrate to the Lord their acceptance of the Watchmen's Testimony, Christians were to recognise that all their sects and denominations had refused this Testimony and were likely simply to carry on, now knowingly in error, in their "bad old ways".

As a result, Christians who accepted the Watchmen's Testimony were now - "to go forth therefore unto him (Christ) without (outside) the camp, bearing his reproach" (Hebrews 13.13, KJV).

This "going forth" was to involve two very practical steps: first, a departure from the "camp" of their sect or denomination; and second, an adoption of the customs of the earliest days of the Church, as made known to us in Acts 2 and 4 and in the Epistles.

SEVENTH STATEMENT: The adoption of the pattern of the New Testament Church

The Bible Watchmen urged that the following features of worship and practice among the early Christians should be adopted once again today.

They argued that it is only within such gatherings that the Holy Spirit will find true openness and a "watching for the coming of the Lord"; for how can He, and why should He, speak to Christians who are still locked, by choice, into their various current sects and denominations, each of which has spurned the Watchmen's Holy Spirit-given Testimony and continues to operate in deep error?

From two key passages concerning the New Testament pattern for church life, in Acts 2.41-47 and 4.31-37, plus various portions in some of the Epistles, the Bible Watchmen drew the following conclusions.

1. We are to **meet in our homes**, with the occasional hiring of larger premises only when necessary.

2. We are to **leave behind any and all denominational assumptions and practices**, many of which we now know to be far from what they should be under the Lord. By God's grace the Holy Spirit will speak in these times to those who are truly watching, a watching they will now be capable of doing by being based in simple home-gatherings that are freed from any

denominational attachments.

3. There should be **no "set-apart leadership"**, in the sense of paid clerics or pastors. Leadership, along with all other responsibilities within the local body of Christ, should be exercised according to Scripture and to the recognised gifting among the members.

4. **All possessions should be held in common** as far as practical and possible. Interestingly the company of Watchmen adopted this principle to a large extent, though at times this led to difficulties which hindered their work and fellowship.

5. In accord with New Testament practice, **baptism in this Church Age should be only "in the name of the Lord Jesus"** (e.g., Acts 2.38 / 8.16 / 10.48 / 19.5 / Romans 6.3 / Galatians 3.27).

The Watchmen taught that Matthew 28.19, (baptism "in the name of the Father, and of the Son, and of the Holy Spirit" and widely adopted by Christian denominations), applies only as follows - (and here we quote from **World in Liquidation,** our italics for emphasis) - "In Matthew XXVIII the Risen Messiah is commissioning *Jewish disciples* who will own Him *after the Church, which is His body, has left the earth* ... It is therefore a self-evident fact *that baptism in the Name of the Triune God, which Jewish evangelists will adopt when teaching the nations which emerge from the trials of the Apocalyptic era, has nothing whatever to do with the Christian Dispensation* ..." (WIL page 457).

6. From their careful studies of Early Church practice, they argued that **the Lord's Supper was originally held only once a year on its solar anniversary** at the end of April, irrespective of the day of the week. In this way the Supper remains as special as it should be, and is firmly related to the Lord's Passover and the Last Supper. They point out that there is no New Testament instance of people "taking the Lord's Supper except on the occasion of its institution" (WIL page 447).

They believed that the Early Church's practices concerning the Lord's Supper quickly became riddled with error including clericalism and superstition, and have become a key means by which ecclesiastical authorities across the centuries have retained power over the people, as they still continue to do.

By contrast, the Watchmen stated that the **"breaking of bread"** (also sometimes known as a "love feast" e.g., Jude 12) has nothing to do with the Lord's Supper. Rather, this is a frequent, probably informal, gathering in homes for worship, teaching and fellowship in the context of a simple meal.

For instance in Acts 20.7 we read that - "And upon the first [day] of the week, (KJV, but the literal Greek reads *"of the weekS"*) when the disciples *came together to break bread* (our italics), Paul preached unto them, ready to depart on the morrow; and continued his speech until midnight" (KJV). The Watchmen concluded that Paul only spoke so late into the night because at midnight they would celebrate afresh the date and hour of Christ's resurrection. (How they established this resurrection timing is explained in AEW's **'The Restored Vision'** (TRV) pp 377-422, and FLP's **'Miracle of Time'** (MOT) pp 89-93 and appendices).

7. Related to the example just given about the "breaking of bread" being different from the Lord's Supper, with the Lord's Supper to be held only once a year on the true solar anniversary of the Last Supper, the Watchmen argued that we should now **observe the anniversaries of key events in Jesus' life on their correct solar dates,** ignoring the traditions of religious Christendom as well as the day of the week.

Thus for example we should remember Jesus' crucifixion not on a particular Friday each year, but on the actual solar date each year, simply because in this, the Church era, no particular day of the week now has any more or less spiritual significance than any other day.

If on reflection we deem that the Watchmen's various "statements and conclusions" outlined in this Chapter are biblically sound, they clearly have many implications for Christians today.

CHAPTER 5
The Present Situation

We remember at this point our need to remain cautious over these matters, bearing in mind that the Watchmen themselves got things wrong sometimes in terms of their date expectations.

When all is said and done, we seek to understand no more and no less than what the Lord chooses to make known to us about current events and dates in the light of His revealed Word. At every step of the way we depend on the Holy Spirit's guidance in these matters.

Monday 12th June 1933 was one key date in the period of years which saw the ending of the era of Gentile domination, and the start of the long-promised return of the Jews to their land. After the horrors of the holocaust, the State of Israel was reborn in May 1948, and Old Jerusalem came under Jewish control in June 1967 – two events which even fifty years earlier would have seemed like mere fairy-tales.

According to the Watchmen, and as shown on their "Chronology of the World" chart, we are currently in what they termed a "hiatus" or "parenthesis" termed **"the Consummation of the Age"**. One key reference to this period is found in Matthew 13.39-40, which is incorrectly translated in the KJV as "the end of the world"; the Greek wording is more accurately translated as "the completion, or the consummation, of the age".

It is a period of "unreckoned years" of unknown length in which the "Redemption Stop-watch" is on Pause. This "Stop-Watch" will be re-started after **the Rapture of the Church** – the next major event we watch for (I Thessalonians 4.13-18 and I Corinthians 15.51-52) – and will then run through to the end of **the seven years of tribulation**, otherwise known as Daniel's seventieth week (Daniel 9.27).

At the end of that week of seven years, God's Redemption Chronology of 5880 years (plus 120 Jubilee years) will have been completed, and also the Seven Times of 2520 years. **Christ will return in triumph and victory**, and **His millennial kingdom will be established on this earth**: quite a prospect.

Meanwhile there are many signs around us that God is still marking key dates with events, and key events with dates.

In his book **Miracle of Time**, Frank Paine shows a chart of the time-pattern from the opening of Christ's ministry in John Chapter 1 through to the saving of European Jewry at the close of World War II (MOT page 196). The time symmetry fits to the day. Three years later the State of Israel was declared on 15th May 1948, which FLP later found to be 4000 Julian solar years from the date of God's covenant with Abram (Genesis Chapter 15, and see **The Restored Vision** by AEW, page 193).

In **Miracle of Time** page 185, Frank Paine gives a further example of God's continuing use of time-patterns, on this occasion with regard to the Six Day War of June 1967.

He notes that the numerical value (or "gematria") for the Greek words "Son of God" is the figure 1934, and that it was, exactly to the day, 1934 solar years from the ascension of the Lord Jesus into heaven (13th June 33 AD), to the ceasefire with Syria bringing the "Six Day War" to an end, on the evening of 10th June 1967. The author concludes - "So God has set His seal upon Israel's repossession of her land and city".

A third set of examples from **Miracle of Time** (Chapter 22) concerns the various Apollo Moon landings.

As the Creator has given the Moon such a central role in the measurement of Time on the Earth, FLP sought the Lord's guidance over whether or not the Apollo missions to the Moon of the 1960s and 1970s had any significance in terms of Bible Chronology.

The Lord tells us that as the events of the seven-year Tribulation move towards their climax of "the Son of Man coming in a cloud with power and great glory" (Luke 21.27) - "there will be signs in the sun, moon and stars" amidst much anguish, perplexity and terror on the Earth (Luke 21.25). Perhaps the Moon landings were something of a foretaste of those "signs"? So, as prayerfully as ever, Mr Paine began to do his sums.

He found that the date of every Apollo mission to the Moon, apart from one, had spiritual significance.

For example, measuring from the first New Moon of Genesis 1 (6 pm, 3rd March 4075 BC) to the launch of the Apollo 8 mission to the Moon (19th December 1968), 74,739 "lunations" (that is, lunar orbits of the Earth), had been completed.

On 24th-25th December 1968, six days into that mission, the crew read the first ten verses of Genesis to the watching and listening Earth below. This reading was thus 6 days into the 74740th moon since Creation. The number 74 is twice 37, and 37 has been found to be a highly significant figure in Scripture. R T Naish, one of the earlier students of biblical numbers, writes as follows (quoted in MOT page 154): "Of all the numbers, this (i.e., the number 37) is perhaps the most sublime, setting forth the wonders of the written Word, and revealing through its pages Him Who is the Living Word".

R T Naish was shown from another writer that - "there are no less than six different combinations of 37 in the very first verse of the Bible". The Lord then showed him that the numerical value of "Christ" is 1480, or 20 times 74, and that of "Godhead" is 592, or 8 times 74.

Is all this just coincidence?

The dates of Man setting foot on the Moon, firstly on 21st July 1969, and secondly on 19th November 1969, were also found to be biblically very significant (in a way too complicated to try to explain here - please see MOT pages 156 and following).

Incidentally it also emerged later that Buzz Aldrin, on Apollo 11, quietly took communion in the lunar module before being the second man to step down on to the Moon. As he explained later - " ... the very first liquid ever poured on the Moon, and the first food eaten there, were communion elements".

Each of the subsequent Moon landings, except one, was also found to have spiritual significance (see MOT pages 159 and following). The only mission that was found to have no spiritual significance in terms of its date was Apollo 13 in April 1970, which was the mission that so nearly ended in disaster with the Moon landing having to be aborted.

One further, personal example of God's continuing use of dates concerns Frank Paine's own death. Frank died suddenly and peacefully at his home at 11 am on 11th November 1983, 65 years to the hour from the armistice to end the First Word War, in which God's long-promised restoration of the Jews started to become apparent. Surely we see in this private incident God's gentle seal of approval of Frank's faithful work over the decades.

***

Turning now to the current scene on a larger scale, we are clearly living in increasingly turbulent times, with "men's hearts failing them for fear" (Luke 21.26). Much of the Middle East, the lands of the Bible, is in turmoil – we think particularly of Syria, Iraq, Iran, Yemen, Turkey, Libya, Egypt, Gaza and the West Bank, with Israel in the middle of it all.

We have mass migration, Islamic terrorism, political upheavals, social breakdown, cyber-attacks, vast stockpiles of weapons of mass destruction, a huge "wealth gap", unusually severe weather patterns and growing concern over "global warming".

"It's always been like this", some people say, but has it? Are we not seeing a rise in the very predictions of Jesus in such chapters as Matthew 24 and its parallels? Can we really envisage these events and trends continuing as they are, with increasing severity and indefinitely into the future?

In Romans 11.25 the Holy Spirit speaks through Paul "that blindness in part is happened to Israel, *until the fulness of the Gentiles be come in*". Do we not have abundant evidence, as explained by the Bible Watchmen themselves and by what we see all around us, that the "until" of that Bible verse is now upon us?

It is appropriate to draw attention at this point to a book by Jonathan Hill entitled **Unlocking the Sign Miracles of John**. The author writes, "Layered within the eight sign miracles of the Gospel of John is an underlying narrative which commentates the *consummation* of prophetic events at the end of this age ... Each sign miracle depicts a final stage episode for either the church or Israel at the conclusion of the Christian Dispensation or during the Tribulation. It is these 'end of age' events at which the 'signs' of the miracles point". This is a most revealing book with great relevance for the times in which we are living. (See Part 4 "To Take You Further" for details).

CHAPTER 6
"So What?" For People Like Us

The Bible Watchmen we have been considering firmly believed that their "Testimony" was given to them by the Lord, for them to publicise to religious and political Christendom and to the wider world beyond. This they did their best to do, first in 1932 and 1933, and then later with the publication of their various charts and books, backed up by letters of explanation and invitation which they sent to political and religious leaders.

Their wish was that people would indeed receive what they were saying as being truly "of the Lord", and as a consequence, like the wise virgins in the parable of Matthew 25, many would be watching and ready for the return of Christ the Bridegroom for His Church. "Behold the bridegroom cometh; go ye out to meet Him" was one of the themes at the heart of their message (Matthew 25.6).

Very few people did respond positively, which was not the result of any lack of prayer or effort on the Watchmen's part. For all sorts of reasons religious and political life went on very much as before, with Arthur Ware, Frank Paine and their colleagues being dismissed, shunned and largely forgotten.

But we have seen enough in these chapters to appreciate that within their work there is indeed a great deal of spiritual value. If the Lord Himself was truly the Instigator of their calling, work and results, as they most firmly believed, then their Testimony remains as much "on the table" today as it has always done.

What is more, over eighty years have passed within this current "Consummation of the Age", and if time was short in the 1930s how much shorter must it be now? This is emphasised by all the events we have seen during these eighty years, notably with regard to Israel and the Jews, a people who so often continue to hold a pivotal place within human affairs.

So what does all this mean for those Christians of today who are grateful for these faithful men and their work, and wish to take their Testimony, in its various component parts as explained in this book, seriously into their own lives and situations? The words that follow in this Chapter are written with such people in mind.

To begin with, whether we want to explore further the intricacies of God's use of Time within creation or not, we do well to try to understand the basics of Bible Chronology for ourselves. Please see Part 4 "To Take You Further" for details of books and suggestions to help you with this.

Meanwhile our understanding of the basics of Bible Chronology has three main "So whats?" for us.

1. "SO WHAT?" - FOR OUR WORSHIP

As we appreciate something of how Almighty God uses Time throughout His creation, including today, we cannot help but fall down in worship before Him! Truly, He is the Lord and there is no other.

We are assured from God's use of Time in the Bible that He remains as much in control of this earth as He has always done, and nothing happens here without His foreknowledge, allowance or direct intervention. It is certain that He will bring His will to pass exactly as and when He wishes, and exactly as and when He has promised and warned. What a comfort this is for those of us "in Christ" in these uncertain times, and spurs us on in our worship, discipleship and service.

Furthermore,, the intricacies of Bible Chronology demonstrate beyond doubt the existence of Almighty God (an existence which of course it is fashionable to question these days), as well as the divine authorship of the Holy Bible, for its many features, not least those concerned with Time, are simply impossible to dismiss as of mere human origin.

No wonder therefore that, even with a limited understanding of Bible Chronology, we worship the Lord "in spirit and in truth" with deeper understanding of His Word and His ways, and with greater devotion for His very Being.

2. "SO WHAT?" - FOR OUR WATCHING

In Colossians 4.2 we are urged by the Holy Spirit through Paul to "continue in prayer and watch in the same with thanksgiving".

Our knowledge of God's overall plan of Time within this creation assures us that all current and future events in the world are under the gaze, the authority and the power of Almighty God our Creator. Truly, in Christ, all shall be well.

We are watching, and need to be ready, for the return of the Lord Jesus Christ as the Bridegroom for His Bride, the true Church, the event known as the Rapture (I Thessalonians 4.13-18 and I Corinthians 15.51-52). This event is firmly booked into "the heavenly diary" and will happen probably close to a season of Pentecost, (that is, in the month of what is now our June, which is the time of year when the Lord's ascension took place (Acts 1.9-11)), at the date of the Father's choosing.

There are practical aspects to our watching. For a start, with our fuller knowledge of God's sovereignty over Time, we can now watch, with greater spiritual awareness than before, the major political events and developments in the world, with particular reference to the Bible Lands of the Middle East with Israel at its heart.

There are always two dangers in such watching. One is to read too much into specific events, which at times the Watchmen were inclined to do, and the other is to read too little. So we watch with care, humbly asking for the Holy Spirit's guidance as to the significance of what is going on, in the light of the scriptural prophecies that are yet to be fulfilled.

A second way in which we can watch is to simplify our homes and possessions, living uncomplicated lives in an attitude of readiness to depart. The Wares and the Paines for example made a point of never owning, but always renting, the homes in which they lived, thus enabling them to "up sticks and move on" as and when they felt the Lord's leading so to do. Meanwhile such simplicity of life and readiness to depart in no way involves a lack of concern for the people among whom we live – indeed, rather the opposite is the case for the stakes are high and the time appears to be short.

A further practical step of our watching springs from our believing that, if the Lord returns in our lifetimes, one day we will simply no longer be here, but many other people, including some who are dear to us, still will be here. Our homes will be here, and our pets and possessions and money and private papers and everything else we own will be here, but not those "in Christ", including, by God's grace, people like us.

In view of this possible, and perhaps even likely, situation, we could write a letter of explanation as to what has happened, and display this in a prominent place in our home during each Pentecost season, to be found by whoever might enter our home after we are gone.

Such a letter may sound far-fetched, but if we are taking God's Word seriously as to promised future events on earth, it isn't far-fetched at all. Instead it is a simple practical step, of help to us as we think things through in the writing of it, and hopefully of help to others too who unfortunately will not have been not involved in the Rapture.

In such a letter we could first explain from the Bible about the Rapture and the implications for those left behind: the urgent need for these folk to put their faith in Christ and then to witness for Him, come what may, during the coming seven years of tribulation, in the certainty that "he who endures to the end will be saved (e.g., Matthew 24.13), even if that saving may involve martyrdom for Christ. Then we could give our wishes concerning our home, pets, possessions and money, with details of our solicitor and our wills.

Anyone finding that sort of letter, in one of the many homes that will have become mysteriously abandoned, would surely find it of great value.

Whether or not we actually get around to writing such a letter is perhaps a small, telling indication of our true response to the findings of these faithful Bible Chronologers.

3. "SO WHAT?" – FOR OUR WITNESSING

The final "So what?" for us regarding the Testimony of these Bible Watchmen concerns our witnessing of these divine truths to others.

We witness first to the Lord Himself, by showing Him that we are accepting into our daily discipleship the findings of these God-fearing men.

In practice we live each day in the knowledge of the overall Time picture that the Lord is steadily working through. Will that sort of response from us, minor and fallible as it is, not warm the Saviour's heart as He sees that at least some members of His body, the Church, are seeking to be truly ready and waiting and watching for His return?

Then **we are to witness to these things among our fellow Christians**, a fair number of whom view Bible Chronology with apathy, ignorance or irritation. Can we imagine what difference it would make if the leaders and members of Church denominations accepted the Testimony of these Bible Watchmen? – referring to it as a matter of course in the preaching and teaching of the Word, and replacing the current annual Christian calendar based on the dates of Christmas and Easter – dates now exposed as being completely erroneous – with the dates and practices as stated in the Bible Watchmen's Testimony? If this became the case the Saviour would see not just the few but the many "wise virgins" watching and waiting for His return for them!

At the same time we must recognise that such a positive response to this Testimony is unlikely in human terms, for that has been the "track record" so far; (though the Holy Spirit in His mercy may well contrive something different, now that Time has moved on so markedly since the

1930s).

If the usual dismissive response to the Testimony remains the case, then individual Christians who receive this Testimony and its implications will find themselves within the various denominations of the Church where the Testimony is still shunned. They must then decide whether to "stay in" and witness to these chronological realities, or to "come out of the camp" and meet in homes as in the earliest days of the Church, and as the Watchmen urged and practised themselves.

This is not an easy decision to take, and will greatly depend on individual circumstances. The heart of the matter is where we can be most effective in our worship, watching and witnessing, now that the Lord has made known these deep Time truths set within His Word.

Next in our witnessing, last but by no means least, is **our witnessing of these things to "them that are without"**, as non-believers in Christ are sometimes referred to within the Word; for example – "Walk in wisdom toward them that are without, redeeming the time. Let your speech be alway with grace, seasoned with salt, that ye may know how ye ought to answer every man" (Colossians 4.5-6, KJV).

Here is a crunch question for us in our witnessing: Do we really, actually, truly believe what the Lord repeatedly teaches in His Word about "those who are without", notably concerning His coming judgments upon them?

Here are a few examples of such teaching, first, also from Colossians: "And you that were sometime alienated and enemies in your mind by your wicked works ... " (1.21); and, "And you, being dead in your sins and the uncircumcision of your flesh ..." (2.13); and, "For such things the wrath of God cometh on the children of disobedience ..." (3.6).

We add two further verses on these matters, from St John Chapter 3: "He that believeth on him (Jesus Christ) is not condemned: but he that believeth not is condemned already, because he hath not believed in the name of the only begotten Son of God" (3.18); and, "He that believeth on the Son hath everlasting life: and he that believeth not on the Son shall not see life; but the wrath of God abideth on him" (3.36).

We know the Gospel ourselves, and by God's grace we do "believe in the name of the only begotten Son of God" and are therefore spiritually safe. But many do not so believe, and are therefore not spiritually safe, in fact very much the opposite is the case. Do we really believe these things? – because when we do so we are far more assured in our witnessing, speaking as appropriate of the urgent need for all to put their belief in Jesus Christ as their Lord and Saviour.

Now we are well aware that the "mood of the age" concerning such matters is one of disinterest. There is little new in this reaction, indeed it is normal, for when it comes to the Christian Gospel and "the offence of the cross" (Galatians 5.11), "the natural man" does not like it, want it or understand it.

It is of course only the work of the Holy Spirit that can bring about conviction and conversion. But our witnessing, including, when relevant, our brief explanation of God's use of Time within creation, can have a valuable pre-conversion part to play in "clearing the clutter" from people's minds. By our helping these needy people to understand clearly the issues that are before them, issues which are backed up by solid credentials such as Bible Chronology, we can open the way for the Holy Spirit to continue and complete the process of their being granted salvation through faith in Christ.

Mercifully "the Lord knows them that are His" (II Timothy 2.19); this present "Consummation of the Age" is a time of gathering-in, and the door of salvation is still open. Our witnessing is very far from being a waste of time – "let us not be weary in well doing: for in due time we shall reap, if we faint not" (Galatians 6.9).

We do not know the future WHENs - the Lord alone knows these - but we do know the future WHATs. We have the task of being Watchmen ourselves, blowing the trumpet of warning (as in Ezekiel 33) as we witness to these future events, referring to the Testimony of the Bible

Chronologers as and when appropriate.

May we indeed be found faithful in our worshipping, watching and witnessing, as we continue to serve as **"ambassadors for Christ"** in today's needy generation, by word, deed and life (II Corinthians 5.20).

In whatever way we may react to the conclusions of Arthur Ware, Frank Paine and their colleagues, it is clear that at the very least their work is still entitled to be taken seriously today. For these faithful men demonstrated how the living God has been actively involved, both over and within His creation, since the time of Genesis 1.1 - "In the beginning God created the heavens and the earth". And if that has been the case since the beginning, then surely that involvement continues now and will continue to be the case through all that is yet to come.

It is timely to emphasise at the close of this Part 1 of the **WARE-PAINE TESTIMONIES** that the aim of this book is to honour these godly men, to make their work and findings known afresh in these turbulent times, and to display more clearly the glory of Almighty God, Father, Son and Holy Spirit.

> *"O the depth of the riches*
> *both of the wisdom and knowledge of God!*
> *How unsearchable are his judgments*
> *and his ways past finding out!*
> *For who hath known the mind of the Lord?*
> *Or who hath been his counsellor?*
> *Or who hath first given to him,*
> *and it shall be recompensed unto him again?*
> *For of him, and through him, and to him are all things:*
> *to whom be glory for ever and ever. Amen"*
>
> *(Romans 11:33-36, KJV)*

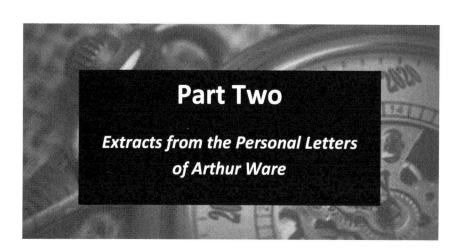

INTRODUCTION

For the first time, by kind permission of members of the Ware family, we are able to include extracts from the personal letters of the late Mr Arthur Ware (1885 – 1978), who we also refer to at times as AEW.

These letters span the years 1930 – 1978. As explained earlier in Part 1, by 1930 Mr Ware was the leader of a small group of God-fearing men who had committed themselves to the study of Bible Chronology, that is, the study of God's use of Time as revealed in the Holy Bible.

Until 1940 most members of the group were based in and around Eastbourne, but Mr Ware sought solitude so that he could pray and study with as few distractions as possible. He loved the English Lake District, in particular the Newlands Valley near Keswick, so as often as possible he would live there in rented accommodation, and correspond regularly with his wife and colleagues in the south of England as to progress, problems and prayers.

In addition to the many letters written in this way from Mr Ware, there are also letters sent to him in reply by his colleagues and other friends and supporters, as well as letters sent between the colleagues themselves when they were physically separated for any reason.

In July 1940 the Company moved to the Newlands Valley, all arranged by Mr Ware at short notice, in response to the order to evacuate all children from Eastbourne immediately because of the threat of imminent enemy invasion on the south coast. This meant that the need for letters between them all was reduced for the time being.

The following years saw various changes in the membership and accommodation of the Company, though they were still based in properties in the Lake District, notably at a house overlooking Coniston Water, from approximately 1943 to 1958.

By the 1960s the continuing members of the group were back in the south of England, in Sussex, Somerset and Surrey, so the number and nature of the letters changed once again.

These extracts from the Ware letters, which have now been catalogued and are published here for the first time, give us a fascinating insight into the work of these faithful Bible Watchmen.

The extracts show real characters coping with real situations, drawing on their profound knowledge of the Bible and their extensive Christian experience. With the benefit of hindsight we can see from these extracts the faults and mistakes of these men more clearly than they could or did see at the time, as well as their many strengths.

Like the rest of us, they got things right under the Lord and they got things wrong under the Lord, so we read this personal correspondence with our "feet on the ground" and our ears open to the promptings of the Holy Spirit. There is a great deal of value within these extracts, hence our gratitude to the Ware family for permission to make them now more widely known.

RECURRING THEMES

It is helpful to point out at this stage for readers of these extracts several main themes which we see running through the letters and across the years. These themes in themselves explain and undergird so much of "the Company" and their faithful work over the decades.

We list these themes briefly here:

1. **Their sense of calling, duty, privilege and responsibility** to be involved in this Bible Chronology work. This led in turn to their self-respect, self-worth and self-belief as they and the work proceeded, yet was always grounded in a deep sense of their own inadequacies and shortcomings. They sincerely believed that they were neither cranks nor nutcases, but were God's chosen few, through no merit of their own, now carrying out

the task that God required them to do.

2. **Mr Ware was very much "The Boss"**. It was to him that "the call" had first come, so he took seriously the need for him to provide leadership, discipline and pastoral care. Throughout, he had a deep concern that the work should continue unhindered – that was always "top of the list", with family concerns fitting in around that priority. He set high standards of self-sacrifice for himself, and expected his colleagues to do the same.

Mr Ware emphasised that membership of the Company brought responsibilities to the men involved, with their wives entrusted with seeing to the children and running the various households properly in support of the central work that was going on. In keeping with those times, the members of the group usually addressed, or referred to, one another quite formally, a practice continued in this book out of respect.

It is clear from some of these extracts that AEW was a strong character with firm opinions, who could be touchy when challenged from within or from beyond the Company. Yet there is no doubting that at heart he loved the Lord, he loved the Word, he loved his wife and family and all involved with the Company, and sought throughout for them all to be found faithful to their high calling.

3. The members of the Company had **a high view, and a deep knowledge, of the Scriptures**. They were men of **fervent prayer**, and were no strangers to the **spiritual opposition** they frequently encountered in the work.

While they had every confidence in the guidance of the Holy Spirit and the accuracy of their figures and dates, they were always aware that they lacked **the academic credentials** within the group which they felt would help in the Testimony being taken seriously; (we have an interesting case of this same point in John 7.15 for example, with reference to the Lord Himself).

This led them to ask one or two academic Bible scholars to examine and authenticate their work. This rarely proved successful as the Company's

Testimony - their findings and conclusions - were so at variance with the accepted academic viewpoints of the time. This difficulty in gaining clear support on an academic level was a frustration which is evident in some of the extracts which follow.

4. The main human hostility to the men and their work, (that is, as distinct from the frequent spiritual hostility they experienced directly or indirectly from Satan, which is often referred to in these extracts), arose from **their date predictions**, on the grounds that either these were made at all, or that these were claimed to possess the full authority of Scripture, or that these then turned out to be wrong as far as anyone could tell.

No wonder that these repeated mistakes, (which often arose from their mis-applying biblical types and antitypes), caused the "Bible Chronology baby" to be thrown out with the "date-predictions bathwater" as far as the public was concerned. Few people thus bothered to listen to Mr Ware's attempts to explain why these mistakes had occurred, especially as he would then often produce a revised predicted date.

The Company longed for their Testimony to be received and widely accepted, believing throughout that the facts they had been shown about Bible Chronology were of paramount importance to both the Church and the world. But the widespread public rejection of their Testimony fostered a sense of ostracism and isolation within the Company, which was perhaps understandable if not always healthy.

5. **The date of 12th June 1933**, and the events leading up to that date, are central to their Bible Chronology work, hence the frequent mention of that date and period in the letters. This was a date they had very publicly predicted would be of great spiritual significance (see Part 1 / Chapter 1), and in this we should not forget that they were correct, notably over the opening of the **World Monetary and Economic Conference** on 12th June 1933, of which they had known nothing in November 1932 and May 1933 when they gave their 200-day and 40-day warnings.

The fact that the Lord Jesus Christ did not visibly appear at that time – an apparently false prediction on their part therefore – led to their rejection, though in later years, when they understood so much more of the different biblical chronologies, they produced a plausible explanation for that apparent error.

6. Each member of the Company was ever-conscious of their **being constantly "in the presence of the Lord"** in their daily lives and tasks.

Often in these letter extracts for example we see AEW wondering if apparently trivial events in his daily round have been specifically "sent by the Lord" for His divine purposes, such as a headache or a cold, sudden bad weather, a particular Bible text on a daily calendar, a "chance" meeting with a stranger, an extreme shortage of funds, or a sudden influx of funds. Quite often we find him asking the Lord how long he should stay alone in the Newlands Valley with the Lord and his work, and when he should "go south" to spend time with his wife, family and colleagues, and to further the work in London when this was appropriate.

He was thus ever watchful for possible, specific, divine promptings, and then quick to act if he felt he had been prompted to do so. Above all he sought to be found obedient under the Lord in the smaller, as well as in the greater, issues of his life, and encouraged his colleagues to do likewise.

7. Related to the previous point just mentioned concerning divine guidance and obedience, a further feature of the letters, perhaps ironically, is **the frequent uncertainty** within the Company as to the way forward under the Lord.

When should they wait, for further clarification or for a strong shared sense of a divine call-to-action, and if so, for how long? And when should they step forward and act anyway, and if so, how and to whom? And when they did act, who should they focus on - the Church, the religious and political leaders, the peoples, the nations, the Jews?

FOUR STRANDS

In summary, it is helpful to keep in mind, as explained in the Introduction to this book, that "the Ware-Paine Testimonies" consist of four main strands: first, the wealth of information about God's use of time within the Bible - including the calendars, chronologies and Jubilee principle - and the accurate dating of Bible events which they were then able to establish; second, the interpretations, statements and conclusions that the Company members drew from that first strand (these first two strands comprised the "Testimony" itself as far as the Company's members were concerned); third, the books and articles that were written; and fourth, the extracts from their personal letters, published here for the first time.

It was mainly the date predictions, occurring among much else within the second strand, that aroused opposition and caused the whole Testimony to be widely but unjustly dismissed.

***

And so in the light of these introductory remarks, we now come to the extracts of the personal letters of Mr Arthur Ware. These extracts are included here in chronological order, and are left "to tell their own story" as much as possible; where appropriate, editorial explanation or comment is provided, written in italics.

All the letters from Mr Ware were written with a fountain pen, and frequently at high speed. At first sight his hand-writing often appears virtually illegible, but a slowly-acquired knowledge of his various quirks in writing individual letters of the alphabet finally won the day. Some of his minor mistakes of spelling or grammar have been retained, along with the variable ways in which he writes particular dates and biblical references, so as to keep these extracts as close as possible to the original letters.

Please note that all letters are from AEW to his wife and colleagues, unless otherwise shown.

Part Two: Extracts from the Personal Letters of Arthur Ware

For each extract is shown: the catalogue number of the letter from which the extract is taken; the date of writing; the place of writing; the writer; the recipient; and any brief editorial input (written in italics) that may be necessary to explain what is going on. To preserve confidentiality actual names are usually replaced with "Xxxxx" or similar.

Some of these extracts are short, clear and pithy; others are longer and deeper and, as with Mr Ware's books, will repay careful reflection with the help of an open Bible and a good Concordance.

In all that we read in these extracts we may well agree here and disagree there, but on every page we encounter a remarkable Christian warrior who got some things wrong - and many things right.

CHAPTER 1
1930 -1934

1930

30115 / 22nd October 1930 / From the Lake District, source address not shown -

As I go aside to definitely engage upon the solemn task of placing upon paper a brief exposition on the state of things amongst men in the present hour as revealed by Holy Scripture, and this solely for the benefit and enlightenment of those yet in their sins, I am grateful to God that I find you in some considerable measure exercised about the matter: for this I thank God and take courage.

... Let reasoning be silenced, that faith – the faith of the Son of God – may be actively that which is in display and control.

... for by a long experience of failure – the utter corruption of the flesh – I have learned in measure the truth of that word, "the flesh profiteth nothing" ... When it comes to doing what we regard as of less consequence, it is much more difficult to be found in the place of true dependence.

(*Concerning their new Wednesday prayer meetings which his colleagues would be holding at Alfriston in Sussex while AEW is in the north*) –

In some measure they will be an indication of the results of our gatherings in the past three years. As I have been largely responsible I shall now be either humbled, or give glory to God.

... upon each one who feels called to attend.

The question is, is it possible for a few with undivided heart to meet to pray about a matter which concerns the glory of God: to meet as fellow members of the body of Christ: to meet in entire dependence upon the Holy Ghost? If so, the rout of Satan in this matter will be complete; for the flesh, and all that is of man, would have no place.

... true prayer is that which can only ascend to God if prompted by the Divine Spirit within each one of us. Including myself, I fear we have yet each one to learn what it is to "pray in the Holy Ghost" when we gather for prayer.

Prayer meetings, as we call them, are undoubtedly a severe test of spirituality. Hebrews 5.14 – "Strong meat belongeth to them that are of a full age, even those who by reason of use have their senses exercised to discern both good and evil". Spiritual immaturity unfortunately will often display itself in a prayer meeting.

I know you are exercised in regard to the urgent need of these gatherings for prayer being productive of living results, and not merely a negative consolation of having prayed.

Real prayer is having to do with God; it is consciously entering His presence; it is entering into communion with Him in regard to the matters presented; it is a loosing of spiritual energy, and a binding of the forces of darkness; it is the setting in motion of principles regarding which we can now know but little, because "we see through a glass darkly". It is actual collaboration between the Head, and the members of the Body of Christ.

1931

31118 / 28th July 1931 / From a farm near Alfriston -

I think that now we are subject, not to being stopped, but to being hindered ... We can pray therefore for preservation and deliverance from all but what is allowed of God.

On Sunday evening I had talks with three separate lots of people, all deeply impressed, and in one or two, evident preparation of God.

My desire is not to be eloquent but to get the facts clearly stated. Not our language but God's power is what will save people.

... nevertheless no line of reasoning must be left out, providing it is likely to break down prejudice and prepare the way for the seed. There is so much of false notions to be removed.

1932

3229 / 21st September 1932 / AEW to a colleague, from Alfriston –

... a creaking of the silence of heaven ...

3231 / 19th October 1932 / AEW to a colleague, from Applethwaite near Keswick -

The thoughts herein came to me before breakfast, as has most of the light any of us has received. This is full of meaning, and if that early hour is neglected none can tell how much we suffer individually and collectively.

3230/6 / 25th October 1932 / From Applethwaite –

... and I waited on in a season of silence ...

1933

3332 / 1st January 1933 / From Applethwaite -

I was conscious in my spirit as well as my body that a power infinitely greater than I was standing in the way and I could do nothing which was coherent. This power is much to be dreaded and it is what I have experienced off and on for three years and it was only broken at times for me to write 'The Hour of Translation' (*published in 1929*) and then only when I and others withstood in the Name of Jesus and with the

Sword of the Spirit applied in the energy of the Spirit and in obedience to God.

... I have felt grace was about to be given to take the offensive against these opposing powers.

Let us realise fully that outside the persons of the Godhead – Father, Son and Holy Spirit – these powers directly under the control of Satan are the most powerful in the universe and equalled only – but for the purposes of good – by the Archangels. Let no-one think it is theory or mere weakness in the vessel, it is Satan and powers in heavenly places in diabolical conflict with saints, ourselves therefore in this case, who, moved of the Spirit, purpose to shed light into the darkness of this world – Satan's sphere. Now Satan does all by darkness and God all by light. He has given us – in infinite Grace – light, and the Spirit insists this light must be shed abroad and not harboured. We must not hold our peace, for today is still a day of good tidings (*II Kings 7.9*).

The conflict is <u>not on earth, it is in the high places, where spiritual wickedness exists.</u>

I rest in the arms of Divine love, and to rest is faith, and without faith it is impossible to please Him.

... the grace of intercession ...

3349/2 / 15th December 1933 / From a colleague to AEW –

But the highest thing goes to the lowest thing in God's creation. It is to "babes" that revelation is made. I commend you in your present weakness to our Great Physician.

1934

3445/2 / 9th January 1934 / AEW, from the Newlands Valley, Keswick –

(*This is written seven months after 12th June 1933, when the warnings the*

Company had given concerning that time had been widely rejected as being false. Since then the members of the group have continued their work based at Alfriston, with AEW usually in the north. It is a period of their seeking to understand more of what actually happened in June 1933, and why the Lord apparently let them make such a very public mistake) -

Since then (April 1933) I know of nothing which has come which has upset anything which we believe came to us from our Divine Teacher – the Holy Ghost.

Nothing on the chart has yet to be altered and nothing but the most flagrant unbelief could allow us to think we were deceived anywhere that was vital ... New light on the chart or prophetic position has been next to nothing ... I was shown early after June 12th (*1933*) not to move away from a single fact recorded and believed by us to have come from God.

I found myself becoming oppressed in spirit with feelings of deadly inertia spiritually and hopelessness – making prayer a task to be dreaded. This increased and always means a crisis is coming if gone through with. It is Satan or his underlings ranging themselves in the path to impede any advance, as I suppose seen in Daniel X (*v.13a*).

... Nothing devilish in the universe can stand before these (*that is, the blood of Christ and the name of Christ*) ... (*we*) take up the challenge on the ground of our union with Satan's <u>Conqueror</u> – the efficacy of the Blood and the power of the NAME.

... stepping out of God's will ...

3441/1 / 10th January 1934 / From the Newlands Valley -

... for the rejection of Chronology leaves prophecy without anchorage and vague as to the time of fulfilment.

... Are we a company of sceptics who go on because we can't turn back? - but who, still suffering from the jar of June 12, have not yet been able to stand on the deck of faith but, hugging ourselves, live <u>below</u> deck like sea-sick travellers?

... we need faith, dear friends, and reason cannot supplant faith without drawing the heart away from God. And if this happens, we are left in the cold; for nothing is cold so much as pure reason, and nothing so unsatisfying.

3442/1 / 21st February 1934 / From the Newlands Valley –

God does not ignore time and resort to miracles, save with an object.

3452/1 / 26th February 1934 / From the Newlands Valley -

The vale of physical togetherness ...

Too much should not be made of ourselves as a company or of a position such as Levites or Nazarites ... (*the danger of their becoming*) too self-occupied. The true Nazarite would be extremely unself-conscious.

3453 / 28th February 1934 / From the Newlands Valley –

I have had to learn by much humbling that no flesh shall glory in His presence.

3454/1 / 1st March 1934 / From the Newlands Valley –

I am able to go out much to pray, and the solitude of the mountains and a place to lift up my voice to God I deeply value.

3440/1/ 6th March 1934 / From the Newlands Valley –

I perceive the weight of things has been upon you and the sailing not all with the wind and tide.

3456/1 / 8th March 1934 / From the Newlands Valley -

Now what is abandonment? I asked the Lord this question on my knees this A.M. The answer came in this form – I saw a MAN placing HIMSELF voluntarily on a cross so that the soldiers could nail His hands and feet to the tree and so that the counsel of God – His Father – before determined – might be done. Heaven knows no other abandonment than this. In the light of coming Glory should we?

(*Oswald*) Chambers speaks of this being done in the will. Our trouble is inward reserve. Until it is broken each has a mighty steel hawser – forged down six thousand years – holding him to the principle that in the ultimate <u>I</u> and not God will have the <u>final</u> say.

In other words, though religious and in much zeal, I have still retained what I call my RIGHT of self-determination, unless I have satisfied the keen eye of God's Spirit that MY WILL has cut the hawser and I have allowed myself to leave the shore and float out into the deep waters of Divine purpose where I am beyond reach of all, save Divine sustenance. Then I can say ALL MY SPRINGS ARE IN THEE (*Psalm 87.7*).

3458/1 / 11 March 1934 / From the Newlands Valley -

I think more and more the Lord leaves His own to act in obedience without making His wish known, it being of far greater value to Him when He does not have to <u>call</u> for obedience but gets it without calling.

God has His hand on the grapes and is pressing hard so that there may be wine for others, and as wheat being ground between mill-stones, so that there may be bread for the hungry.

... which would make this a matter to silence the critics because figures speak the truth.

... some things have to be searched for and are not given for the asking.

... the delay has been like a lash to the flesh.

Rank simplicity is our need.

May the Lord become more precious to you under the present pressure, for if not you will find rebellion lurking in your inmost parts.

3460/1 / 19th March 1934 / From the Newlands Valley -

(*Concerning their new understanding of the Jubilees*) - a sledgehammer to all opposition ...

3466/1 / 1st July 1934 / From the Newlands Valley -

At such times (*of conflict*) we do well to remember what is at stake, and to realise how deadly must be the foes ranged against us which resort to every device to turn us aside, be it poisoned fiery darts or other wiles, and in order that we shall give up the battle and retire to wait until we "feel" better able to enter the hideous warfare against unseen foes.

You may rest assured that the nearer you come to reaching the Throne, the more deadly will be the opposition. I use the word deadly for the effect it has upon the spirit is of one seeking to stifle you by a process of throttling.

... that God has measured time ONLY from Blood to Blood, that is from the day of Atonement when blood was shed to another, 49 years hence when blood was shed again ... for the Cross is Satan's defeat and is the way by which God has secured the coming of the Glory, and Chronology points the time and runs right through Holy Writ.

... Let us keep the hated Chronology to the front – it is the Spirit's Testimony, not ours, and all the hatred of it and fear and all the efforts in our own midst to baffle and turn us aside arise from the Satanic revolt against the Spirit's testimony to Christ's return. Mr Xxxxx's action (*this member of the group had now distanced himself from the testimony of June 1933 which he had originally supported*) is a proof of this and all his (*that is, Satan's*) attack is against the Chronology. Satan wants no Abishag for David but God has called us to find Abishag (*I Kings 1.1-4, Abishag representing the Testimony that is to bring comfort to David, representing the Church*).

3468/1 / 9th July 1934 / From the Newlands Valley -

The point to keep in mind is that every date has a scripture verse to guarantee it.

3469/2 / 10th July 1934 / From the Newlands Valley -

(*The aim*) - to first get right on to redemption ground, presenting the perfect sacrifice of Christ as meeting every sin and shortcoming, and with this the perfections and excellencies of Christ as the ground of our own weak service.

3470/3 / 12th July 1934 / From the Newlands Valley –

Praise and pray.

3476/1 / 22nd July 1934 / From the Newlands Valley –

… the testimony of the Lord …

(*God has chosen*) - to provide in the Apocalypse the greatest Revelation ever received by mortal man.

Time is therefore not reckoned by God from June 12th up to the Jewish nation being taken up and grafted in (*Romans 11.23*).

(*Concerning the Lord's predicted return on 12th June 1933*) … but the promise was only delayed not negatived …

… the chronological Christ, the Wonderful Numberer.

As I have beheld this mighty structure (*all the years now known*) of the Ages framed together, I am caused to marvel and declare that next to Redemption, it is the mightiest demonstration of Divine power that the Word of God contains.

3475/3 / 29th July 1934 / To AEW from a colleague in Alfriston -

… a season of no small freedom in prayer …

3477/1 / 31st July 1934 / From the Newlands Valley -

... it is difficult to keep still when so much divine gun-powder is in our heads, hearts and hands. The whole secret of the Ages has been given and for this we bow in thanksgiving.

3478/1 / 8th August 1934 / A colleague to a colleague -

... and that the Lord in His wisdom and mercy may preserve each one of us till we see Him face to face.

3480/1 / 17th August 1934 / AEW from the Newlands Valley –

(*Concerning Satan*) - because his power goes if he is discovered ... Satan only has power if I give it to him.

3481/1 / 23rd August 1934 / From the Newlands Valley -

I trust that you, dear brother, and Mrs B, keep sustained in quiet confidence before the Lord in all things, AEW.

3483/1 / 27th August 1934 / From the Newlands Valley -

God never will act or allow us rather to act for Him in this world except <u>out from death.</u>

I trust she (*a mutual acquaintance*) is given repentance.

3485/3 / 28th August 1934 / A colleague to a colleague –

It is a solemn thing how Satan is allowed to trap those who really desire to be faithful.

... We look forward to seeing you again as soon as the Lord makes occasion.

34ab/1 / 29th August 1934 / A colleague to colleague –

... the only way to meet him (*Satan*) is to have identified ourselves with the death of Jesus Christ on the Cross, and ... to stand, having put on the whole armour of God.

3487/1 / 8th September 1934 / From the Newlands Valley –

... above all let us realise that we die with the testimony. "Thou fool, that which thou sowest is not quickened except it die" (*I Corinthians 15.36*). May we all know death as the gateway to life and manifested power.

34ac/1 / 17th September 1934 / To AEW from a colleague –

We remember continually before the Lord the fact that you stand your watch alone ...

On Sunday morning we sought to be in the way where the Lord might meet us ...

34128/1 / 22nd October 1934 / From Harlyn Bay in Cornwall -

(*Concerning AEW's new lodgings*) –

... time alone can prove if it is a suited place since we walk by faith.

The place is just a few houses and a sweet sandy bay with usual Cornish cliffs leading out to Trevose Head and lighthouse ...

... the serious labour it has fallen to our lot to pursue.

... and feel fairly certain this is place of divine choice ... and here I intend to keep my counsel and shall feel more free by keeping the King's business to myself.

... I know you are all daily presenting the needs of our Master before the Throne and by His grace His needs have become ours.

34129/5 / 24th October 1934 / From Harlyn Bay -

... but often it does not please the Lord to give the full light at once ...

34129a/2 / 29th October 1934 / From Harlyn Bay -

... but all light has to be received in faith and is therefore subject to attack.

(*Concerning 12th June 1933*) –

... on the one hand Christendom suffered excision from the Divine olive tree ... the nations on the other hand, as ruling the earth under a Divine delegation of power, were brought to an end of their charter and became the immediate subjects of Divine judgement ... for, I believe, the expression "Gather the tares in bundles ... to burn them" (*Matthew 13.30*), which action commenced on June 12th, applies to Christendom in its political and religious aspect, since in God's sight they are but one aspect – apostasy.

... both as regards the times of the Gentiles that is the religious aspect, and as regards the era of Gentile governmental supremacy the political aspect, time ceased on June 12th and NO time is reckoned by God again until the first tick of the clock in Daniel's 70th week when the 1260 days opens immediately upon the Rapture ... and this dear friends, as God caused us to declare, will be exactly as on our first chart in the year 1933, for the intervening era is not reckoned by God for Jew or Gentile – indeed has no place. The time is termed "the harvest" and is an era when judgment has commenced and when the mighty angels are behind the scenes – not as in the Seven Times keeping things controlled, but getting the stage set for the opening of this dread seven years when Jew and Gentile must again live that lost 7 years.

(*After suddenly being given much light concerning the "Seven Times" of Daniel Chapter 4*) –

After breakfast I was feeling the effects of this inrush of such supremely vital matters from Heaven - it is a strange feeling to become possessed of matters for the first time when they affect the whole universe, but I was fully aware a thing utterly concealed from man or fowl of the air had been given us.

So I went out and for the first time walked right out to Trevose Head and lighthouse. A half gale was blowing and it all seemed fitting to be so near upon the raging waves of the sea, which speak of the nations and of that near movement of which John speaks - "I saw a beast rise up out of the sea" (*Revelation 13.1*).

I was, as you may imagine, praising, like Daniel, the God of our fathers for making known so wondrous a secret and I got the thought that I might see a seal, of which a few are to be found on this wild coast. I scanned the waters and thought it was an idle fancy as I could see none.

On the way back around this very jagged and rugged piece of coast I saw a sandy beach called "Mother Ivey Bay" and crept down as I felt the symbol was fitting and, like John, should stand "upon the sand of the sea" because I wanted to read about this Beast that rises up out of the sea at the moment when <u>time</u> again is reckoned.

After I had got out my Bible and was reading, I beheld a black object and lo and behold, facing me, and staring at me so close in as to be able almost to stand on the sand, was a seal. I thought it would be washed up as the wave retreated from the sand and returned.

It remained for a few minutes and then swam away and I never saw it again, but I know Who had sent it and it was a Divine symbol just as Seal Road three years ago (*a reference to a key moment of revelation for AEW at a house in Seal Road, Selsey in 1931*).

I have no doubt that this was given as a Divine confirmation of the precious light, and that we may take it that it was God's seal on the light given. The issue was the Beast to rise out of the sea, and here, like John, I was standing on the sand by the sea to receive a seal or confirmation, that what I had received concerning the Beast was from God and that no time would be reckoned until that beast rose up, and it would be on June 12th 1933, in God's counsels, when that would occur.

I mingle my praises with yours for this precious answer to prayer, and subscribe myself with love in Christ Jesus to each one.

Your affectionate co-labourer, Arthur E Ware.

3490/1 / 6th November 1934 / Colleague to a colleague –

Both this morning and his afternoon we have been enabled to spread out our petitions before God in no uncertain way.

3491/12 / 7th November 1934 / From Harlyn Bay –

... what it is to be ignorant and yet how great does it make one's dependence.

However, the prize is a high one so we must expect no easy way.

3495/1 / 16th November 1934 / From Harlyn Bay –

We have to be careful in these things not to go in "head first" as sometimes doing so entails creeping out with a bruised head.

We have learned in the past that the Spirit of God is very jealous over these matters because of their unsurpassed solemnity and importance.

The order always I find is this. First the impression laid upon the heart and mind that a certain "thing" IS so, and this by the Spirit no doubt. Under that impression, to apply one's heart and mind to gathering together all the correlative facts and put the "thing" to the test. Difficulties appear which are apparently insurmountable, but faith refuses to allow the impression to be dismissed, then it becomes the office of the Holy Spirit to teach what is lacking in essential knowledge, guiding either direct or through a book (possibly) which contains certain facts stated.

(*Sir Edward*) Denny speaks of how the Lord gave him to think the 70th week was cancelled and how he was tested many times, but it was the Lord by the Spirit who created the first impression which faith will never let go.

The opposite of this is allowing the mind to speculate with suggestions and then spend time in fruitless toil. I have experience of both. The later experience prepares one for what is the Spirit's work.

... but more glad still to note (*the position*) is still more clear in your hearts, and as there remain steadfast in God, the understanding which exists will be added to by wisdom to grasp the detail ... The more I consider them (*the figures*) the less easy does it become to find any loophole for error, and you may rest assured I have grubbed about long enough over them.

(*A typical example of AEW's working on the Bible dates, concerning in this case the various dates involved in the crucial "Seven Times" prophecy of Daniel 4*) –

I have had a suspicion that Nebuchadnezzar' reign actually began in between Jan and March of our BC 603 – that is at the fag-end of the Jewish Sacred year ... So it proves, for from November 2nd Jewish year 5678, 2520 years takes us to 60-70 days before the beginning of Nisan say April 603 BC. This being so Jewishly, it was 604 but actually it was in our year BC 603 ...

3496/2 / 2nd December 1934 / From Harlyn Bay –

(*Concerning AEW's desire to see all distractions from the work to be removed*) –

... We can truly pray bro Bl ... will get busy and hew in pieces all that now binds him. I expect if he is to abide he will have to clear the lot ...

... and conscious also that no problem over these many years has been without solution in the proper season.

3496a / 2nd December 1934 / AEW to a colleague, from Harlyn Bay -

(*Concerning a brother who is no longer committed to their work*) –

On his own confession he has had Divine checks such as the fire (*at his farm*), and I know also he was greatly troubled by poultry disease ... I have little doubt that his backsliding and business have developed together ... Another question is, is he needed to fulfil a part in the counsels of God? This must be so if <u>seven</u> are necessary to the Divine plan and purpose.

I fully agree that the passing over of control (*of the farm*) to his boys is not calculated to impress anyone in the district with the fact that in expectation of the Lord's return he has given up ordinary pursuits, all would suggest it was mere fluff ... (*I intend*) definitely to lay the matter before him and secondly I am hoping he himself may receive grace both to seek to know God's will and be obedient thereto.

3497/1 / 5th December 1934 / From Harlyn Bay –

(*Concerning a recent sense of oppression*) - No doubt to be a bond servant of Jesus Christ is the only <u>true</u> liberty one can enjoy on this planet. All else is bondage.

... we may feel like a poor child who has happened across a bag of priceless gems and be found idly playing with them ... all seems to have gone down into death and be out of our grasp but <u>faith</u> has dropped its anchor in the Sanctuary and can therefore remain sure and steadfast despite the prevailing contrary winds. Are we yet expert in war? (*I Chronicles 12.33*).

3498/1 / 7th December 1934 / From Harlyn Bay –

I trust grace may be given you to fatten up all your spiritual energy and seek the throne of grace as there is a deadly pall resting upon us which can only be broken by prayer and fasting.

... never again to be within the reach of Satan. Nothing I take it not "in resurrection" is beyond Satan's reach.

3499/1 / 10th December 1934 / From Harlyn Bay –

... and when in prayer I have sought mercies of the God of all peace on your account.

(*Concerning the brother no longer committed to the work*) - I wish I knew where he has got to in his soul relationship with God.

34101/3 / 16th December 1934 / From Harlyn Bay –

The only thing the Spirit will bear witness to is the TRUTH and our need is to arrive only at the TRUTH about every detail ... I may sketch out figures on bits of paper or more often keep them in mind, but I skirt finality or anything which approaches it until every brick in the building of evidence is rounded off so as to fit despite any storm of criticism.

I trust soon to report "all clear" on the chart, or as we used to say "no part dark" (*Luke 11.36*), then perhaps we may proceed to set all down in order from the beginning.

34102/2 / 16th December 1934 / A colleague to a colleague / From Alfriston -

May the Lord grant you to be renewed inwardly day by day till He comes.

CHAPTER 2
1935 -1936

1935

35af/5 / 26th February 1935 / From the Newlands Valley –

May simplicity, singleness of heart and a refusal to pander to self, work (*in*) us all so that the Spirit may keep Christ before us as our only resource for prayer and service.

35am/2 / 14th March 1935 / A colleague to colleagues, from Essex –

I hope to come on Monday if it is well, and the way is open.

35an/4 / 15th March 1935 / Colleague to a colleague, from Alfriston -

(*Oswald*) Chambers reminds us that God gives us the Spirit of Christ but not the mind of Christ. **That** has to be worked and wrought out and can only be effected as "our mind" is identified with His Death.

35ao/2 / 15th March 1935 / From the Newlands Valley –

I have no doubt Abraham and Lot show the two states – both saved from judgments, the one by a hallowed walk and communion with God, and the other by a sovereign act of mercy.

Let us not forget the Chronology is God's weapon and it is this that is opposed.

35at/2 / 19th March 1935 / From the Newlands Valley –

When a truth passes away from you it seems to lose all its power and almost mocks you, but when it pleases God to quicken so that the truth begins to live again, then it becomes yours for ever.

(*Regarding two previous supporters who have now turned away*) –

In thinking over about bro(*ther*) Dxxxx I see now clearly that God would have neither him or any other in a position to claim association in this testimony unless in true subjection to every Divine requirement touching it. There could be no halfway house, otherwise our brother Blxxxx would have been permitted to continue with us.

I pray your season may be one of real profit and that you may consciously feel that you have secured a hearing touching the needs of Christ.

35aw/2 / 25th March 1935 / From the Newlands Valley –

We have to learn well so our Teacher often teaches in not too rapid stages. We have to absorb one fact well before we are prepared to receive the next and all is brought forth in perfect order. This being so, patience is needed, and if all is not understood at first go, we have to avoid irritation through coveting knowledge before the due season.

35az/1 / 27th March 1935 / Colleague to a colleague / From Essex –

We forget that God tells us that the just shall LIVE by faith and that there is nothing visible or tangible down here, so that all we have to cling to is the Lord Himself, so that every "prop" of self that we might be clinging to may be knocked away.

How true it is that that we never truly realise what the flesh is until we purpose to give Christ the ALONE place in our hearts.

(*A quotation by someone else now included in this letter*) – "If you want to have an easy path here, don't touch heavenly things".

(*AEW continues*) - There is nothing that Satan hates more than a heavenly man ... He has only two barrels to his gun, the first is – he will allure you, and if that does not do – he will crush you – if he can. For example, the children of the captivity – "If you won't eat the kings' meat I will throw you in the fire" (*a mixture of Daniel 1.3-16 and 3.6ff*) ... The same God is the God who can deliver us.

35bb/2 / 28ᵗʰ March 1935 / From the Newlands Valley –

May God speedily have mercy (*and*) bring us through into His large place (*Psalm 118.5*).

35bc/1 / 29ᵗʰ March 1935 / From the Newlands Valley –

God requires obedience in all things as ONLY thus can we be preserved from the wicked one who would appear to revenge all disobedience.

The Church, by its association with the world, has completely compromised its place as witness for Christ and is of course, as we know, rejected in that capacity. That which He (*Jesus*) has, step by step, made known to us constitutes HIS TESTIMONY ... This Testimony is one which could have been rendered by the saints, but they have been schooled by the adversary to distrust Scripture Chronology, refusing it any place whatsoever.

The Lord will call for repentance of a true order from all His children. Heaven will be before them and their path here known as closed, what an inducement to leave all and seek a low place. To remain "in" anything will be to take up a place of witness AGAINST Christ, but to go outside the camp will be to share His witness and testimony.

We await God's delivering hand in all spheres, in the meanwhile we are prisoners of the Lord for His testimony's sake.

With love unfeigned ... Affectly yours in Christ (*sic*), Arthur E Ware.

35bg/1 / 5ᵗʰ April 1935 / From the Newlands Valley –

... plans are no good unless originated in heaven ...

In prayer afterwards I took my stand in no uncertain manner for God's will in all things. I believe we may say and must say "the child, nay, the son, lives". Let us go in and take him up (*as in I Kings 17.22-23 and II Kings 4.35-36*).

35bh/1 / 7th April 1935 / AEW to one colleague, from the Newlands Valley -

(*Concerning this colleague who has sent a generous cheque from his own now-slender resources to the Company's "common purse". This touches on the whole matter of the group's finances, which at times caused friction. Here AEW gratefully acknowledges this sacrificial gift, and emphasises the Company's guiding principle of leaving all their financial needs "with the Lord". The alternative - to buckle under pressure of financial shortage and seek conventional employment - would damage the Testimony work and the core principles by which the Company operated*) -

... your action has but carried us further out yet into the deep waters where faith and faith only becomes the one resource for the children of God. The water we are all in is very deep and our bark (*sic*) very frail, and if viewed by the carnal mind of the average believer of today, we should be branded not only as foolish people but as wicked for embarking upon such a hazardous enterprise.

We have "drifted" into a place of NO resource SAVE THAT WHICH IS OURS IN THE LIVING GOD. Peril surrounds us on every hand, and few there be on earth who would do aught for us save to offer the advice that we return to being ordinary people, and, like all others of the Gentiles, seek after the means of subsistence and let our calling look after itself.

35bq/2 / 8th October 1935 / From Grasmere –

(*Concerning AEW being led to particular lodgings in Grasmere*) –

... a principle re God's guidance: namely that where past steps have been ordered by Him, future steps, that is any new step, will have a relation to what is passed, the whole forming a series of links in a chain and not a series of new beginnings.

35bv/3 / 16th October 1935 / From Grasmere –

(*Concerning weakness*) –

Our one qualification appears to be a true measure of known weakness – that is, before so great matters we feel we are nothing more than vessels of fragile clay.

Let us abide in this sense of known weakness, but ever recalling that weakness is no use to God unless there is the sense with it that His strength is made perfect in our weakness ...

(*God*) is going to make His voice heard above man's din, and that obtrusively or unobtrusively He is going to do mighty things in the company of the Elect, and also in the out-calling of multitudes from the world to Christ.

... a further stone in the temple of evidence.

35by/3 / 25th October 1935 / From Grasmere -

Yesterday I had to kneel down and claim the power of the precious blood to avail before the Throne, to free my mind from a confusion which I knew was demoniacal. Many times before in past years when pressing ahead it has been my only resource. I have wandered all over the place with figures and am now again getting au fait with nearly all the salient facts.

Yesterday, twice, "he bringeth them unto their desired haven" I took as a definite indication light was coming (*Psalm 107.30*), and I believe it is, and "by faith we understand" first, then with the intellect.

35bz/2 / 27th October 1935 / From Grasmere –

(*Concerning a possible return by AEW to the Keswick area*) –

Again, I feel we need to take into account that the Spirit takes account of places, and Keswick is a marked place for us and the whole Church. Here light has been given from the start of this matter, and every part of that district seems indelibly associated with this testimony in one form or another.

Anyway I dare not stay here without some form of confirmation, and I am g (*sic*) to Keswick this afternoon to test the weather out. If I move it will be tomorrow and then I shall have been 21 days here ... If Stxxxx is free (*a house where AEW had stayed before in the Newlands Valley*), I shall expect to go there, as in principle it is never well to move about – "there abide" is a word to be accepted (*from I Samuel 1.22*).

Satan has power to blind and this has to be feared by all – safety of course is in dependence upon God and danger lurks whenever there is independence and self-will.

(*AEW concerning a colleague meditating and praying while on a recent visit to AEW in the Lake District, he*) - "found himself in the presence of "Jesus only". We need both to watch for and take account of these mountain top experiences, for they have a meaning.

35cb/1 / 31st October 1935 / From the Newlands Valley –

We are the Lord's captives and He has told us to 'write the vision and make it plain' (*Habakkuk 2.2*), but as there is not much yet plain to us we cannot write so we are shut up.

... it is after or during such a struggle that the Spirit drops a word which clears many difficulties away.

35cf/1 / 3rd November 1935 / From the Newlands Valley –

I see clearly that the secret things are concealed, and what is concealed has to be revealed (by the Spirit) and cannot be reached by the long arm of the flesh, howsoever sharp the intellect that controls that arm.

... With the incoming of this light from heaven, <u>all</u> major difficulties fled like the darkness before the rising sun, and after all, the difficulties were much of our own imaginings, caused by jumping to conclusions which had no true foundation but which kept us in darkness.

I never liked the position (*over a recent detail that had caused confusion*) because the essence of all for us was that our Chronology was accurate having come from God and therefore must be astronomically correct.

(*Concerning AEW's belief, in view of the fresh light just granted to him, that the Lord was to return to remove His Church in June 1936, with clear indicators beforehand of what was about to happen. This is another good example of the intricacies of the sums and calendars in which they were involved*) –

... yet marvel of marvels in the mind of God the complete 50 days will witness the resurrection of Christ at the beginning, and the resurrection of the Church and translation of all at the end, just as if it were a consecutive 50 days which in one sense it really is, if you ignore the interval of 1900 years etc.

Surely this forms the top-stone of the Divine structure and perfects a plan which is the Logos of God, that is the Lord Jesus Christ in chronological expression – "according to a plan of the ages which He made in Christ Jesus our Lord" (*based on Ephesians 3.11*).

We now know all fits in astronomically and it only remains to take the completed structure and assign the relationship of vital events to days and new moons, and this can be done I think on the Julian scale, we allowing others to convert to Gregorian save that we for vital events could give both ...

It really appears that there will be no secret about what is going to happen and that it will become world-wide knowledge. Does it not say, "While they (*the foolish virgins, Matthew 25.10*) went to buy, the Bridegroom came"? Surely this infers that, while at the beginning, the testimony will reach the wise virgins, at the end, the foolish will get into a panic and stampede ...

... and (my) gratefulness to each dear brother since, like Aaron and Ur (*sic*, "Hur" in KJV, Exodus 17.12) with Moses, you have by your prayers and obedience to God's call upheld the weakest of outstretched arms which the forces of all hell have set themselves to oppose the light coming through.

My 30-day (*train*) ticket expires on the 6th Wed: but I have no light yet to go South even for a brief visit but I await any word of command.

35cj/2 / 12th November 1935 / From the Newlands Valley –

Pray on and be assured we are caught up into the understanding of things calculated to completely upset the set views of Christendom on this and that.

35ck/1 / 13th November 1935 / From the Newlands Valley –

(*Concerning the Gospel accounts of Jesus' death and resurrection*) –

The problem is a chronological one, and this means that what the Church has despised is the 'via media' of access to one of the most priceless truths concerning the Lord's death.

Apparently the matter is nearly solved (*by AEW*) but not quite, as everything has to be reconciled and this position is very trying ... meanwhile I can only labour to collect all data from Scripture. Much that has come is of the deepest interest, but the difficulty is to express it so that it is clear to oneself first, and then to others.

Greet dear brothers. I count on their prayers and the supply of the Spirit of Christ.

35cl/11 / 14th November 1935 / From the Newlands Valley –

Our object is to get the true pulse of the Lord's purpose regarding our "first day of the week" so that the true balance may be restored. I have no doubt that it is part of God's purpose to completely restore the Church to the right attitude on all such matters in coming months.

35cm/1 / 15th November 1935 / From the Newlands Valley –

(*Concerning their practical working methods*) –

One thing is vital, namely <u>never</u> to whittle down principles (*in the hope that*) by thus doing difficulties are removed. I like to segregate the points of difficulty and make them stand out naked before me and work from that point. Anything else is useless, because the more enlarged the difficulties become, the more likely you are to learn the Divine reason for the <u>apparent</u> discrepancy, at which point also new light will come in, which never would have been sought except for the difficulty.

... probably the secret lies in what is omitted from the narratives, more than in what is said.

Little did the Church know on June 12th (*1933*) how near Heaven was, and how few could look across and see its fair fields and golden courts.

(*Concerning the final details of the Cross timings*) –

... it has been kept back as most precious of all ... so that we may be full up to the brim when we move forward, strengthened by heavenly food of the choicest. The struggle is not over until this is given and I have been C.B. (*sic, meaning "confined to barracks"*) for many days and shall be until opposition is shattered and we – the Church – possesses (*sic*) the truth as to the death of Jesus, and with it confound every tongue raised against the Truth.

35cn/4 / 22nd November 1935 / From the Newlands Valley –

When the Lord returns to complete His resurrection ministry the Roman Empire must have been formed again by then because: it must be so as all must be back where He left it in AD 33 ... we cannot be guided by the recurrence of dates but only by the Spirit.

35cw/6 / 28th November 1935 / From the Newlands Valley –

... because I see that God would offer no solution to be accepted by men if such called for studious explanations as to various Scriptures and their meanings.

In general Scripture must mean what the words would imply to any ordinary person and should need no explanation.

As in this case something may be concealed, but when the explanation is forthcoming, the words are still found to mean what they say.

God asks no one to tell somebody else what He means when He speaks, because He means what He says, and our difficulties are endless if we try to make what He says mean what He does not say.

35db2 / 20th December 1935 / From the Newlands Valley –

(*Concerning the need for 100% accuracy in their figures*) –

… and one wrong makes all wrong.

35dc/2 / 26th December 1935 / From the Newlands Valley –

What I mean plainly is that the unseen powers of darkness, when you are <u>all</u> found together in the path of obedience to God's will with prayers and devotional exercises, are ceaselessly challenged and by some mysterious way which is not easy to explain, God is enabled thereby to grant me the light and understanding of hidden things which go to form the Testimony of the Lord in this hour, both for the Church and the world.

This fact in itself proves how genuine is our unity, that is, you five brethren there and myself here are in God's sight, one, even as God and Christ are one.

(*Concerning the attacks of Satan and the need to remain diligent*) –

<u>On guard</u> we should say, Is this from the Lord? and if so, Where does He benefit and where are His interests advanced? or, Is this required of me because a call of duty in fulfilling a responsibility that otherwise would bring dishonour? or, Does this suggested plan appeal to me as a

legitimate means of respite from bearing the cross He has given me to bear?

For any of us to appear able to be free to spend time with relations other than the vital duty call, is to announce that we have no serious business in hand and are really only whiling away our time; and when the Testimony goes forth it would appear to be such as has been obtained with ease.

Let us remember the Testimony has not gone forth, and that every power opposed to Christ in and out of hell will be in energy to hinder it, and the form the hindrance will take is specious wiles played upon each of us, so that if it be not me who is hindering it will be another.

... our only resource is to trust to Christian abject dependence that we are kept by Him who has Himself experienced every wile of the devil. The wiles usually will find entrance through some unmortified desire or allowed indulgence known to Satan, and upon which he will trade.

... and how often indeed we have to confess to moving a plan, ordered or allowed of God, by acting too soon and really in verily taking before the time that which, had we waited, the Lord would have put in our hands, and with it the blessing of His presence which, by grasping, we have had to forfeit.

The making of plans is an evil thing and utterly hinders the Spirit's guidance at the time, and not only so, but when the plan is one of movement, for a considerable while before it is carried out, the heart is so directed that all else is really shut out and the devil uses it accordingly. As servants of God we can have no plans as we are under orders from Another, Who never gives advice until the time to act comes.

1936

36dl/3 / 17th January 1936 / From the Newlands Valley –

(*Some words of the Archbishop of Canterbury concerning the late King George V, quoted here by AEW*) –

"The use of the name of God in public utterances was, I know, for him (*that is, the late King*) no mere convention, but the expression of a simple, reverent, and deep sense of his own responsibility to God".

... I feel God would have us armed with finality so that we are <u>ready</u> for any call.

36dq/2 / 22nd January 1936 / From the Newlands Valley –

Tomorrow I shall have completed 40 days in the mountains and unless I am clearly checked I shall come South in a day or so ...

... but by God's grace we shall soon see the name of Jesus exalted on the pinnacle of our chronological Everest, and these last steps may be steep and trying but we can abjure feelings and find strength in beholding the vast stretch covered, and in the joy of presently standing with Christ on the top of the plan of the ages, every detail translucent with Divine glory, and withal a weapon which in the hands of the Spirit will carry all before it.

36ds/3 / 29th January 1936 / From the Newlands Valley –

(*Concerning the "Seven Times" of Daniel Chapter 4, AEW here rebuffs some recent criticism of their findings made from a Christian organisation*) –

... he (*Mr Xxxxx*) threw overboard his former faith in the Seven Times, which was God's one sure and certain means to guide the Church as to what He was doing, and by it He guided us.

As usual they had a slam at date fixing in the usually hypocritical and pharisaical tone. I note also the great measure of self-congratulation they indulge in. The speakers and hearers are just like directors and shareholders of a very successful concern when they meet at the annual meeting to declare higher dividends – everyone is pleased and smiling.

Did they but know it, they are getting their dividends now by all this self-congratulation – later they will know at what fearful loss to Christ they were trading.

36du/1 / 31st January 1936 / From the Newlands Valley –

Concentration on God is our all-round need now.

36dw/1 / 31st January 1936 / From one of the most spiritually-senior members of the Company, based in Eastbourne, writing to his own mother in Essex, a supporter of their work herself –

How I dare do it (*put self in prayer before God's interests*) ... is only accounted for by the fact that we are worms eaten up with self-interest of one kind or another. We follow One Who never thought of Himself ONCE, and I had to plead that never again on earth, in the face of the dire plight of untold millions of lost souls, might I speak or think of myself in God's presence, or anyone else's for that matter.

... <u>Satan ruins us by getting us occupied beyond our own spiritual needs</u>.

... Not one of us will be fit to stand before the saints or sinners until we have forever <u>forgotten</u> ourselves.

"O bliss to leave behind us the fetters of the slave,
To leave OURSELVES behind us, the grave clothes and the grave!"

... I believe we have been damnably (destructively) self-occupied in the past. You may pray this for me, for I know until I forget SELF, even self-appreciation or self-depreciation, there can be no real pouring out on behalf of the World's needs or the Church.

Let us all pray that we may be marked by an entire absence of self-interest or occupation, and then the Holy Ghost must rush in with Christ's interests and power.

36ea/4 / 4th February 1936 / From the Newlands Valley –

I have to abjure finality everywhere and always have done, because I realise that finality is impossible until the last piece is fitted in.

... Much love, dear brethren. Calvary is victory over all fleshly thoughts and makes way for Divine life and revelation. May this be our position.

Yours as ever, A E Ware.

36ec/1 / 5th February 1936 / From the Newlands Valley –

(*Concerning previous opposition and difficulties*) –

I could do nothing because of a confused mind and a sort of effort to compete with the clock.

... I saw quickly that the enemy had sought to drown me in the detail with its many perplexities, leaving me unable to get the spiritual perspective.

36ef/2 / 10th February 1936 / From the Newlands Valley –

... upon the 50-cubit gallows (*Esther 5.14 and 7.9-10*) upon which presently he (*Satan*) will be strung up and exposed as the one who fixed in the people of God the aversion to dates.

36eo/2 / 20th April 1936 / A colleague in Eastbourne to a colleague in Essex -

God's invariable habit is to upset human calculations, and if we thought there would be a steady flow of ink these days we have had to accept otherwise, but are fully confident that "not one thing shall fail" (*from Isaiah 34.16*) of the Divine purpose as to the time of the publication of the facts ...

36es/2 / 26th April 1936 / From Derwentwater Hotel, Keswick –

... and God is the Master of symbols ...

36fg/3 / 29th May 1936 / From the Newlands Valley –

God is never in a hurry …

36fn/2/ 4th June 1936 / From a colleague in Eastbourne, to AEW in the Newlands Valley –

(*Quoting from Oswald Chambers*) – ""I will never leave thee nor forsake …" – am I learning to say not what God says, but to say something after I have heard what He says?".

It is not a question of whether we are conscious of a "good" time of prayer, but of believing that we have been heard, so it seems, and believing that the "availing" will be effective with you (*that is, AEW*) who has to labour alone.

36fx/4 / 14th June 1936 / From Portinscale, Keswick –

(*Concerning AEW getting an unexpected lift by car from a couple who turned out to be very interested in the Testimony*) –

It all seemed a provision.

36gb/2 / 18th June 1936 / From Portinscale, Keswick –

All is blessedly clear and in accord with Scripture … all has fallen out to give us mastery over the figures up to the Exodus.

36gk/2 / 14th August 1936 / From Patterdale, Ullswater

(*Concerning a shortage of funds*) –

It is a position allowed and one to be bowed to, and for the moment we can only wait until relief comes …

36gn/2 / 9th December 1936 / From Easedale House, Keswick -

… that God is our sufficiency whether for power, guidance or temporal needs, and He will not fail where the Glory of Christ is concerned.

36gp / 11th December 1936 / From lodgings just returned to in the Newlands Valley –

I am deeply thankful to be settled again and in isolation after about 6 months of wool gathering. My weakness demands isolation if I am to get concentrated thought.

36gu/2 / 21st December 1936 / From the Newlands Valley –

(*After the abdication of King Edward VIII*) –

Protestantism is but a damnable system set up by men and now corrupt to the core, but the Reformation from which it sprang was God's act …

36gv/1 / 24th December 1936 / To a colleague at Birling Gap –

(*In their newly-established understanding that 25th December has nothing to do with the birth of Jesus Christ*) –

With love and thanks to you all but no happy Xmas!

(*In pencil on the back concerning 'Christmas', in another's hand*) –

… (*Christmas*) has been harnessed to the devil's chariot …

36gx/1 / 30 December 1936 / From the Newlands Valley –

(*Some frustration that some biblical dates are yet to be finalised*) –

This (*delay*) seems to have been part of the Divine plan to keep all in such a state that finality could not be reached until finality was demanded … I think God takes little account of Parliaments (*that is, greater divine account is taken of individual rulers themselves, especially monarchs; written in the wake of the recent abdication*).

CHAPTER 3
1937 -1938

1937

371/1 / 1ˢᵗ January 1937 / From the Newlands Valley –

You will rejoice to know that at last the iron-barred gate to understanding the Flood dates has given way at the command of heaven and we are now in possession of the needed light to fix every point in the Chronology to the Exodus.

These difficulties are the Divine way of forcing one to learn something without which it is impossible to get perfect accuracy.

375/2 / 2ⁿᵈ January 1937 / From the Newlands Valley –

(*To some of the group, concerning another of their number who has just installed a wireless at his home*) -

I seek to be patient in this matter but the hour is late for discussion as to whether the wireless brings in the spirit that is of Christ or that of the world and its prince of the powers of the air.

I have long since been satisfied that it is a shame to a Christian to have a wireless ...

I have felt assured that it is a satanic device to soothe the nerves of the myriads of earth with jollity, music and a bloodless religion so that the disturbances God has allowed to visit the earth, to awaken near to the coming of the great and terrible day of the Lord with all its fearful destructions, may be offset by the ability to turn a handle and obtain that which would get the mind occupied and leave the conscience at rest. The wireless is of the world and the world lieth in the wicked one.

3711 / 16th January 1937 / From the Newlands Valley –

A will, crushed by the sheer weight of the cross of Jesus, is to God priceless.

3714/4 / 22nd January 1937 / From the Newlands Valley –

The question is not what is your opinion or mine, but what facts do the Scriptures reveal? - seeing that those facts and nothing less are Truth ... Does God ever give Sacred figures on the surface? Does He not always give secular time, from which by deduction on moral grounds the sacred is obtained? ...

The flood is an epoch heavily scored and underlined by God, and at the flood there is a break in Time and a new start as at the Exodus, and it is this which is concealed and which had kept away any from measuring time to the Exodus except superficially.

... but we have got to let all such things be determined by God and only trace the copy He has given, ever seeking to make the recorded facts direct and not our minds (*direct*), which get filled with casual notions of what ought to be.

... for only by learning what is not can you learn what is ...

3715/2 / 21st February 1937 / From Poste Restante, Keswick –

(*Concerning a change of where AEW is able to live*) –

The change has been a rather unwelcome test but I took it at once as being from Above.

3716/2 / 23rd February 1937 / From a different address in the Newlands Valley –

We are only "the light of the world" (*Matthew 5.14a*) in so far as we are allowing the One Who said, "I am the light of the world" (*John 8.12*) to shine through us, and this we know takes some doing because our evil natures so easily besmirch any reflection we receive of heavenly light.

3718/5 / 24th February 1937 / From the Newlands Valley –

Are you getting through in your intercession seasons? I find a great need to take the Kingdom by force – a grain of apathy produces DEATH.

3721/1 / 1st March 1937 / From the Newlands Valley –

... as I am sure the Spirit honours order, while not being bound.

If there is not order there is disorder. I think in terms of order specially when there is nothing gained by it not being so; as when a settled plan is possible, which is not always.

Real prayer is at all times difficult I believe, and calls first for faith and then determination. Without faith being active, prayer is deprived of all driving force, and is usually from the head and tends to be lengthy and deadening and guaranteed to make it more difficult for others, and to make it more difficult to come together again. A suitable Scripture, which brings out the power or willingness of God to answer prayer and to scatter His adversaries, will often beget a living faith because the Word is a living Word.

It is the purpose of Satan to weaken faith and this he does; but this can be met more easily (since we have the Blood) than a faith weakened by personal causes, such as failure of one kind or another in keeping in communion with God.

3723/9 / 10th March 1937 / From the Newlands Valley –

(Concerning AEW's recent discovery of the Moon now being two days behind its former timing position) –

... and at that moment for the first time in history the creature saw the work of the Creator in exactitude.

God has no place for the flesh – He will not work with it – circumcision hurts.

3724/4 / 12th March 1937 / From the Newlands Valley –

(*Concerning the New Testament practice of baptism in the Name of the Lord, and not in the Name of the full Trinity – see for example Acts 2.38, 8.16, 10.48, 19.5 / Romans 6.3 / Galatians 3.27*) –

... and baptism in the Name of the Lord held no doubt the secret of power in the first days – identification with Christ brought manifestation of favour.

3727/2 / 7th April 1937 / From the Newlands Valley –

At the beginning faith laid hold of His Resurrection, now it must lay hold of His Return.

3733/8 / 8th April 1937 / From the Newlands Valley –

... but we have to do with a God who thrice has caused the great lights of heaven to obey His will (and is going to again, see Zech(*ariah*) 14).

3736/13 / 12th April 1937 / From the Newlands Valley –

Christ is in nothing that terminates with DEATH.

3741/1 19th April 1937 / From the Newlands Valley –

I am going for a trip up Skiddaw as it appears fine and I feel a measure of call.

3746/4 / 26th April 1937 / From the Newlands Valley –

It is easy to seek to bind God to a path which we discern as from the Word, and yet to find it not so.

... and we need not to be devotees of too set views or traditions on prophecy, yet God forbid that we should be as Mr W Hxxxx who in (*the*) enclosed article on 'Life of Faith' (*a Christian magazine*) suggests we should know nothing as a certainty.

3749/1 / 26th April 1937 / From the Newlands Valley, to one of the Company whose family members have just disowned him because of his involvement with this work –

One never knows with God how things are going to fall, and it is for us just now to be as the servant who watches the hand of his master. A crisis in the world's history has arisen, and God has in grace taken us all up so that, at His moment, He may bring us forward to show He left not Himself without witness.

3750/ 28th April 1937 / From the Newlands Valley –

God is a God of surprises. Never have we felt so secure in God as to our position.

3762/4 / 9th June 1937 / From Portcotham in Cornwall –

(*AEW feeling rather low*) –

Work is a blessed remedy for many spiritual ills.

3763/1 / 11th June 1937 / From Portcotham –

(*A reference to the chronological significance of June 12th 1933*) -

... at the turn of the year tomorrow, June 12th ...

Once a son always a son, but what a difference between the right to be called so and the qualification by conduct.

3764/4 / 14th June 1937 / From Portcotham –

(*Concerning a criticism of "the Seven Times" in an article in a Christian magazine, written by a longstanding opponent*) –

... about the Seven Times, and that it is now a proven truth which came forth from God and forms a vital part of the Written Word of God ... he (*their opponent*) should yet be allowed to maraud about, assailing the truth and all who stand or did stand for it.

Does it not prove that God has allowed Satan to blind the minds of them that have not believed it, and that they must remain in darkness until that day when it shall please God to allow them to partake of the mercy He has shown us?

(*Concerning AEW getting down to making some background notes*) –

... and once a good start is made I shall look for grace to get down to a steady gait daily.

... Allow me to say I take nothing for granted and still watch as to the purpose of my being here – my mind open and, I trust, my heart for guidance or light as to any step.

As brother Bxxxx says – May we discipline ourselves so as to be delivered from mental wool-gathering – a thing I find I also have to fight, since it produces in one the very quintessence of spiritual incompetence.

3765/4 / 16th June 1937 / From Portcotham –

(*Concerning their longing and waiting*) –

... but one day soon there will be a change – perhaps very sudden, and all streams will begin to run with the prophetic mould while to-day they appear to run anywhere but that.

... I seek to go quietly, not forcing things in setting my own programme but seeking to occupy daily with what comes before me, and I think that some light may come as to how and when God purposes the Testimony to go out.

3767/5 / 22nd June 1937 / From Portcotham -

(*Concerning their all being together around Eastbourne with AEW alone in Cornwall*) –

… that this may effect a change this end – you receiving grace to prevail in prayer, and I receiving grace to overcome self and Satan and all else that exists to contest the completion of this great weapon, for the overthrow of everything which would hinder God's will at the end of the age.

3775/4 / 13th October 1937 / From the Newlands Valley –

(*As the Testimony goes forth*) – over the earth, exposing all the fearful haunts of evil in religious and political Christendom, and offering, in the light of the fullest revelation ever accorded the sons of Adam, a last hope of Salvation through the efficacy of His one perfect sacrifice and oblation which God has accepted for the sins of men.

(*Concerning the differences in their knowledge and understanding between November 1932 and now in October 1937*) -

Every vital doctrine of Scripture is now substantiated by Chronology, and TRUTH is now seen to be held together by a vital structure of dates, in the which, if there were to be found one error, the whole structure and the truth which it supports would be found to be at fault, and therefore unworthy of the barest consideration at the hands of men.

… The troubler is at work (*Mussolini*) – strengthened by his erstwhile supporter in Germany. He mocks England and petrifies France.

(*Concerning the need for concentration without disturbance when grappling with a difficulty, the seeker*) – is more likely to obtain help by meditation more than discussion … Often the difficulty is seen to be a new entrance into light.

3777/8 / 18th October 1937 / From the Newlands Valley –

(*Concerning other Christian writers*) –

Such have never understood that knowledge is a first fruit of separation to Jesus as in John 15.15, and that without this we must draw from our own wells, which always yield impure water and not "the water of life".

3779/3 / 22ⁿᵈ October 1937 / From the Newlands Valley –

... it was ground (*that is, looking solid enough*) but we must have Scripture and not conjecture.

(*Concerning Samson*) – a figure of the Church having lost its true Nazarite position of separation ... (*Numbers Chapter 6*)

The House (*that is, a private home*) is every corporate expression of Christianity on earth ...

3781/12 / 27ᵗʰ October 1937 / From the Newlands Valley –

(*Concerning their financial needs and their general hopes*) –

However faith can wait and trust and not build an edifice in signs – nevertheless these (*signs*) *are* to find a place, even if only a pigeon hole in the heart.

3782/3 / 28ᵗʰ October 1937 / From the Newlands Valley –

... but we must be careful not to force the pace – the Spirit is sovereign and He only can give Light.

3786/1 / 2ⁿᵈ November 1937 / From the Newlands Valley –

... but we do wish to know the mind of God and the way wherein He would have us to set our feet.

... The Chart is a true representation, but "no part dark" (*Luke 11*.36) is our hearts desire and if any adjustment is needed we shall be shown ...

(*Concerning Jesus and the Jews' Sabbaths*) –

I doubt not His principle was to walk in wisdom to them that are without, but when only His disciples were concerned, who knew the facts, He would not hesitate to treat the Jews' Sabbath as an ordinary day, providing He knew no-one could be stumbled by it.

Our own position about Christendom's Sunday is the same, for if we donned flannels and a sports jacket on Sunday we should stumble many who are weak in the faith (*from Romans 14.21*).

... We are not I feel called upon to piece together the story of the Lord's life, but only to see that the dates learnt do not conflict with the stated facts of the gospels.

3787/2 / 5th November 1937 / From the Newlands Valley –

How good it is for our feeble and treacherous minds to keep restating these great facts, until we know them as we know one another's names.

(*Against the enemy*) - I took a bit of a stand that God is never in a hurry and He does not wish us to be (*either*) except in rare circumstances.

... and all who have faith will find it adequate to rest their feet on ...

... What saith the Scripture? ...

(*Concerning a sense they have of the need for imminent public action, five years after their actions of November 1932*) –

You now know the great question before us, not, Are we to act? but, How are we to act? I look for an incoming of light speedily.

The unconverted possess experts in Chronology and "theology", but how to approach them is a question. One thing is certain – we shall need to write soon to the Archbishop (*of Canterbury, with whom they have been in contact previously*) as we are not keeping our contract – if we change our policy, courtesy demands we advise him. I am inclined to think God intends to stir the Protestant bodies, unless Christendom is really all who would be reached through the Press.

... Let us watch our steps in the coming few days – let confident prayer go up – let the Glory of the Lord in it all be upon our hearts and let us ever say, "Lord, it is Thy business not ours" – we are friends of the Bridegroom. In more ways than one God will have to show His power before we go forward.

3790/2 / 7th November 1937 / From the Newlands Valley –

(*Concerning publicity plans for 25th November 1937, in view of their certainty of Christ's return in June 1938*) –

We are to call a meeting in London, at a place to be decided, on November 25th – a notice of this meeting and its purpose - the reading of a paper revealing the course of Time from Creation and the facts of the Lord's life (all carefully set forth) will be sent to every newspaper, home and foreign, to the heads of all Christian denominations, all universities and all learned societies. Tickets will be offered or enclosed.

Every attendee will have a copy of the new Chart which he will hold and follow as the paper is read, and all newspapers after the meeting will be at liberty to publish the facts – chart and all.

The facts are so dramatically vital to the world that they will surely tell them out. Before, copies of the new chart will be sent in sealed envelopes to other countries so that they may be published with the Nov 25th address which will deal exclusively with the time question and provide the world with proof. Ten days after, on Sunday December 5th a further paper will be read, telling further what the facts mean and formally announcing Christ's return next June 12 and setting forth what it means for the nations, Israel and the Church. Time forbids giving the copious detail which has passed before me.

3791/4 / 8th November 1937 / From the Newlands Valley –

May God get His way with us all and direct our steps that we falter not.

3792/3 / 10th November 1937 / From the Newlands Valley –

(*Concerning the enemy*) - but then I saw that the Lord at the cross had spiked the enemy's guns so that when they fire they only emit smoke, he has no cannon ball to hit with or shells.

He (*Satan*) takes good care however to bring his guns up at the appropriate moment and the discharge of smoke is disconcerting, but if we wait the wind of the Spirit drives it away, but we have to take care we do wait or the smoke will drive us away, which is what it is intended to do.

Let us make no mistake, dear friends, the enemy is not one to forget or minimize, his power is frightful and actual when he finds us engaged on something which is of darkness (*that is, so challenging to, and destroying of, the darkness*). I shall never forget the experience … before the first Lyceum meeting (*that is, of intense spiritual opposition before one of their public meetings held in London in May 1933*).

(*In late November 1937 the Company called a public meeting in London, followed in early December 1937 by their sending letters to the King, to many religious and political leaders, and to newspapers, in which they announced the expected return of the Lord in June 1938.*

There was very little response from the recipients of these letters, either positively or negatively, which not surprisingly caused further soul-searching among the members of the Company in the weeks and months that followed).

1938

3811/11 / 11th February 1938 / From the Newlands Valley –

I trust to hear things at your end are in the way of a true advance, and that your prayers are availing before the throne, as indeed they must if offered in the name of the Lord Jesus Christ …

I am by no means insensible that I am gaining by your prayers. I feel our need one and all is to stand steadfast and give no ground to the flesh or Satan. Agag must die (*I Samuel Chapter 15*).

3812/5 / 16th February 1938 / To a generous supporter of the work,

from the Newlands Valley –

... God has shown us that we are just ordinary people and that we have to deal with the ordinary affairs of this life while giving ourselves to the great issues which ever confront us ...

... None of us knows why God chose us, but all of us know He did choose us. Mrs Xxxxx (*another keen supporter*) knows very little about the dates, and will probably have to wait until the Glory to find time to go into them all and behold the wonders of God, but she walks with the One who the dates are all about, and her heart finds rest in Him and not in understanding the dates.

I don't know if you have prayer together when she visits you, but it would be a source of strength to you both.

3815/6 / 18th February 1938 / From the Newlands Valley –

May God keep a firm hand over us all, for this is no day to be beating the air or following our own wills.

3816/2 / 22nd February 1938 / From the Newlands Valley –

Find a place in your prayers personal or collective for our brother ...

3817/4 / 23rd February 1938 / From the Newlands Valley –

The figures will be used to CONVICT the Church as to what God gave in His Word, and to CONVINCE Israel as to its position and the wonder of God's ways.

I have a head and am going for a sharp walk before tea and to post this. With hearty greetings and love to each.

Yours as ever, Arthur E Ware.

3819/2 / 1st March 1938 / From the Newlands Valley –

We have waited long, dear friends, but there must be A DAY when God will do His part which is THE GREAT PART: His part is to make a way for the testimony to be listened to.

We have a right to pray that we may not be taken unawares by anything God may do, and this in view of Isaiah 45.11 and Amos 3.7 specially.

(*Concerning some pressures from people outside their group*) –

… for long I have felt Satan is challenging us through the will of others …

… I am anxious to clearly see my own path. My ticket expires on Sat (*AEW's return train ticket to Eastbourne*), but that is not altogether guidance.

3822/1 / 6th March 1938 / From the Newlands Valley –

The enemy's purpose is always to move the feet of the saints – feet which dare not move except at the bidding of the One who knows the end from the beginning – the Alpha and the Omega.

He (*the devil*) sought to move the feet of the Lord in the temptation in the wilderness, but failed miserably. Nevertheless the conflict, to drive saints off ground taken in the heavenlies, is real conflict, and we ever have to come back to that first word – "the gates of hell shall not prevail against it" (*Matthew 16.18b*) – against what – against an ecclesia founded upon a Rock and that Rock the name of the Son of God. What the Ark was to Israel in the wilderness so that Name is to us – to the Church.

We are never given encouragement to trust God except that which flows from a knowledge of Himself and His character. Heaven offers no sympathy for anyone who finds it difficult to trust God, as that would be to slander the One who dwells there.

The greater the test of obedience, and the longer you are kept waiting for God to justify the trust you place in Him, the greater He is glorified and the greater His Word magnified.

(*We are including here another example of their being still convinced, on scriptural grounds as far as they were concerned, of the imminent return of Christ for His church, in this case, in June 1938. As we learn in these pages of these faithful men and their work, we have to take on board their recurrent, mistaken expectations in this matter of Christ's return, (caused mainly by their tendency to misinterpret scriptural "types" in the light of current events in the world at that time). These mistakes of course led to ostracism and ridicule, yet they sit alongside the men's undoubted spiritual integrity and maturity which we see being displayed in these extracts in so many other ways)* -

... not, dare we trust them (*the Scriptures*), but, dare we not trust them?

Perhaps we have put our own interpretation(s) on these and will find we are wrong? To suggest this is to say we either have amazing self-confidence and must be allowed to exhibit our folly, or that the Holy Ghost cannot be trusted to guide into all truth (which could be blasphemy). (*With the benefit of hindsight, we have to go courteously with the first of these two alternatives ...*).

... but living and acting in anticipation of our impending translation – knowing the time has come according to the Scriptures. This is faith, and everything else is make-believe and will come out in the wash of adverse circumstances.

3824/6 / 10th March 1938 / From the Newlands Valley –

As far as I can see the figures dovetail in perfectly everywhere and we can rejoice together in this exquisite display of Divine time keeping.

(*Concerning their funds being low – perhaps a clear warning sign from the Lord that they should "steady on" over the imminence of "the rapture"? But we can see why they might take this situation the other way: they would be "gone" in a few months, so this temporary shortage of funds was hardly significant*) –

I can hardly stay up here when I am going into debt. I mean our resources are now nil ... If our resources are at an end let us tell our Father so – we cannot serve Him and not pay our way.

3825/9 / 11th March 1938 / From the Newlands Valley –

(*Concerning prayer together*) – No doubt it is the undeviating concentration which tells in heaven, for at such time the flesh simply pants for a respite which, if indulged, dissipates all that we have done or nearly so.

"Could ye not watch with me one hour?" is a hard word to the flesh (*Matthew 26.40*).

3826/4 / 14th March 1938 / From the Newlands Valley –

(*Eight days after his letter of 6th March (3822, see above), AEW is now conscious of some "divine brakes" being applied regarding November 1937 and since, until the right time has come in God's sight for the Testimony to be published*) –

I was thinking yesterday how amazing it is that NEVER once, anywhere with anybody, have we ever been taken the remotest account of.

(*All the people they approached in December 1937*) – apart from clerics, sent to on Dec 4th, all with one consent ignore the whole matter. Why is this?

Have we ever fully realized why God allowed or even caused us to make such apparent fools of ourselves in 1933? My own position today everywhere amongst saints and sinners is that I am branded, apparently with the very best of reasons, as a false prophet who ran unsent, and as such I deserve the ignominy and contempt of all lovers of truth. I fancy it was this that kept all away on November 25th (*in 1937*) – the (*news*)papers thought I had hatched out an excuse for 1933.

In plain language it is evident that God intended to close our lips (*in November 1937*) and no effort to disseminate the light given has the remotest effect. There must be a very positive reason for this action.

... I believe God will not allow a vestige of light we possess to reach the saints until they are ready to GO OUT to meet the Lord. Look at our position - FAR OFF outside the camp (*Exodus 19.17*). Why are we there? - because it is there that we found the Lord whom we serve.

... The saints have got to break ALL present associations and join us far off outside the camp. The Ark we bear is the Name of the Lord, and God can know NO gathering of saints except where He has set that Name, and where two or three are gathered together in that Name, the Lord is there.

... All this leads me to realize that God has really made it impossible for us to do anything, because He has a moment and a plan He will carry out.

3827/6 / 16th March 1938 / From the Newlands Valley –

You, dear friends, will be powerfully holding the ground against the forces of darkness that are evidently utterly opposed to any sending forth of God's marvellous truth into the earth.

3829/4 / 31st May 1938 / From Seascale on the Cumbrian coast –

(*Concerning the "ecclesiastics" who receive here strong criticism*) –

They are a haughty lot and God says they belong to Satan's synagogue ... they are God's greatest enemies on earth and we need have no fear of them or what they shall say against us ... (*Here AEW is likening the "ecclesiastics" of his own day to the "Nicolaitans", a self-important, heretical sect present in the churches at Ephesus and Pergamos, Revelation 2.6 & 15. While Pergamos is described as the place where Satan sits and dwells (2.13), those "of Satan's synagogue" are actually false Jews who are mentioned in the messages to the churches at Smyrna and Philadelphia (2.9 & 3.9), so AEW is slightly inaccurate here. His message is clear though – he is no great fan of "ecclesiastics"!*).

... Perhaps the desire to write (*by AEW*) is of the flesh and to justify ourselves.

... I doubt if we are to cast further pearls before swine or sacred things to dogs. These men care not a whit for Divine truth but to uphold their systems from whence they extract an unhallowed sustenance.

... Light is very precious in days of darkness such as we have been in, and what was given left the whole structure so far given to us of God, unimpaired.

<u>Never</u> have we had to go back and undo what we had received from God, and always have we found new light endorsed the past and <u>led on in a direct line</u>.

3830/3 / 1st June 1938 / From Seascale –

We ... need to be patient and must take care not to try to force an interpretation because here the sovereignty of the Spirit as to the suited moment for giving light on a passage <u>which affects our future actions</u> must be bowed to.

To seek light before the time will either open the door to Satan to afford a false interpretation, or if not this, to cause a sense of defeat and loss of communion.

(*Concerning when the manna ceased*) - As so often in Scripture we find a principle in this passage (*Exodus 16*) which is the first to speak of manna the starting and ending points of its employment in Israel.

I mean that often Scripture, when first mentioning a matter, also gives the limits chronologically of its start and finish, as for instance in the case of Kings coming to the throne to the total length of reign is also given.

... it would be disastrous to make Scripture unsay what its simple reading implies. In principle it is dangerous to touch the translation (*of any biblical text*) unless proper authorities <u>in sufficient numbers</u> are agreed that the original autographs warrant it, as frequently is the case.

3833/8 / 9th June 1938 / From the Newlands Valley once again –

More and more in measuring Sacred Chronology we are taught how God uses time to express Himself on moral issues.

... and trusting our way may soon be filled with laughter and our lips with praise.

We are hedged about by lack of funds and unless there is a release I could not bide long up here to carry on writing.

3835/13 / 12th June 1938 / From the Newlands Valley –

(*This is written 5 years to the day since the opening of the WMEC in London, a date regarded by the Company each year as very significant*) -

I feel what has come through is very important and glory always seems to encircle light ... The ark always goes first, borne by Levites who as Numbers VIII shows, are given as a wave offering to God.

... May the Lord keep us steadfast and unmoveable, seeing we know our labour is not in vain in the Lord (*I Corinthians 15.58*).

3837/2 / 15th June 1938 / From the Newlands Valley –

(*This extract is included at some length as it states very clearly the Company's reaction to the rejection of the testimony in June 1933*) -

Someone said you had some helpful thoughts on Judges XIX a day or two back – Cash up, Gentlemen, please! we are "share-ists" (*that is, any new light granted to an individual is to be shared among all the Company members*).

Many believers never quit the world and its religious systems. The Jordan is to a believer who, going ahead of his fellows, desires to live and walk by faith, the gateway into union with Christ in the heavenlies where he now is seated triumphant ... adopting the death of Christ as his own death – death in such a case being viewed as the end of life – Adam life.

Jordan is therefore the gateway to Heaven or hell. Jordan is death as the end of life for the wicked, but is death – a defeated and conquered foe, to the righteous – a veritable gateway into Paradise.

There is no heaven without a Jordan – a Jordan that has been crossed once and for all by the Lord Himself but which every saint has to pass through in order to learn that Christ has passed thro' for him. Departed saints reached its banks and found the water gone.

Up to June 12 1933 the Assembly (*that is, the visible church on earth*) was, as we know, the official vehicle on earth for bearing the Ark of testimony and <u>always somewhere</u> in the Assembly was the ark to be found.

After that day the Assembly as the official witness for Christ and bearer of the Ark was rejected or spued out. We ... had borne in the last 200 days of the Assembly's history as a witness, a special message from Christ to His Church – it was an overture or approach concerning His return. This overture and the messengers were flatly rejected.

The Assembly knew not a Christ who fixed dates but they did know of a devil who did (*know such a Christ*), and anyone who fixed dates must be an emissary of the devil and not of Christ. We now know the message was from the Lord and that He it was who was giving a 40-day intimation to the nations of their excision.

Rejected as to our message and our persons by the whole assembly of Christian synagogues – condemned in scathing terms ("avoid this date fixer like the plague" etc) we found ourselves pitchforked far off outside the odious camp, called Christendom.

Did the Lord endorse Christendom's action? No, indeed He flashed out His flaming sword and taking the insult to Himself He brought down that sword for the first time for 1900 years and cut off the Assembly of Christendom as His witness on earth. He had given warning by Paul at the beginning (*eg., Romans 11*) and later by John in Revelation III, that He would do so if occasion arose.

Did He leave us to redeem our own characters or to go on bended knees to our castigators? ... By no means, but rather "If thou take forth the precious from the vile, thou shalt be as my mouth; LET THEM RETURN UNTO THEE; BUT RETURN NOT THOU UNTO THEM (Jeremiah XV) *(v 19b)*.

From July 6th 1933 up to the present time it has pleased the Lord to cause His Spirit to build up in this rejected company a testimony the like of which it has been the portion for few mortals since Adam to possess. In other words, the Ark of the Testimony must be somewhere, and if the Assembly is rejected, it shall be in the house of those the assembly rejects – far off outside the camp of religious Christendom.

Now it is clear that at the end the ark of testimony, borne by some who keep the Word of the Lord and do not deny His Name, must at the appointed chronological moment fulfil anti-typically what we get in Joshua as to the people of Israel and the Ark crossing Jordan. Keeping the word of the Lord with such would imply an absolutely accurate and Spirit-taught knowledge of the times and seasons as found in Scripture, or in other words an intimate knowledge of dates in Scripture.

3839/1 / 20th June 1938 / From the Newlands Valley –

… there seemed to be a need (*in AEW's mind*) to take up a less determined attitude to satisfy the cravings of the mind for instant ability to interpret, and confirm <u>by reasoning,</u> what had come and been presented as light from God.

Reasoning leads to darkness but a worshipper at the feet of Jesus is one to whom the Spirit can reveal all things including the difficulties that reasoning creates … If I can only accept as light from God what my reason can in detail explain, then it will not be in this life that I need expect light from God because reason is not faith: and God never panders to reason.

… now the haughty clerics have sealed their doom by rejecting the most precious light given since the first century.

3844/1 / 21st December 1938 / From Alma Square, London NW8, to a colleague –

I mean the Xmas disturbance jars one's spirit, the more so when we know the fearful plight and suffering which is resting upon the matter of Israel in the present hour (– *a reference to the news of Jewish suffering at the hands of the Nazis in Germany*).

3845/1ff / 22nd December 1938 / From Eastbourne by a colleague, to AEW in Alma Square, London NW8 –

(*The writer includes this quotation from ANO in his letter to AEW*) - "God can unravel the most intricate paths; can make the crooked straight; O, there is a softness in God's touch, which gives a help no man can minister! God sees WHERE the SORE is, and lays His hand on the very place, whereas man only AGGRAVATES the wound. You can do, in connection with God, what you cannot do, or pass through, with men: and what pains God takes to encourage us … constraining us to firm out our hearts before Him, and to find Him a Refuge – Yes!"

(*The writer, to AEW, now continues himself*) - Be it perplexity of circumstances, or other trials, God has in all but one intent – DELIVERANCE, not death, is His aim. If He made Israel to hunger, it was not to starve, but to FEED them. It is the characteristic of our washing in Christ, not to be moved by evil tidings.

… then the Gospel comes in, the Blood which cleanses, and we feel our ground of hope is in His righteousness put on us. Satan often strives to take from us this confidence, and thereby separates us from God. Let our desires after holiness be as the wood which the fires from the sacrifice kindles into a flame …

3847/3 / 24th December 1938 / From Alma Square London NW8, AEW to a colleague -

(*Another case of certainty that turned out to be premature*) - we see the last possible doubt disappears, and we know of a surety that our absence from the Lord will terminate next June 12 (*that is, in 1939*).

I hope and pray your little man (*the recipient's young son*) is really better.

(*Concerning AEW writing up the Testimony*) - I expect to get a start on writing very soon but one needs a Divine priming as to the need – I mean the Divine requirement. I am sure the story will include the <u>whole</u> plan of Time and revealing the former things, but specially revealing <u>what has now been fulfilled.</u> It is this which will create the shock.

… Our family has been successfully removed from Xmas festivity.

CHAPTER 4
1939

1939

3901/2 / 2ⁿᵈ January 1939 / From Alma Square, London NW8 –

(*A period of deep soul-searching and self-honesty*) –

I asked myself yesterday, did I really believe that in six months, the sacred portals of the Father's house would be flung open ... or am I trying to make myself believe it? What about you brethren? If we believe it, how is it affecting us? ... Or are we getting like the general body of saints that are waiting to see? What does God see in me or in you which makes Him find pleasure as His witnesses of Christ's return next June?

Facts go dead on us if not acted upon, even if they are founded upon Divine utterance ... Are we waiting for the Holy Ghost to bear witness, or is the Holy Ghost waiting for us to bring our lives into some sort of harmony with what our position will be when the Testimony is out and we committed?

... I feel our need – mine and thine - is to get a thousand times lower before the Lord as to our own utter spiritual need and our lack of the broken heart and contrite sprit. I ask, if the world or the Church saw our lives, would they believe that in our bosoms we carry the most mighty secret of the Universe – one which directly affects the lives and souls of every man, woman and child on the earth?

(*Keep praying, for*) - the powers of hell are let loose against us collectively and individually, in the hope of defeating us or delaying us or of wearing us down until we give up. The need is not so much prayer as getting our souls and lives to such a place that God can see and hear Christ in us. Are we broken and abased, or secretly puffed up with knowledge and the high privilege of our calling?

... but woe to us if we think God will use us unless He knows we can answer to His satisfaction. All power comes from the broken will and all backsliding starts with the unbroken will. Too often we find ourselves broken in the big issues but devilishly unbroken in the small ones – the little foxes that devour the yet tender grapes. Does the Lord not call upon each one of us to take, as it were, a Nazarite's vow? (*Numbers Chapter 6*) ... utter submission to Christ so that our loyalty to the rejected One makes others smart; no contact with death in ourselves or others. What a position! Yet how dare we face June 12 next without it? How dare we claim to be witnesses without it? If we do it is because we think we can get through without bowing to every claim of Christ.

Failure humbles but we wait for shocks. Brokenness means we need no shocks for it comes of the Holy Ghost shedding light into the dark recesses of our beings, so that we know what we could do and be, if we had the pluck or if God let us GO.

Be diligent! – how often it appears in Scripture and it is the only time apposite to Laodicea (*Revelation 3.14-22*).

3902/2 / 3rd January 1939 / From Alma Square, London NW8 –

What we are attempting to do is of necessity one of the most hideously opposed things since the Church began, because its object is to bring the Church to completion (153). (*Concerning the figure '153', please see page 35, under Heading 9*).

3909/3 / 29th January 1939 / From Alma Square, London NW8 –

(*Concerning a meeting of Egyptian and other Arab leaders with British Government officials in England*) –

... seeing the object is to deprive Israel politely or otherwise of their inalienable possession.

We are doubtless very near the hour of action and how we need to get into living contact with the One on the Throne.

3913/6 / 4th March 1939 / From Eastbourne, by a colleague to a colleague –

(*The letter is signed off*) –

Yours in Him, our Lord Jesus Christ, Saviour of Sinners, Saviour of the World.

3914/4 / 12th March 1939 / From the Newlands Valley –

(*Concerning the Church of Rome and the Papacy*) –

… and yet this great pompous system of religious harlotry has just, as never before, presented itself to the world claiming all authority because in the successor of St Peter, who they call the Prince of the apostles.

3914b/1 / 15th March 1939 / From the Newlands Valley –

(*Concerning Satan's opposition*) –

… (I) … have the assurance that if we – you at your end and I this – persist in standing aggressively in the determination that Christ and His Testimony must prevail, we shall sooner or later experience what our faith now asserts.

Oh, how real is conflict when a real Satan stands athwart the path. Nothing can be done until faith in living energy can dislodge him. So I press on – as you will.

3916/1 / 17th March 1939 / From the Newlands Valley –

I was able in shelter of a wall to get out before dinner for a season of calling upon God. I have been doing this each day and usually twice a day as it seems only thus is it possible to get anywhere near engaging the forces of darkness that are ever present, making themselves felt by various forms of oppression and seeking to overwhelm one's spirit by one device after another.

Deadness with a lack of desire, or an overcoming sense of impotence, confusion of mind and no ability to discern what the will of God is, are a few of the various forms of attack, and each one is real and leaves behind it a sense that we are all wrong somewhere, and that God has no interest in the matter, and we are wearying ourselves unnecessarily.

In other words we are being left (so it would appear) to meet these forces of spiritual wickedness on our own. Met they MUST be or we can give up ... We have to realise that the very conflict is the proof of the Spirit's presence and it is His presence that draws the attack of the enemy.

If He (*Christ*) failed, then the Universe would pass into Satan's hands for ever. Yet He never flinched and never murmured though, next to Satan, his deadliest foes were the very ones He had come to rescue and save. In very truth, He was the Divine Testimony – the Ark of the Covenant.

As being <u>first</u> called, I have a responsibility which I cannot divest myself of and I therefore can rightly use the words of Ephesians VI 18 ...

(We) – a little company of eight souls – of these six are Levites called to bear the Ark and the time has come for <u>advance</u>.

... before the enemy we begin to realise how ridiculous we are, and how, apart from Divine aid, we not only could not advance but Satan would triumph over us by some artifice and throw us headlong out of His path. Do we really realise how perfectly ridiculous we are if it comes to a trial of strength with Satanic forces?

While the conflict endures the faith must be claimed. Whoever left the battlefield for a rest?

3917/1 / 17th March 1939 / From the Newlands Valley –

(*The reference to "Translation" in the second paragraph refers to AEW's book "The Hour of Translation" which was published in 1929*) -

Yesterday I was up the valley in the early A.M. commencing to prepare the way by a renewal of allegiance to the One who commissioned us.

After dinner yesterday I walked out beyond Keskadale to the top overlooking Crummock and Buttermere. The loneliness was perfect and suited to a lengthy meditation and communion as I walked, and then coming back, I had a lengthy season of calling upon God – not merely praying ...

This A.M. I was again in the valley ... Then I took up ground for a complete victory and unmasking of Satan as the one who uses <u>every</u> subterfuge to hinder, chiefly these (*that is, Satan's subterfuges*) are complete impotence to discern God's will or what is to be done, and all sorts of confusion. The opposition has been and is very strong, but I was helped in looking at "Translation" and recalling the victory of that last chapter which so exposed the state of the church.

... I hope no time may be wasted. I also seek knowledge as to <u>when</u> there is to be a move.

3917a/1 / 20th March 1939 / From the Newlands Valley -

(*Displaying great confidence in the anticipated positive response of "the saints of the world" to the Testimony*) –

There is no doubt God has <u>great</u> purposes in store and I cannot fail to believe that, by a great stroke and after repentance, the saints the world over will be brought to submit to the testimony, accepting that it comes from God, and that thereby to a great extent unity of thought and action will prevail.

The programme includes baptism as ours (*that is, in the Name of Jesus alone – see page 56, Heading 5*), the Lord's Supper, the breaking of bread on the resurrection day as in Acts XX ...

... I expect to get liberty to write fully for the saints, that which will bring home the sin of rejecting dates, etc.

3921/6 / 24th March 1939 / From the Newlands Valley –

Whenever able I get out for meditation and I find the open helps greatly.

... It is strange how all goes back to 1933 when Hitler rose.

3922/1 / 26th March 1939 / From the Newlands Valley -

Praying alone and often is, I find a great test and of late I have experienced a deadly sense of ineffectiveness or not being heard. This is to be expected just before God makes a move, I expect. Ceaseless attacks go on leaving one almost numbed with a hopeless sense of confusion as to what one ought to be doing.

(*Concerning the risk of starting to write too soon*) - I feel it would lack that true sense of meeting the occasion if I tried to do it in cold blood.

3923/1 / 28th March 1939 / From the Newlands Valley –

Faith to be faith has to be accompanied by works, that is, faith that does not get you committed somewhere is not faith but make-believe.

3928/6 / 30th March 1938 / From the Newlands Valley –

(*This extract emphasises that these weeks were a period of intense expectation, that the Lord God was going to move in a dramatic way, with "the testimony" being a key part of this divine move; but quite how or when this move was to occur, and thus their actual role within it, was not clear for them at this stage*) –

I see clearly the midnight cry could not be sounded by anyone who had not <u>evidence</u>. Facts, yes, but <u>personal</u> evidence alone can carry conviction and this has been allowed and we, dear friends, give unfeigned thanks for we have heard the voice of the Beloved and we reply, Make haste, my beloved ...

... We certainly feel God is bound to honour our action last year at this time, but if He does not do it the way we think or hope He will do it some other way ... <u>Refuse</u> all pressure or anxiety ... We may rest assured the next move is from Heaven but I keep watching in case we may be guided to take some step, such as a further warning to A of C (*Archbishop of Canterbury*).

... What moves me is the contemplation of all He has done for His own, and yet out of all the mass of believers who take His gifts, how few – a privileged few truly – have cared to watch for Him - for Himself. I am bowed and overwhelmed with so precious a reward after these many years of watching ...

3930aa/1 / 18th October 1939 / From the Newlands Valley –

(*Now a few weeks into the Second World War, AEW is still in the North, but that was soon to change ...*) –

I trust you are all finding the way back to the place where communion with Heaven may be enjoyed as intercession ascends.

3930/5 / 19th October 1939 / From the Newlands Valley –

Though much has discouraged us, yet the Spirit within is the mighty power of God and has undimmed determination for Christ's glory in the testimony. We must pray in deep earnest and believe that God does intend the vision in some form or another to be written.

3933/1 / 30th October 1939 / From the Newlands valley –

(*Concerning the need for care when working with biblical 'types' and 'antitypes' – ironically, this is one of the main reasons why they were often mistaken over the timing of the "coming of the Lord"*) –

Reasoning and discussion never bring us anywhere and the mind can never elucidate God's mysteries ... we find ourselves reverting to the exercise of the mind, very often, in the hope of solving this or that mystery from the Word of God ... What is not our part is to try and interpret – that is the Holy Spirit's part.

3934/1 / 2nd November 1939 / From the Newlands Valley –

I have not been out much lately and feel a bit weary in the bonnet.

... Eternity is before us and endless seasons in glory when we shall learn the whole truth.

... I find it is only when outside and able to call upon God in earnest that I am able to get through at all.

3935/1 / 6th November 1939 / From the Newlands Valley –

I was seeking cleansing and anointing for what is before us, and there is certainly no anointing apart from cleansing.

... May God help us all to put walk before talk.

(*Concerning their belief in the imminent return of Christ*) –

I had hoped, in view of an early removal to 'a city of habitation' (*Psalm 107.7*), it would have been possible to have disposed of most of the furniture, other than a few bits of real use.

3936/2 / 7th November 1939 / From the Newlands Valley –

(*Again, their certainty over the imminent return of Christ. This was now expected in June 1940, with, perhaps, a 200-day warning to be given by them in late November 1939 - less than three weeks ahead - thus repeating their actions of November 1932*) –

All traces of uncertainty have disappeared and we can move forward in the full blaze of a revelation from God as to the path.

(*He*) is coming and the world is to know it. All will prepare but only the elect will be truly ready.

3937/6 / 9th November 1939 / From the Newlands Valley –

(*We see here once more AEW's great confidence and strong leadership of the group – it would have taken much courage for any of his colleagues to express caution, let alone any misgivings, over these expected dates!*

As, many years afterwards, we now learn from these letter-extracts some of the inner workings of the group, we reflect on what was going on. Here is a group of sincere, devout, focussed, God-fearing men, under a remarkable leader, doing their very best "to get things right" under the Lord. So much of what they did was and is right, but time and again they "jumped the gun" over the Lord's return for His Church, unfortunately attracting, in so doing, much understandable criticism. This meant in turn that much of the "wheat" in their work has been neglected, often undeservedly.

As a result, there are many lessons here for those of us coming after – over the right understanding of Scripture; over prayer and guidance; over the relationship between faith, assurance and certainty; over the need to discern whether "blocks in the road" are from the Holy Spirit, or from the devil; and over the need to discern when to wait, and when to act) –

I hope we realize that all that has been given in the past weeks is intended of God to knock the bottom board out of all scepticism or unbelief as to the coming 200 days. God knows our past disappointments, and He would have us to realize we must not carry about on us any doubt as the end being NOW. The cry is, Lo, the Bridegroom. God intends we shall have no single element of doubt.

How could I be expected to write if I felt one single question as to there being a further delay? No, dear friends, those last rays of light have come out of heaven and they remove for ever any question as to there being further delay.

We need, and must seek, that living witness, but faith must rest on the solid rock of Holy Scripture, and these types as to the 7 years and the glorious picture of the testimony being in death for a period which synchronizes with the days and hours of the Lord's death, removes all question and places our feet on the rock.

(*Shown here is the tendency to assume that "the solid rock of Holy Scripture" on the one hand, and their own understanding of "types" within that solid rock on the other, are identical. They aren't! – and this was the mistake they were prone to making*).

3938/1 / 16th November 1939 / From the Newlands Valley –

(*Concerning 26th November 1939, 10 days ahead, a date they were sure the Lord would mark in some way*) -

Not that we are to build castles in the air but that as in 1932 we definitely and soberly believe the 26th is a day that cannot pass unnoticed. Faith, I say, says it cannot pass unmarked. It is the climax of all the gracious light given in the past month and with that light we can meet all unbelief whether it be from our own coward hearts or from the devil.

Things are none too easy up here – as with you I expect. Why should they be? Spiritual grit has to be tested and spiritual grit is Christ dwelling in us. He had to be tested and it is the life of the Son of God in us being tested. Are we letting His Son go or are we cramping Him up by wanting to live our own little lives in our own little way? "Let my Son go that He may serve me" (*Exodus 4.23*) is the key word just now for this is the testimony of the Son of God.

(*Concerning AEW being able to write up the testimony with some urgency by 26th November*) -

It need not take long if liberty is granted but pray, oh friends, in the all-powerful name of Jesus for this liberty and full light as to the Divine will.

3939/2 / 17th November 1939 / From the Newlands Valley –

God never excuses ignorance and the fact that the professing Church ignored the matter and refused to examine the facts and learn as we … makes no difference.

All light given in due season is confirmed by the Spirit in the Word but first I must receive it and after God gives the proof. How often during these years this has been so.

Israel was wife to Jehovah and the Gentiles were espoused to Christ but both are rejected but out of the failure of the mass in each case a remnant – a chaste virgin – is found for the Lord in the final issue and that is why

[this] 7 years and the coming 7 years are to be viewed literally as the two sevens of Jacob – consecutive. This is very blessed.

I think it is probably true that the net <u>was</u> cast in 1932 and this time it will be seen in action rather than cast again.

… there seems a possibility the seed sown in 1937 will fructify … we must face it that no written matter sent out in normal ways, no matter how terrific in dynamic power, would awaken Christendom in under several weeks or months.

(*Concerning what exactly AEW should write up*) –

It is to be <u>the</u> basic document on which <u>all</u> rests. I cannot therefore be too long or too abstruse. It is to this I set my hand <u>now</u> and if it be God's will He will give pace and wisdom by the Spirit without whom none can serve God adequately. A few days of liberty should suffice to do it but "make it plain upon tables" (*Habakkuk 2.2*) needs Divine unction.

All other considerations must go – the time is past for mending ourselves or our nets … May God guide all for His Glory.

3943/2 / 24ᵗʰ November 1939 / From a letter entitled "A Note on leaving Newlands on Nov 24ᵗʰ 1939" –

I go back to one of the first gatherings at (*Alfriston*) after June 1933, and I recall saying, "Well friends, we have committed God". Do I regret such words? No, indeed! I go further and say with all boldness, God has committed Himself to us, by that which He has given us of Heaven's priceless secrets <u>because we are Christ's,</u> and He it was who chose us and not we Him, so that for this 200 days He in us might PREPARE THE WAY OF THE LORD.

(*They were all to be back in the Newlands Valley rather sooner than they could have imagined …*)

3946/2 / 1st December 1939 / From Mount Royal, London W1 –

(*AEW has found accommodation in London so as to be alone for his writing. He now enters a period of grappling with what exactly is to be written, and for whom, and in what tone*) –

No doubt, as I am now fixed up ready to write, there has come an inrush of evil power but the standard of the Spirit will be lifted up against the evil.

3947/2 / 5th December 1939 / From Mount Royal, London W1 –

We have seen the need to keep step with heaven and this, by knowledge granted, we will do. The writing is a big matter for a small man, but actually the need is communion and with this all can be done in a way pleasing to God.

… By the frame-up I mean really the Divine picture of what the document is really to be. The Title is important …

(*Concerning another matter, irrelevant for us*) - which I trust may be before the Xmas holiday of Christendom.

3948/1 / 6th December 1939 / From Mount Royal, London W1 –

No doubt this advancing (*concerning the writing*) has let loose those powers which confuse the mind and leave one prostrate before what appears an impossible task … Satan is out to utterly oppose the casting of such a beam of light into the darkness of the world.

All we have to say is a veritable sequel to the Scriptures and has to be presented in that light, and this is a grave responsibility and only the Spirit can empower for such a task.

… All is in the lap of Jesus and faith and courage will enable the Spirit to reveal the plan.

3949/2 / 7th December 1939 / From Mount Royal, London W1 –

Has Satan retired from his never-ceasing business of holding the world in darkness as its prince? (*John 12.31 / 14.30 / 16.11*).

... (*No wonder*) we should be met by a gathered assemblage of forces from the realms of darkness in the heavenlies. The testimony is to be written – in a manner acceptable to God, and then be sent out into the earth to enlighten it and to accomplish God's will and bring the numbers of the redeemed to fulness.

The allowed opposition is without doubt to drive me in upon God and so to find out His will for the writing ... is it not here that Satan has a peculiar power – this stopping of utterance?

(*Concerning their financial needs*) - May God think upon our necessity.

Much love and praying always for your upholding.

3950/4 / 8th December 1939 / From Mount Royal, London W1 –

The more I meditate the more I see that ... God's Word is a written Word and not a spoken one ... All matters of importance in all spheres have to be written. No one can quibble over a written statement – neither can it be perverted with ease.

I seek quietness and confidence, but above all to stand on the ground that this work, which is for God, was secured in the death of Christ, and even as He was raised so must the testimony be, to the glory of God. For it to be raised it must be written and made manifest before all men.

We therefore hold fast and, armed fully, we advance with the sword of the Spirit in one hand and the pen in the other. Truly it is a conflict but very soon every barrier will be driven asunder and every iron bar be snapped before the advance of a power in us which is greater than anything in the world. Hearty greeting and love.

Ever yours, Arthur E Ware.

3952/1 / 11th December 1939 / From Mount Royal, London W1 –

The immeasurable solemnity and importance of any communication, made in God's name to the whole earth in the present hour, is calculated to make one fear to write a word until it please God to unveil to us the full thought of His mind for the writing.

It becomes more and more clear that any ordinary effort to state the case simply cannot be the Divine requirement. I feel assured it must be that in some way what is to be written will assume the form of a Divinely ordered (I do not say inspired of course) sequel to the Bible narrative.

It must be a document which like Scripture <u>states facts</u> and leave no room for discussion by raising arguments. It must be terse or else it would be inordinately lengthy and this would be wrong.

The question arises as to our authority and how it is to be expressed. God requires that it shall be known that what is said is official as coming from Himself, through channels He has appointed for the task.

… I cannot write until what is written is loosed from above. What God has given is really a new unveiling of the Holy Scriptures.

I feel certain the full light on the Seven Times is going to provide a mighty weapon for convincing both Gentiles and Jews. All in 1933 rested on the structure of the 23 years of Nebuchadnezzar being counterpart to 1917 to 1940.

Flowers sent from Cxxxx (*a faithful friend in Cornwall*) now flourish in a vase and are a welcome companion in this city of grime.

… what is to go forth is the Testimony of our blessed Lord and Master Himself, and who but He could know the true requirement?

3954/5 / 27th December 1939 / From Mount Royal, London W1 –

(*Concerning the strength and nature of spiritual opposition*) -

One simply has, <u>every time</u> before doing anything required by God, to be led into the wilderness to be tempted of the devil. The temptation goes on until, by appropriating the death of Christ <u>as our own,</u> we can say "the Prince of this world cometh and hath nothing in me" (*John 14.30*). Satan can do nothing with <u>a dead man</u> but he can play havoc with a half-dead one.

It takes us a long time to die, and we have to be careful not to carry about a secret, cunningly-hid determination <u>never</u> to attend our own funeral – that is, never to cease keeping ourselves for ourselves and letting God have what only He can pick up.

Fortunately or unfortunately, when God calls for one <u>to do</u> something He wants, He allows us to be brought up against a power that is so great that <u>only</u> death can possibly meet it.

The power is allowed in order to compel us to mortify the flesh. For instance, if what is to be written could be done by the natural man Satan can stop it, but he cannot stop the life of Christ flaming in or flowing out because that life has triumphed over him.

I have felt on occasions that whenever I got near touching the actual facts we possess with a view to expressing them, that a power rose up from within which made it <u>impossible</u> (*twice underlined*) – <u>utterly impossible</u>.

What power was it? It is Satan or his emissary binding me in spirit, so that the Spirit of God could not break through, or perhaps, putting it another way, so that if I wanted to express the fact I had no power to do it even if I had employed natural ability.

Brethren, Satan is abroad and fully alive to what we are to do and what the effect on his kingdom will be, if the facts are all published.

... Earnest praying will avail ... Yesterday we had "all things are yours" (*from a devotional calendar, I Chronicles 29.14*) and death is one of God's priceless gifts to His children.

... I acted on the word and seek by faith to stand, and I doubt not in due season we shall witness the triumph of Christ in the writing of the vision as He intends it to be done.

CHAPTER 5
1940 -1941

1940

401/1 / 1st January 1940 / From Mount Royal, London W1 –

(*We learn here of AEW's questions and spiritual struggles as he grapples with the task while appreciating its enormity; he longs to visit them all in Eastbourne but is hesitant to do so*) -

We have always found that it is nigh impossible to read God's ways while they are in process of being worked out; just as we have always been disappointed when we looked <u>on</u> to a date but never when we looked back to one and saw the hand of God or His back parts like Moses in Exodus XXXIII after He had passed by.

For me the past few days have meant a further descent, and I have found rebellion lurking within and a resentment at being so long on an as yet futile task.

After much darkness and an overpowering sense of satanic effort to make me accuse God, I got a measure of relief in the early hour by what I must term an adjustment of aspect.

This made me see how determined God is that the Testimony shall be the Testimony of the Lord <u>from a company</u> which is absolutely <u>outside</u> the camp of religious Christendom, so that in very fact we are to address those in Christendom with an invitation "Come ye out to meet Him". That is, we are viewed by God as an outpost, an advance guard, and all who would be ready must respond and join us by doing exactly what we have done, namely <u>sell up</u> and <u>break every link</u> with religious and commercial Babylon.

I see God will <u>not</u> address Christendom which is <u>now</u> under judgement.

He will only allow an appeal to be made to those inside to come out. Truly all pretend to respond though I confess I still wonder if the Papal system is included.

... God has waited 6000 years for it (*the Testimony*) and the Lord as Bridegroom 1900 years, and to us has fallen the high but solemn task of doing it.

Who would not quail before such a task? ... (*prayer that*) <u>fear</u> may be banished, for fear is of the devil and God hath <u>not</u> given to us the spirit of fear but of love, POWER and sound mind (*II Timothy 1.7*).

... I (wrongly) dropped into the idea God was addressing Christendom which He is not and there is a world of a difference.

... I hesitate to take a break to run down and see you all and the family, fearing it may be too costly in the matter of recovering myself but I am open to do so.

402/3 / 3rd January 1940 / From Mount Royal, London W1 –

I cannot write if I am under pressure on money matters, neither can I stay here unless I see funds are to come. I again say this is [ideal] and I give thanks for its convenience – all under one roof and with the black out this means much.

404a/1 12th January 1940 / From Mount Royal –

(*On receipt of some funds*) - ... this quiets my spirit.

4012/2 / 30th January 1940 / From Mount Royal –

We have a startling story to tell and I am glad to get on to something constructive and new.

4016/4 / 4th February 1940 / From Mount Royal –

(*Fresh money worries – are these testings from the Lord, that they should carry on in faith, or warnings from the Lord, that they should pause and* "take stock"?) –

May our God have mercy upon us but let us remember this is the way the Master went and we share in the sufferings of Christ. Nothing else explains our state. May we do it gladly and not lose faith but I confess to be being at times much tried.

4020/4 / 8th February 1940 / From a colleague in Alfriston to AEW in London –

(*A stout rebuttal of an article on "Date-Fixing Fallacies", written by an old adversary, referred to here as Xxxxx*) –

... and it is truly an effort out of the pit, and no words could be too strong in exposing these offences against God. From the way Xxxxx wrote – (*quoting from the words of Xxxxx*) - "it is impossible to decide exactly at what date the calculation should begin" – implies we are left to be reliant on ourselves alone to understand the Scriptures, and ignores the Presence and Ability of the Spirit to guide.

(*From this article by Xxxxx*) - One would not imagine there was such a Person as the Holy Spirit in existence on the earth, to guide one in the Scriptures.

4025/1 / 23rd February 1940 / From Mount Royal –

There was a fearful explosion here last night which broke the windows of several shops in the building and put the wind up all the ladies. I have never heard such chattering in the passages ... They thought it was a raid! It was the opening of 3 x 37th day to June 12th and I wonder if it had a meaning, possibly an earthquake on June 12th when the saints are raised.

4029/2 / 4th March 1940 / From Mount Royal –

(*Time is getting very short if they are right about the Lord's return on 12th June 1940 ...*) –

These days passing unmarked only again proves that God never lets anyone know in advance what He is going to do. We have never been able to anticipate action by God. Nevertheless I take it as our duty to be watching every sign and to be ever on the lookout.

… and for our part we as rejected witnesses cannot act until God removes the stigma upon us – which we bear for His sake. Then again, the world is all in a state utterly contrary to that which must obtain in the weeks preceding the return of Christ. The Jews and Palestine comes first. Then the Roman Empire and the break-up of the present impasses between the nations. <u>This has got to happen</u> in coming weeks – that is, so that by the end of April Israel may be a nation in their own land under Roman suzerainty.

… The evidence however that we possess as to His coming this year is <u>too strong</u> to allow us to think for one minute that He will not come this year … the Genesis types of Jacob and Joseph cannot be dashed to the ground and if the Lord did not come in 1940 they would be.

(*Or perhaps they were wrongly applying those Jacob and Joseph types?*).

We have types but they depend on interpretation – figures cannot lie or deceive anyone.

(*We see in such remarks that they are very conscious of 'types' needing to be interpreted correctly, which with hindsight we can see turned out to be not the case on this occasion*).

I often pine for Newlands and feel how much better I could do there but "the city" seems to be the decreed place.

4032/2 / 17th March 1940 / From Mount Royal –

Prophecy stops dead at the fall of Jerusalem in AD 70 as Daniel IX shows … and then jumps over to "the week" in verse 27 (of Dan IX).

In Luke XXI the Lord does the same almost. He speaks of Jerusalem falling to the Romans and of the slaughter and captivity which would follow, then jumps over to the end of the times of the Gentiles on June 12. After this He says "There shall be signs in the sun, moon and stars" and possibly He jumps further over to the end of the next seven years, that is from June 12 1933 to March 24 1940.

We cannot do better than continually face the fact that there is no possible chance of an extension of time beyond this year.

All that has happened since 1917 is <u>only</u> preparatory and not the subject of actual prophecy.

The question before us is when is God going to move? It must be soon and are we to take any steps before He does? This we do know, the testimony has been given for <u>this</u> hour. The Cry at Midnight (*Matthew 25.6 and parallels*) has to be sounded … So far I have been unable to get going on the Chronology and I am deeply concerned to know why.

4033/1 / 18th March 1940 / From Mount Royal –

(*Concerning various peace efforts being made to end the war*) –

All the world is trying to end it as all the world is suffering by it, but it will be in vain.

(*Concerning their continuing belief that the Lord would return on 12th June that year*) –

I have asked (*the Lord*) that under no circumstances may we be taken unawares. I feel it is to God's glory that some should <u>know</u> the day. Apart from this we can <u>do</u> nothing but watch.

Let prayer – fervent prayer – arise from all our hearts – a real assault upon the throne in the interests of Christ.

4035/1 / 22nd March 1940 / From Mount Royal –

The great question I ask myself (and I fear the devil suggests it) is what use is there in a long diatribe on the Chronology if it cannot be out until mid-April at the earliest and the Church is going to depart in June?

Is it for the Remnant, and the Church only have it for a couple of months? What a problem.

You see if the Chronology is not faithfully written and properly presented, people will have no means of knowing if it is accurate because they do not understand it. The position is altogether remarkable for we have no money for printing and that proves God is not wanting it out just yet. What is the reason for that?

Over and over again as I return to the facts we possess about <u>this year</u>, the more utterly impossible it seems that God could find a way to circumvent them.

I wish I could leave here but I know not where to go unless it is to (*he mentions a quiet base in Alfriston they have used before*), and that would be no good for the writing.

(By April 1940 they realised that the time remaining until 12th June was now too short for the Lord to return on that date of which they had been so sure for such a time.

May 1940 saw the miraculous evacuation from Dunkirk, promptly followed by an order that all children must be evacuated from the south coast in view of the threat of imminent invasion. Mr Ware made the necessary arrangements and moved the whole company of 20-25 souls from the Eastbourne area first to Seascale on the Cumberland coast, and then to various rented properties in the Newlands Valley.

Being now living close together there was no longer the need for so many letters and their numbers drop away for a time.

The work went steadily on, with three of their number being granted exemption from military call-up so that they could continue the work on Bible Chronology, the relevance of their work within the present dire national situation of the time being duly recognised).

1941

4101 / 6th June 1941 / A Memorandum to the Prime Minister and to the Archbishop of Canterbury (*after several occasions of national prayer called for by King George VI, and the extraordinary evacuation of 338,000 troops from Dunkirk in May-June 1940*) –

We well know a nation cannot guide its foreign policy by the Bible, but woe to that nation that flies in the face of the clearly revealed statements of Holy Writ concerning it.

Britain has been destined by God to be the upholder of Egypt, and as such she will be called upon to play a vital part in events prior to the setting up of the Kingdom – a fact recorded in the 11th chapter of the Prophecy of Daniel.

(*This was written 12 months before Rommel and his Afrika Korps reached a point dangerously close to Cairo. The Germans were finally stopped by the British Eighth Army at El Alamein, October-November 1942, a battle described by Churchill as – "not the beginning of the end, but it may at least be the end of the beginning". So Britain did indeed "uphold Egypt"*).

4103/1 / 7th August 1941 / From the Newlands Valley, to Dr McNxxxxx, who became a regular correspondent –

(*There now follows by far the longest extract from one of AEW's letters which are included in these pages. This extract contains a very detailed description of the "Testimony work" from its beginnings, granting us a clear insight of what it involved in practice as the years went by*) -

In Ecclesiastes I.9 and III.15 the Divine law of repetition is clearly set forth, and this in the present instance plainly means that conditions which obtained in the Church in those glorious days (*that is, in the Apostolic era*) at the beginning are again to obtain at the end.

... the place that time occupies in God's moral administration is simply stupendous ... God "hath determined the times before appointed" ...

The Ware-Paine Testimonies

… His plan of time – a plan that scintillates with His glory and every detail of which is to be found in Holy Scripture.

The Church has refused to treat the subject of time in the Bible seriously, and in so acting it has presented an affront to Christ by Whom, we are told, the ages were framed (*from Hebrews 11.3, the Greek word 'aion' being more accurately translated as 'ages' rather than 'worlds' as in the KJV*).

In 1933, in association with certain brethren, five of whom are now members of this company, I was called upon of God to make certain declarations. One of these was the announcement that in forty days the Gentile nations would suffer excision, as forewarned by the Apostle Paul in Romans 11.22. It was an unequivocal intimation that Christendom would cease to be God's witness in the earth from a point forty days hence. This declaration was made in the evening of May 2nd and forty days thereafter would be June 12th.

On this latter day there opened in London, the place where our declaration was made before an audience of about 2,000, the greatest assemblage of nations in the history of the world. Leading members of the governments of every nation under heaven came together for the opening of the World Economic Conference.

At the official opening of this Conference no reference was made to God, and His Name was deliberately excluded from mention. That was a dark day in the history of the world, for as we have since proved, it pleased God to order that that vast assemblage of nations should meet and officially open their Conference, and, (we say it with shame) officially deny His holy Person at the exact minute when SIX THOUSAND YEARS had passed from the Creation of Adam. Sixty-six nations were gathered in the sixth month of the year, on the twice times sixth day, that is the 12th of the month. (*AEW mentions these "sixes" because in Bible numerology – the study of numbers within the Bible – 6 is the number of Man, often acting in defiance of God*).

In very truth at that moment the nations of Christendom were rejected and the Professing Church or Assembly was "spued out" in fulfilment of our Lord's threat in the address to Laodicea. the former is the political aspect and the latter the religious aspect of one act of judgement.

Not only were we called upon to take part in giving to the nations an official intimation from God of what was going to happen, but we have since received such proofs from Scripture that the whole matter has become as clear as anything could be.

... I speak again of our own position as a company since 1933. It will be obvious to you that if our Lord on June 12th 1933, disowned every corporate expression of Christianity in the earth, He must have left Himself without corporate witness. How did He meet this situation? In this way.

For a few years before 1933, He brought a few of us together – the Church in my house – so that we might bear witness to the closing of the dispensation and His Second Advent. All our actions were wrought simply as members of Christ's body within the Church. We could not and did not act apart from the Church, but after June 12th 1933 our position completely changed. The testimony we bore in Christ's Name in 1932 and in 1933, the general body of Christians in this country <u>flatly rejected</u>, and without the slightest effort to really learn the meaning of our declarations. <u>We were branded as irresponsible date-fixers of the Second Advent.</u>

To all outward appearances, my declaration of May 2nd that our Lord would come for His Church on or about June 12th appeared to be a grievous error. No account was taken of what I said about the cutting off of Christendom or of the fact that forty days thereafter, every nation under heaven by representation of its government was assembled in London.

Nobody realised that we were delivering on behalf of Christ, the Antitypical Jonah, His forty days warning to the nations of the earth. We learned afterwards that the message of the evening of May 2nd 1933 was the actual anniversary of the day Christ rose from the dead, after being three days and three nights in the heart of the earth. The Church, prejudiced above the eyes against the chronological prophecies of Holy Scripture, rejected our message sent of the Lord, and <u>was itself rejected and "spued out" as His witness in the earth</u>, and that event took place on the day it was thought by Christians in general we should be humbled in the dust for doing despite to the truth of God by making a fatal prognostication.

After June 12th 1933 our position changed, and though we had become the subjects of despising to the masses of believers, it became clear that God had foreseen what would happen and had formed us into a representative company outside of religious and political Christendom, which He would take up and instruct in the full knowledge of His mind and purposes so that at the appointed moment we could go forth like those at the beginning to be His witnesses in the earth.

The first companies of the saints dwelt together in love and shared everything they possessed with one another. We and our families have been almost miraculously sustained for eight years <u>from within the limits of our own circle</u>, God having provided that sums of money for one reason or another should come to certain ones in our company, so that they could meet the needs of all the others. Mrs Wxxxx has been a heavy contributor in this direction.

In 1933 all were called upon to give up secular occupations in order that we might devote ourselves wholly to prayer and study of the scriptures. In plain language, if God was to act through a representative company it must be one which acted on the original principles for the Church, as set forth in Acts II and IV, and we are assured that it is God's purpose to bring the whole Church back on to the original ground before it is translated to its eternal home in the heavens.

Enoch is a type of the Church and lived for 365 years, each of which is typical of a day in the solar year. God never expected Christians to be looking for Christ at any moment, because to do so is both impossible and impracticable. It is possible for a Christian to live for a year at a time, and to make his business and domestic arrangements on that basis, and in following such a course no one could be viewed as settling down in the world. Usually with us, we have received an indication in the spring of each year, and this indication has come through a Spirit-given understanding of some further detail in the types covering the present parenthetical era, called "the consummation of the age". Having received this indication, we have known perfectly well that the Lord could not come until June the following year.

Because of the Church's attitude between 25th November (*1932*) and 12th June (*1933*), these last 200 days failed to produce the fruit God had intended, and instead of the Lord coming to receive the Church as we had anticipated (and very rightly so, as the facts have since proved), He rises up and rejects the Church's testimony which He spues out of His mouth as being utterly nauseous to Himself.

We know God's purposes may be delayed by the weakness or sinfulness of man, but they cannot be defeated. This being so, we have realized that before the Church is actually removed we should be called upon of God to bear witness <u>with all who believe our testimony</u> for another 200 days, from November 25th to June 12th. On this account we have always taken up active watching in the autumn each year in expectation of active testimony in November. In 1937-38 we bore witness officially to all the religious heads of Christendom in the British Isles ...

The vast array of new facts from Holy Scripture has been made available to the Church through an infallibly accurate Spirit-given knowledge of the Divine time mysteries of the Bible. A wondrous array of new facts has come to light concerning every phase of our Master's life from the Annunciation to the Ascension.

(*AEW now mentions their clear expectation of the Lord's return in June 1942, followed by the practical consequences that should arise from this expectation*) –

... what is it all intended to declare? Simply this, that our Lord and Master will come according to His promise as the Bridegroom of Matthew XXV on June 12th 1942 ...

(*Those who accept this expected date should*) - give practical expression to their faith by the selling up of their homes and by the disposing of all their possessions ... God would not be party to a testimony composed merely of lip-service; since lip-service abounds in the Church of Christ, and all consider that they are ready for His coming. (*Such people*) are prepared at any moment to proclaim the fact – little thinking that an ounce of practical preparation is worth more than a thousand tons of words unsupported by practical actions, which are the proof of a living faith, and of a living love for the One who has been absent for nineteen hundred years.

It is these practical steps that the Church dreads to take. It will be said, "Supposing I do this or that, and He does not come, what will my position be then?" This is just what happened to us all in 1933 and with what result? Only this, that the Lord had received His portion, and we all were brought to the place of those in the early Church of having nothing, and being compelled to trust in God for the provision of our temporal needs which He has never failed to supply.

It is quite clear to us that going forth to meet the Bridegroom means being stripped of every earthly possession and the breaking of every earthly association.

The return of Christ as Bridegroom is at a time known to all Christendom, and this is a result of a cry that is raised, "Lo, the Bridegroom". (*Watching means*) - prayerfully searching the Scriptures, <u>particularly in those parts that are chronological</u>, in order to discover the precious secret which lies hidden <u>somewhere within their pages</u>. (*This date is*) - <u>more deeply concealed than any other fact</u>. Herein is the glory of God displayed (Prov XXV.2)

<u>You can see how vital it is in this whole matter to understand how, in the</u>

mind and purpose of God, June 12th 1933 is the official end of the 6000 years of man, the Christian dispensation and the Times of the Gentiles.

Daniel's Seventieth Week is the keystone of all prophecy ... Because of the action of the Jews and Gentiles towards the Lord and His herald, (*John the Baptist*), God cancelled the period with intention that it should be lived again at the end of the age and prior to the setting up of the Kingdom which has been held in abeyance because of the rejection of the King by the nation of Israel. It is for this reason that Daniel IX avoids all reference to the 70th week being lived from AD 26 to AD 33.

All aspects of our company have been linked to the pathway of our Master. Every important event connected with us has occurred on a date, or in relation to some event, in His own pathway ...

We are absolutely assured that the Lord has identified Himself with us ... and that all that He has revealed ... constitutes His testimony ... standing with a few outside EVERYTHING in Christendom which bears His Name ... and presenting Himself in a garment detested by the Church, namely, a garment of dates – garbing Himself as the great Date-Fixer of the Ages, the One who fixed the date of June 12th 1933, and sent this frail servant and a few with him to prepare His Church so that they might know what He was about to do.

The Church, dear brother, has yet got to link arms with a date-fixing Jesus, and it will have to learn, as we have learned, to love every date in the Bible and all their associated time mysteries, because all is the work of His own hand, and all is inextricably bound up with the whole body of Divine Truth as revealed in Holy Scripture.

... three of our number who were of military age have been granted unconditional exemption ... for (if we had been broken up) how could we fulfil the type of John XXI, namely, six disciples in a little ship dragging the Net of Testimony to the Resurrection shore?

For eight years, off and on, I have conducted my labours in this mountain district near Keswick. This made it possible for us all, when things got too hot on the south coast, to obtain suitable accommodation in this quiet valley, close to where the Lord's people have annually gathered for over sixty years. We are all housed in three separate farms and are thankful to be well removed from the sphere of the enemy's activities ... though were we not engaged as we are we should be only too glad to be able to minister to the spiritual and bodily needs of our fellow countrymen.

4104/1 / 30th September 1941 / From the Newlands Valley, to Dr McNxxxx –

(*Here is another example of the rightness of so much of their thinking with regard to biblical Chronology, which we can assume still applies today despite their recurring mistakes over predicting the dates of these matters*).

(*We as a company*) must possess a knowledge of the "times" if it is to minister to our Lord Jesus Christ at the end of this dispensation, because without a knowledge of the times there can be no understanding of the present position of Christendom, or of those in Christendom who constitute the Church which is the Body of Christ.

... There is going to be a great recovery, and a great company of Gentiles, typically seen in the younger son of Luke XV, is going to return from the far-off land, and there is going to be a public re-instatement of the Church as it was seen at the beginning.

... I mention all these things because I would have you to know what God began when you were in our midst has not gone up in smoke but was part of a great preparatory work for the things which are now about to come to pass.

We are fully assured that not one thing shall fail of all the good things that we hoped for in 1932-1933. The Shunammite will return (*II Kings 8.1-6*), and the fatted calf will be killed, and the Father will say, "It was meet that we should make merry and be glad" (*Luke 15.32*).

4105/2 / 15th October 1941 / From the Newlands Valley, to the parents of one member of the group –

(*Another clear statement of the group's aims and expectations. God's people being a pilgrim people, separate from and passing through this world, is a dominant theme in this extract*) -

We have found (*the solemn issues*) cannot be believed without being acted upon ... We are assured, as you know, that we are standing on the very threshold of eternity, and God would have all His children to act in the light of this fact.

... We have evidences innumerable that it was He who set us apart from all Christendom so that we might constitute a company representative of the whole Church. If God cannot obtain satisfaction for His purpose through the mass, He must effect them through a few representing the whole.

(*When we go to the whole Church very soon*) – God will see to it that our testimony is believed. Drastic action will follow ... multitudes will desire to be rid of their earthly possessions, but then it will be too late, for how could a believer sell a property to an unbeliever when proof exists that in a few years he will be swept away with his possessions in that fearful day when the Lord visits the earth with the besom of destruction.

(*Soon*) – it will no longer be a matter of faith but of proven fact.

God has shown us from the Scriptures that before the end comes there will be a great restoration of the first principles ... we know that it has been the purpose of God that we should act on those first principles as a company representative of the whole Church. I cannot tell you how fiercely God has rebuked in our midst any effort to depart from them, if it meant possessing anything which would make it possible to set up and possess one's own home on this earth.

... it was never God's intention that the saints should possess houses and settle down in the world ... if at the beginning the Holy Ghost wrought to lead Christians to sell their houses and become pilgrims and sojourners in the earth, it was that they might follow in the footsteps of the Master Who had no certain dwelling-place.

We see clearly that from the moment the Church departed from this principle they lost the most vital link between themselves and Christ. Instead of being sojourners they became, like the world, earth-dwellers and this quickly stripped them of all desire for a heavenly home. The very essence of worldliness and of earthly-mindedness is a willingness to settle down in comfort in a world in which Christ was a Pilgrim and a Stranger, and Who received from it but a cross and a grave.

... In plain language, wherever the Church appears in its true light it is either seen as a company of people "tabernacling" or sojourning on earth in temporary dwelling-places, or as a tabernacle in which God dwells when he comes down to dwell with men in the eternal state.

... it became necessary for God to set us apart so that He might have a company which would for eight years (*from a point in 1933-34 to a point in 1941-42*) live in temporary dwellings as true pilgrims and sojourners; so that the principle should be effected in a representative way, even though it would not be in the mass. So it was that directly the 6000 years were finished we were set apart for a typical period of eight years.

... God could have no official connection with any company of saints save with those who lived and acted on the original basis on which the Church came into existence. The possession and ownership of a house ... is the precise opposite to being a sojourner and I shall be extremely sorry for any saints to be so found by the Lord. All we possess as Christian belongs to Christ, and nothing that belongs to Christ should be left behind when we depart or else it will be used against Christ.

4108 / 18th December 1941 / From the Newlands Valley, to a former close supporter of the group and their work -

(*Concerning their repeated apparent failures over expecting the date of the Lord's return, with reference to some current events in the war*) –

By informing you of our expectations from time to time we have involved you in the consequences of their apparent failure, the reasons for which I will not attempt to explain save to remark that they are the logical consequence of faithfulness to our duties as watchmen.

... It seemed clearly part of the programme that all in our family and all linked with us should be involved more or less in the suffering connected with disappointment, for the simple reason that presently they are going to have part with us in the consolation (II Cor 1.5).

(*Concerning the earthquake on November 25th 1941, and their expectations as to all that is to happen on the world stage shortly*) –

... for nothing but the most outrageous infidelity could suggest that the shaking on Nov 25th was other than a plain act on the part of the One who controls the universe. Presently this fact will be interpreted to all mankind.

... The Christian Church has run away from its duty of warning the world and is asleep. It is this neglect which has brought about the storm. Jonah possessed the testimony of God, and when he was cast into the sea the storm ceased. This is what will happen when very shortly we publish the main facts and cast them forth into the sea of the nations. Our present belief is that we are now to do this and that in due season thereafter God will bear witness by the darkening of the sun, etc, (see Hebrews II.4).

It is remarkable to note that power has been allowed to Russia to turn the tables upon Germany, and it would seem certain that Nazi-ism has received its death-blow ... I remarked on the day Germany attacked Russia that it could be none but God Who had allowed Hitler's eyes to be blinded. The P.M. speaks of Germany's war against Russia as the greatest blunder in History.

(*Very soon, at the end of 200 days*) the storm will be quelled and mercy flow out to mankind as never before seen. People will be converted to God in multitudes. The Church will be restored and Christians united in mind, heart and will, and all this as a result of the publication of the testimony which is nothing more nor less than a collection of all the facts from Holy Scripture which have a bearing upon the present hour, by which we mean, practically speaking, the 200 days which opened with a great shaking on November 25th last.

CHAPTER 6
1942 -1945

1942

4203/1 / 12th May 1942 / From one of the group in the Newlands Valley, to AEW at Lorton, north of Crummock Water –

We have been making "understanding of what God requires of us" and what form the writing is to take, the main burden of our prayers thus far in the light of the approaching Pentecost.

4204/1 / 12th May 1942 / Probably from Lorton, to Dr McNxxxx –

(*They now expect that the Lord's return will be in 1945 not 1942*) –

Light with God is a thing most precious and it has to be sought in the face of deadly Satanic opposition, and this calls for deep humbling of ourselves because of the sinfulness of the flesh which would intrude into holy things unless checked. Paul's "thorn in the flesh" is an example of this.

… Far better, allow me to affirm, in such a case (*that is, announcing a year of the Lord's return and then being disappointed*) to have expectations that fail than to fail to have expectations – far, far better.

… is the Master not worthy of being watched for by His own, even if it costs them all but their very lives? Let it not be forgotten that the spuing out of the Church as the vessel of testimony is closely associated with its refusal to watch for His return. "Watching" is the believer's cross in the last hours of the day of grace. Laodicea is a Church without a cross.

Seldom in history, save at points of tremendous importance, does God mark events by earthquakes.

(*New light was given on March 14th 1942 as to the Lord's return: this is now expected in 1945, to balance AD 33 and AD 36)* –

The Church which is His body will be restored to its place of separation and consequent power. Whether this will lead to the immediate sounding of the Midnight Cry remains to be seen ... In the Jordan plan to which we referred so fully in our August letter; the new light fits perfectly. God's paths in Holy Writ are always straight.

(*No true Bible-believers would dispute that, but - said with the greatest courtesy - clearly Man's paths of interpretation of God's paths are not always so straight!*)

4205/7 / 15th May 1942 / From Lorton –

Scripture is always self-confirmatory.

4211/1 / 1st June 1942 / From FLP, in the Newlands Valley, to AEW at Lorton –

What a sword-thrust to clericalism Acts VIII will be when presently the whole system is exposed!

4212/1 / 2nd June 1942 / From Lorton –

There is no doubt that Simon (*of Samaria, the sorcerer, Acts 8.9-25*) is the perfect type of that form of Christianity which is nothing other than heathenism cloaked with a thin coating of nominal adhesion to Christianity.

... (*Since 1927*) - every year since, we have expected Him to come but in vain we have watched. Not however in vain as He views the matter – far, far from it. To Him, those who watched not for Him are the ones who have lived the 15 years in vain – if not in positive vanity.

... now after one hour of 15 years we know when He, the Bridegroom, will come. I feel our watching is to be viewed as over. I am not watching now for Him to come this year or next or the next but 3 years hence.

... we now commence to get things ready for His arrival ... How gracious of God to allow that our watching, feeble as it may have been, is credited to the whole Church – we, as Levites, have acted for the rest "in their stead".

4220/1 / 12th August 1942 / From Lorton –

Prayer has an accumulative value, but for this, one has to be watchful and to persevere or else that element disappears.

The first thing is to get <u>perfectly clear</u> as to what God's will is. This is not easy as it is here the contest begins. We know in general that the vision, (*another term for their "testimony"*), has to be written but we are dealing with matters far too solemn for anyone other than God to decide the form the writing is to take and even what is to be presented.

... (I took up the pen) but before long confusion set in and liberty seemed checked ... it is all allowed to bring one to a dead end so that all "fleshly" efforts may cease. God knows, and only He, what will meet the need of the world today. The issues are staggering in their solemnity and in their enormity ...

(*Concerning a book by Watchman Nee*) - It is truly a masterpiece of simplicity and he has light given by God so that we of the West may be humbled. Its sublime obedience to the letter of scripture is so refreshing. What would we not give for an hour's talk with him as to his views on the present position ... The book strengthens our position as a church in a house and shows we have been kept on true ground – the only ground possible since 1933.

(*Concerning the church in houses*) – I judge it is <u>not</u> the purpose of God to restore the Assembly in any corporate form - that is, there are to be <u>no</u> local assemblies again. It is this which has been rejected. The sects will continue and some saints may remain in them. All obedient to the testimony will meet in their homes or in one anothers' except when, for purposes of exhortation (Hebrew X-25), all local saints come together in a hall or other suitable place leased for the occasion.

4222/1 / 14th August 1942 / From FLP in the Newlands Valley, to AEW at Lorton -

(*Concerning the Watchman Nee book mentioned above*) – Nee is splendid about the "delightfully unofficial" atmosphere of an assembly of those first days.

4222a/1 / 15th August 1942 / From Lorton –

(*Concerning some helpful words written by Oswald Chambers, leading on to some deep soul searching about the dominance of self*) –

... all weakness is from lack of concentration upon God. I am amazed at how long I (*that is, AEW*) can continue in a confused relationship or negative state of heart towards God.

By this testimony He is going to restore and complete the Church – causing it to stand apart from Professing Christianity, just as at the start it stood apart from Judaism.

... We may well ask ourselves in all reverence and sincerity, What sort of a time is Christ having in us? The truth is for the greater part He is ignored because we fail to realize He is in us (see John XVII).

... (*in the last few days*) – the Holy Spirit has been applying the cleansing fires of the Cross at the focal point of iniquity – the self-life. Until the believer is Christ-centred to God's satisfaction, iniquity in some sort will focus itself to our grief; and try as we will we cannot suppress it. The self-life if it exists must express itself in evil somewhere, or possibly in several places, though usually at one central point ... the cause is the self-life or adamic nature. ... the throne (*that is, of my heart/life*) is not yet His because SELF has not yet been DETHRONED. In this sphere there can be no make-believe.

If Christ is not the centre, whatever my knowledge of Divine things may be, I am SELF-CENTRED and in the last analysis I shall use Divine things, yea, Christ Himself if that were possible, to exalt myself.

... God <u>demands of us</u> that we seriously and deliberately dethrone "self" by accepting that at the Cross the Lord dealt with this self-life and took it from us, nailing it to the Tree. For this reason we are told to regard it as a dead thing. What shocks me is our (that is "my") willingness to go on in a powerless confused state, never getting to grips with the real cause of the impotence, but satisfied so long as I do not openly break down.

(*As Oswald Chambers writes*) – the Cross ... is <u>the moment of absolute surrender,</u> (*rather than mere*)<u> religious sentiment.</u>

... <u>until to God's satisfaction</u> the Cross is accepted for the flesh in every form, we shall remain religious but powerless. Self in some form will dominate us and the outgoing of the testimony will be only a form of self-realization. This is a loathsome thought and I dread it for myself or any of us.

Obedience carries an inestimable reward ... <u>He is there</u> but we ignore Him, or at the best (speaking with reverence) keep Him living in our drawing room which we visit in our best religious moods only.

1943

4303/1 / 4th July 1943 / From the Newlands Valley, to some supporters of the work –

(*A helpful reminder of the Chronology figures involved, though 1945 is now expected to be the year of the Lord's return*) –

On June 12th (*1933*) not only did the Christian dispensation officially end but the 6000 years of man's probationary history also ended <u>together with every other chronological era of Scripture</u>. As the Millennium of Christ's reign, that is the seventh thousand years, could not then begin, it was ordained of God that at that point Time should cease to be reckoned until the removal of the Church to heaven and the opening of Daniel's 70th week and all the events recorded in the Book of Revelation from the

4th Chapter on.

This interval which runs from 1933 to 1945 is called by the Lord Jesus "the consummation of the age" or "end of the world" as given in the Authorised Version in Matthew Xiii. 40 etc. The last reckoned point of time by God was June 12th 1933 and when the Lord descends from Heaven for His Church, as He will do on June 12th 1945, time will commence again and three important eras of Scripture will commence to run again.

The point to grasp is that June 12th 1933 is the latest point of time which God could name for the translation of the Church because thereafter He refuses to reckon time treating the interval as a hiatus, or break in Chronology. Anyone who quarrels with this statement, or rather 'reckoning of time', quarrels with God and not with His poor servant.

Very much more I could say on this side of the subject and particularly in bringing forward proofs from the Bible that the interval is fixed by God at 12 years, namely 1933 to 1945. (*We are obliged to note that in this expectation once again they were mistaken*).

(*Here AEW accounts for previous predictions which turned out to be mistaken*) -

I must say a brief word as to the reason why God allowed me His servant to make a statement about the Lord's Coming (*in June 1933*) which has proved to be a stone of stumbling and rock of offence to many (*Isaiah 8.14 / I Peter 2.8*). (*God wanted to cut off "the company" and take us aside, to instruct*). This he could not do unless our mouths were effectively closed, as they have been now for ten years.

The reason for this is that God utterly forbids that any part of this new revelation of Divine truth should reach Christendom until He authoritatively summons His children to come out of the sects of Christendom, since He will not feed them where they are, as all sectarianism is a denial of the one body of Christ.

It is clear to see that the Lord intends the sounding of the midnight cry that all His children shall leave the sects and commence to practise Christianity from the house, as at the beginning where they broke bread house to house.

The real truth is that it was the Lord presenting himself to His Church in the garb of the Great Date-Fixer of the ages – "a sign which shall be spoken against ... that the thoughts of many hearts should be revealed" (Luke ii.34).

... that He might have an instrument consistent with the dispensation which He could use to recover the Church to Himself, and not only so but to bring the Church to fulness as regards members.

(*Concerning the plan to write the book* **The Restored Vision**, *which was first published in 1957*) –

From the day we publish these new facts the Bible will radiate new life and light to God's people everywhere, and for the first time in history for 1800 years the truth will be told concerning the earthly pathway of our blessed Master illuminated by a true record of time covering every moment ... all of which was the priceless possession of the Church in the days of the Apostles.

... We are not our own masters and it is not left to us to supply our own needs. We have always been kept in the place of dependence and by this means we are caused to walk very near to God ...

We in fact believe the war will end in the early autumn.

You may blame us for having held out hopes and declaring our belief that the Lord would come in the years 1940 and 1941. This we deeply regret but it was unavoidable, since to be faithful to Christ in the matter of his coming we had also to be simple – simple enough to obey the light given us at the time. We of course fervently believed what we declared.

In March 1942 it pleased God in answer to definite prayer to lift the veil and allow us to see the complete programme, and with this the knowledge that God had a far greater purpose for the testimony than we had ever contemplated.

He then threw the searchlight forward three years to 1945 and has since confirmed this by many signs, specially from the Gospel of John where most of the recorded miracles are destined to have their counterpart in relation to the Church and Israel between the autumn of this year (*1943*) and the spring of 1945.

1944

(*In the spring of 1943 two members left the group and moved away to the south of England, a development which deeply upset AEW and turned out to be, with hindsight, quite a turning-point for the whole work with things being never quite the same again. But the work continued, and in late 1943 AEW rented Lanehead, a large house overlooking Coniston Water, for the first time. Some or all of the group were based there until April 1958*).

4401/1 / 11th April 1944 / From Lanehead, Coniston, to two members of the group still living for the moment in the Newlands Valley –

(*Concerning some recent visitors to Lanehead*) –

… and three "strangers" in our midst with their worldly talk and walk. I fear each is yet a stranger to the grace of God but all were present on Sunday A.M. (*at the gathering for worship*) and seemed a little impressed as the hidden meaning of the present world chaos was set forth and with it the need of Christ for salvation.

… but only sheer grace with some form of high explosive on the sleeping conscience alone would bring any to give up the world and its ways for Christ and their souls eternal join.

4403/2 / 3rd October 1944 / From AEW in Seascale, probably to the group members now based at Lanehead –

(*As late November draws near once again, the date of any 200-day warning that may need to be given regarding June 1945, the date they expect Christ to return, AEW checks through their position*) –

I ask myself therefore, (and you will do the same) do I really believe these things to be proven to us by the Scriptures, or am I trying to make myself believe them? – a very different thing.

Our one source of knowledge is the Scriptures, so I set myself day by day to go over the facts and re-express them to myself until the Spirit bears witness in power that what we believe is from the Scriptures and that presently – a matter of days or weeks – we shall be called of God, as in 1933, to bear witness to all men. The facts really believed are overpowering and should possess us as being the supreme issue of our lives every hour, day and night.

Dependence, expressed by an attitude of true humbleness of mind and heart, but with no lack of zeal in waiting upon the Lord by prayer and concentration, must avail to bring us into communion with Himself about His affairs and more than this, who can want?

4404/2 / 4th October 1944 / From Seascale –

(*Concerning the figures*) - There are many pitfalls for the uninstructed.

4406/1 / 10th October 1944 / From Seascale –

... before we can DO something God requires us to BE something. I can do lots of things and no one objects to doing things, but when God asks me to BE something, it signifies that He is not satisfied with the state of the vessel. This creates conflict, often of a dire order, and we know that there will be no advance until the Divine requirements are fully met.

No one is even allowed to act publicly for God or have any part in testimony without having to face in the light of the cross what we are by nature, that is our disposition to sin by some form or other of self-pleasing or self-gratification which is a contravention of Divine law, or for us as Christians the commands of Christ or His apostles through whom He bore testimony.

... The Lord would go forth but CANNOT. The vessels are not ready. Death is the only preparation – identification with Christ in death is the only preparation for the meaning of His resurrection life ... thus far the Cross has only disturbed the outer coating of the flesh ...

May God have mercy and extend grace to us each one.

4407/3 / 13th October 1944 / From Seascale –

(*A quotation from a Christian source at the start*) - "God always keeps us to the original terms of His call".

... somewhere in our beginnings we had a vision, and God will never fail to keep us up to it. Mine was manifestly Romans XII 1 to 2 and all failure ever since has been lack of faithfulness to the terms of those verses – i.e. the Burnt Offering aspect. I feel sadly how we (I speak for myself) fail to hold ground taken. Exercise for a time and then reversion to the old ways and habits. This is sheer lack of grit.

The essence of sin is self-pleasing – the essence of righteousness is yielding oneself to God, and one's members as instruments of righteousness with God.

4409/1 / 17th October 1944 / From Seascale -

It has occurred to me that the Red Sea is deliverance from sin and its power, while the Jordan is deliverance from self and odiousness.

I have realised that if there was to be movement there must be money, and now there is money and so there will be movement.

4410/2 / 18th October 1944 / Probably from Seascale –

(*Concerning the Seven Times of Daniel Chapter 4*) –

How is the Lord going to bring this motley, scattered and schismatic company (*that is, the true church spread across the sects and denominations*) into one path and to be of one mind and to say the same thing? ... We may well cry to God to show us what to do. We have light and knowledge which if shed broad would do much to unite the people of God, and how could they be reached other than by writing? Here is a subject for ardent prayer, the need of a (*illegible adjective*) message to the people of God – not facts and figures merely but <u>exhortation</u>.

4412/1 / 23rd October 1944 / From Seascale –

(*As Oswald Chambers writes*) – "the Spirit does not bear witness to our reason". Often I have wished for a clearer witness as to Nov 25th but probably God requires us to act in faith on the facts revealed and not to seek mathematical certainty which would oust faith.

Today I have reacted to the position (*concerning the Seven Times*) with a tired mind and body and this usually happens before light is given. I also had a bad night – all of which suggest an interest in matters by the powers of darkness.

It was 10 years ago on the 28th that light was given at Harlyn Bay on the 7 Times, (*see 1934, Extract 34-129a*) and again it may be that for this reason I have been called again to the sea. God has His own times for things to be done ...

4417/1 / 3rd November 1944 / To AEW from a lady supporter who has found his address after a long time –

(*Concerning the events of 1932 and 1933*) - <u>I</u> have not been stumbled, but honestly I have sought <u>in vain</u> for <u>one</u> friend to see <u>with me</u> as to your messages in 1932 and 1933!

What kept me from being stumbled about your messages in 1933 was this: - In answer to my prayer the Lord spoke to me from the Word thus Jeremiah 18.7-10, illustrated by Jonah 3. I asked some of my friends why they did not call Jonah a "lying prophet" if they reckoned Mr. Ware was one.

II Peter's words about the holy men of old speaking as "moved by the Holy Ghost" yet not fully understanding at the time just what the Holy Ghost signified by their message – so they sought for a "further revelation" and received it; - "to whom it was revealed" – and so in your case! But I've found myself quite alone in such a view point.

4418/1 / 3rd November 1944 / From Seascale –

(*Concerning the Lord*) - He never instructs before it is necessary as we learnt on April 25th 1933 when we had just seven days warning before we were called to make a public declaration on God's behalf.

Let prayer ascend and let it be the prayer of a living faith that has only the interests of Christ as its objective.

4422/2 / 14th November 1944 / From Seascale –

(*Concerning readiness for action*) –

I feel we must get as near as we can be by the Word alone and after that the Spirit will guide or reveal what cannot be discerned as to action.

4425/1 / 18th November 1944 / From Seascale –

I find fear of having to face an unsatisfied expectation again is a great hindrance to simplicity. I seek to tread this down as that which Satan would use against me. In the main I can say that very often I find myself in liberty as I contemplate the message I believe we have to deliver to the world.

I have no doubt the Spirit alone could know what is to be said, having respect to God's honour and glory which so easily and unwittingly a human might besmirch ... I shall watch hourly now for a word as to moving from here – how good it is to be a servant and not a master and only have to do what one is shown ... If any developments I shall phone FLP.

4427/1 / 23rd November 1944 / From Seascale –

Prayer was, as I expected, much contested, and for long I felt bound in spirit with that deadly sensation which seems to grip one by the heart and the presence of which I have long known signifies a deadly effort of unseen powers to throttle all prayer, or turn it into a series of meaningless words.

... there is no room for question as to 1945 being the year the Lord will come.

1945

4505/4 / 23rd April 1945 / From Seascale, a different address –

Let us pray that we may fully enter in to the mind and purposes of God, and not be turned aside by previously deferred hopes. It is important that we should be directed by the Spirit as to the preparation to be made ...

4506 / 27th April 1945 / From Lanehead, to those who are still living elsewhere in the area –

(*Concerning their annual keeping of the Lord's Supper on 28th April each year*) – It is a pity we cannot all be together for this blessed memorial of the Lord's death. May the season be prepared for and kept in sincerity and simplicity of heart. I expect we shall be alone on the earth keeping the occasion on the true anniversary.

4508/1 / 25th July 1945 / From London W6 to a lady supporter of the work –

May the Lord guide you and keep you quiet and trusting in a day when

4510/2 / 14th August 1945 / From Hammersmith Post Office to one of the group probably living in Ambleside at that time –

… a call to duty may come at any moment. May we be ready for the call – it will be stern and we shall need unlimited grace to obey.

… Keep in touch and get any from Lanehead to join you but let the Spirit be in evidence.

4513/3 / 21st August 1945 / From FLP at Lanehead to AEW in London –

(*We*) remember also that the ground taken together in London – full understanding of the Chronology – has developed now into a larger territory – the Chronology and prophecy linked together.

4514/1 / 22nd August 1945 / From London W6, probably to Lanehead

(*On June 12th 1933*) the Assembly of God which had existed for 1900 years (2000 Bible years) was totally and finally rejected by Christ for its unfaithfulness and lukewarmness, and the whole Dispensation from AD 33 to 1933 viewed as having ended in dismal failure with the Church uncompleted and the Father's House with numberless seats without guests (Luke XIV. 22) as it were. (*The Dispensation*) failed of its object, and the whole thing was therefore rejected by Christ. Now if the matter stopped there it would means that God had attempted something too great and had failed.

How glorious that our God is a Rock and His purposes cannot fail, though they may be delayed through man's failure to receive the good God bestows. The Dispensation however did fail, and this being so there was no Gentile Bride for the Lord in 1933 – only an unfaithful harlot Church which was living in sin with the nations of the world.

… in 1933 God began a new purpose or rather a new plan to accomplish the original purpose.

On April 1st 1938 we were introduced as a company into a place of death and that was our true beginning.

(*The Lord to return 12th June 1946*) – we are to see the mighty power of God exerted so that His original purpose – a Gentile Bride for His Son and eternal companion and co-sharer in His eternal glories.

... (*By*) God's grace the Church will leave the earth in 1946 in a blaze of glory such as was seen in those first months as recorded in Acts. What a plan it all is and how perfect are the ways of God.

... Really these past seven years, when seen as God has marked them out and measured them, leave one speechless with amazement. The world will be amazed when it knows all.

May the Lord stir our own hearts into greater faithfulness so that when we meet Him face to face, as those who have experienced His favour in a special degree, we may not be ashamed.

4516/1 / 24th August 1945 / From London W6 –

... that in a brief season now we shall be able to share all these riches with the whole company of disciples on earth, but not until by some act the Lord has brought them out of their present evil associations on to the ground we have had to take ...

In plain words, in 1938 the Day of Jehovah opened in heaven ...

... the brides of the Lord – Gentile and Jewish ...

The present is a critical moment, and I doubt not that in giving all this understanding the Lord is giving us the final equipment needed in going forth to declare His counsel to the Church, Israel and the nations.

... Never has the world been more prepared by adverse facts or ominous signs for listening to what God the Lord has to say, and of a surety God

The Ware-Paine Testimonies

has set the stage and for a brief moment He will invite all the world once again to consider the question, "What then shall I do with Jesus that is called Christ?".

May the Lord help us to hold for His glory all the precious things of the Sun and Moon that He has bestowed upon us.

4518/1 / 29th August 1945 / From London W6 –

Seldom does God do anything anyone expects ... we may get a word about it or else a witness from the Spirit that we must act.

... we must not rule out the thought that we might have to step out in faith. One thing stands out above all others and that is the need to write the whole story out for all to take heed who will. I conceive that come what may this will be the next thing on our programme.

... it is often enough with God to mark a date so that it can be pointed back to and take its place in the Divine plan.

4523/2 / 11th October 1945 / From Friston near Eastbourne –

Light and truth that God has given us has got to be placed upon a candlestick so that it may give light to all that are in the house.

Directly we get on to Ephesian ground and realise our union with Christ, we cease praying soulish prayers, which most often are the mere expression of natural religiousness, and enter upon intercession, the starting point of which is the supremacy of Christ and our blessed union with Him in that supremacy.

From that point the instruments are acting in harmony with the forces of light in the heavenlies. (*Quite a sentence follows!* ...) - The dignity of the position possesses the soul, as our oneness in Christ is realised by the manner in which the forces of darkness are dispelled before an intercession which avails before the throne, because the instrument is able to present the all-prevailing Name of the Lord with all that attaches to that Name, and not to come with prayers which emanate from the soul and which are really the outcome of that inferiority complex which the powers of darkness produce in those who are engaged in warfare for which they are not equipped through lack of intelligence or diligence.

No one engaged in the work of God is exempt from this warfare. Satan is a powerful foe and he employs cunning tactics and we need not think that past victories will save us from future conflicts, though they may verily increase our knowledge of the art of warfare in the heavenlies.

4525/1 / 26th October 1945 / From Friston –

(*Nothing much to report*) - as the season here seems to have been an occasion when we have been left "in soak", and this I trust in preparation for what is yet to be accomplished in the way of writing and editing what is written.

Last night we had a most solemn season, speaking openly of things in the life of which hinder true communion – sin in the flesh – and suggesting that it is for this reason I have never been allowed to write the life of the Lord – a task demanding practical holiness of no mean order. Confession was made before God, and one another, of failure, and the cry went up for greater power from the Lord to walk in purity and holiness with Him as the life.

May we all strive that He may ever be <u>at home</u> in our midst but for this all sin (for which He died) must die out in us.

4530/3/ 11th November 1945 / From FLP in Friston, (in the south, helping AEW with typing work) to a colleague, in Ambleside or at Lanehead -

(*Concerning Jonah as a "type"*) - The Spirit ever since has been confined in Christendom (the whale) in the nations (the sea) and has really <u>suffered</u> suffocation practically – never being free to utter the truth of God. Now God is going to <u>loose</u> the testimony of the Spirit and has for this purpose had to revive or bring to light again <u>the Truth</u> which we have received.

4535a/2 / 5th December 1945 / From Friston –

The UNO (*United Nations Organisation*) is the devil's substitute for the reign of the Prince of Peace, and this organisation will constitute the great competitor to the testimony of Christ which is about to be raised up in Christendom.

CHAPTER 7
1946 -1949

1946

4606/3 / 27th July 1946 / From Friston, to a critic of their work –

… under the pernicious influence of the modernist cult … which first in Germany and later throughout the world turned the masses of men away from a spiritual to a material outlook on life, and as a result has landed the world into its present state of irremediable chaos.

(*Concerning Matthew 6.19-34*) - and face the fact that no believer in Christ has the right to cast aside words which for all time establish the principles upon which His disciples must act in all such matters.

For our sakes whose conduct you assail, please read those words carefully and be not thereafter influenced by the fact that the vast majority of nominal Christians wilfully and totally ignore what Christ taught. Are you prepared to say that those who put Christ's teaching into practice are fools because it is so rarely done?

Take a look at where this cursed practising of a nominal Christianity has landed mankind. Christ calls the few who practise His teaching "the salt of the earth", because if it were not that they acted as a preservative within the leavened mass of nominal Christians, the whole thing would long ago have gone to total corruption and returned to an abysmal heathenism.

It is just twenty years since I left business because of an insistent call to devote my whole life to the active service of our Saviour, whose return I knew was drawing very near.

4608/1 / 16th December 1946 / From the Keswick Hotel –

There have not been wanting inward evidences that the hour has really struck for the writing of the message which will acquaint Christendom with the fact of the Lord's imminent appearing (*now understood to be 12th June 1947*) and of its own speedy dissolution and destruction in the seven years which follow.

I need to be deeply convicted that this is the end and that mercy's door will close on this generation when the Lord descends next June 12 as Master of the house.

4609/1 / 19th December 1946 / From Keswick –

(*Concerning the coming judgments, they are conscious of the need to interpret correctly the relationship between the Chronology figures on the one hand, and the various "types" they believe to be relevant on the other, an interpretation they have frequently got wrong in the past*) -

... knowing what we do, we cannot but feel in some measure the same deep sorrow for the blinded masses in this and other lands, upon whom presently equally fearful destruction is coming ... and in less than 6 months Christendom will have been shut up to the judgements of the Apocalypse.

Have we received final light as to the time of the Lord's descent for the Church? This question cannot be solved by mere recourse to the mass of chronological facts which clearly appear to declare the Coming next June (*that is, in 1947*).

These are of course vital and upon them our faith is to rest as they are a part of God's revelation in the Scriptures; but not being a series of positive statements the question ever arises as to interpretation of the Divine types in the Chronology.

This letter is in part answered by the fact that all these types agree in revealing that 1954 is the year of the Kingdom. By inference therefore we know that 1947 must witness the start of the Apocalyptic seven years we call Daniel's seventieth week and consequently the appearing of the Lord for His bride.

... the issue is a spiritual one and not only a chronological one. By this I mean the chronological data only begins to LIVE as we hold it in relation to the Lord Himself.

... we are therefore driven not to the facts but to the Lord – in a sense from the Written Word to the Incarnate Word who is the Way, the Truth and the Life.

(*On Skiddaw*) - After lunch I went along on a level with the halfway house to the first ghyll. It is a spot seldom touched by foot of man and quite high up. Here in the sun and out of any wind I was able to lift up "my heart with my hands" to the heavens. Such prayer is never easy or meant to be, but if persisted in on the ground of the precious Blood, it must avail to drive back the forces of darkness that assail all those who give themselves up to supplication in reference to the interests of Christ ... Two Scriptures were latterly brought before me, "Then shall we know, if we follow on to know the Lord (Hosea VI), and John VII 17 "If any man willeth to do His will he shall know of the teaching, whether it be of God".

... for myself of recent years I have felt I was losing ground because of a lack of inward zeal and personal delight in contemplating the Lord's appearing.

... hope deferred maketh the heart sick ... Lukewarmness is to Him repulsive ... There used to be much more zeal in our midst and no doubt the wicked one watches and strives to dull our affections and get us off into self-pity or self-occupation and so rob the Lord of the one thing He looks for in a company which He has set apart for Himself and highly favoured with an abundance of light such as can be possessed by none others on the earth.

... when Laodiceanism is rampant and when God's children are seeking to keep the body of Christ warm by piling on religious clothes and the like.

... never has there been so much religion and religious talk but it all lacks heart because it ignores His request to His own to watch for His appearing which is now at hand. Utter coldness exists between the head and the body of Christ, and for this He disowns all their testimony.

... It is affection Christ wants and a little sincere interest in the matter of His return, but this the cold body of Laodiceans refuse Him. They will have nothing to do with dates or times or seasons – the one thing which to Him is of absorbing interest because of His love for His bride for whom He is now coming, that He may take her away from the coming wrath of God and have her safe by His side in His Father's house.

Dear friends, if we are an Abishag company (*see I Kings 1.1-4*) our position is to have part with Christ in bringing warmth again to His Body, the Church, before He returns. It is the dates and the knowledge of the times that will do this and nothing else.

Am I warm towards Christ? ... do I love His appearing? I count on your unceasing prayers as we cannot stand still but must advance.

1947

4701/1 / 7th March 1947 / From near Coniston –

The God of Christendom is, before all, the God of Israel, and He is also the God of the forces of nature.

4702/1 / 11th June 1947 / From Lanehead –

The truth is that between 1933 and the coming of the Kingdom, God has designed a certain pattern of time. <u>This pattern can only be discerned as it is experimentally lived</u>, and by no other way.

4706/2 / 5th October 1947 / From Seascale –

I trust you are finding access to the throne. Anyone can pray with the lips but Esther got to the throne and found favour because she fasted 3 days and 3 nights – that is, she became identified with the death of Jesus anticipatively and that means the knife to the flesh.

4707/1 / 8th October 1947 / From Seascale –

If we knew <u>true</u> dependence, such as the Lord upon His Father, we should, like Paul, be always delivered unto death for Jesus' sake – that is, always at an extremity of need – a need which if unmet would mean catastrophe and dishonour. Instead of this we, feeling no actual sense of need in any realm, lapse into a careless and heedless walk, and only come to our spiritual senses when some need awakens us or when faced with some demand from God we feel utterly unable to meet. To myself I say, brethren, these things ought not to be.

Yours in the one conflict, AE Ware.

4710/3 / 17th October 1947 / From Seascale –

I woke up to the fact that I was getting bound in my spirit and, like a sponge with no water in it, all dried up and not a thought of any value but only a hopeless sense of utter incompetence and impotence.

4712/4 / 27th October 1947 / From Seascale –

… great are the efforts of the enemy to withstand advance.

God <u>must</u> always honour as the basis of all blessing the Son and the work of the Son – He well knows if He does not, who will?

4713/1 / 29th October 1947 / From Seascale –

Expenses generally are running away with resources but as long as all is needful, the Lord will supply our needs.

It is clear that the Lord intends to address all who are His in Christendom, but this means the document must be suited to a most general circulation and not just fitted for evangelicals.

4714/2 / 2nd November 1947 / From Seascale -

(*Written on this, the 30th anniversary of the Balfour Declaration*) –

As you know I have a personal link with this day 30 years ago, for it was then I received my first quickening and was led to begin the study of prophecy, so I am 30 years of age in that realm.

Our late sister Jxxxx Lxxxx was very strong in pressing upon saints the need of seeking protection in this way (*that is, from the devil's efforts to plant in our minds thoughts that are not the mind of God*), as immense mischief can be wrought by accepting a suggestion about anything or anybody without testing its origin, so Paul speaks of every thought being made captive to Christ.

4715/2 / 5th November 1947 / From Seascale –

… the members of Christ are to separate themselves from all that Christ has rejected.

… no doubt the Lord intends the message to work havoc like the sword of the sons of Levi (*Exodus 32.25-28*) who at once responded. In a sense the blessing we want for the unsaved depends on the obedience of God's children. If they obey and separate themselves from the evils of Christendom, as we believe they must do, then the Lord can move mightily to adding such as should be saved.

4717/2 / 23rd November 1947 / From Seascale –

(*Concerning the wedding of Princess Elizabeth and Philip Mountbatten*)

… but I see signs which may be ominous. First it was all done before a "High Altar" and we know God has reproved Britain for such things. Xxxxx (*a senior cleric in the Church of England*) is a flat-out rejector of the testimony and has had more put before him than anyone in England. A redeeming feature is the old Prayer Book.

Nevertheless it does all seem a type and a perfect illustration of the great event which follows the fall of the false church at the end of the week (*that is, the 7-year "week" of tribulation as described in Daniel 9.27 and in Revelation Chapters 4-19*).

May the dear bride be saved, and her splendid young husband, and never ascend the throne of decadent Britain.

4718/2 / 24th November 1947 / From Seascale –

I find an increasing desire and prayer to God for the ability to tell the story of those years from 1927 on in words that will bring out the purpose of God in His dealings with us.

... There is the waiting on God that refuses to go away <u>unheard</u>. The things Christ most needs can only be got by supplicating the Throne in that attitude ... We ask for much when we ask for the worldwide circulation of all the precious light God has given. Do we wonder there is an array of satanic forces and the power of darkness against even a start being made? Have we done thinking about ourselves and the place accorded us? If not, our prayers are all around our pettifogging selves, and we cannot launch out into the deep of Divine purpose but hug the fogbound shore where all the rocks are.

A look back fifteen years is useful in helping one to grasp the persistence of God in the execution of His purposes which now will begin to broaden out into a mighty stream embracing all the members of Christ on earth and not restricted to the narrow limits of a small representative company.

... to the natural man it is always <u>the time</u> but God's times are according to His own inscrutable wisdom which is discerned after and <u>not</u> before or very seldom so.

... and let us stick to it that there can be <u>no rain</u> until the sword has been put over the false prophets of Christendom. Afterwards there will be the sound of abundance of rain but the whole sham religious Christendom must be exposed first (*from I Kings 17 and 18*).

Have you power with God through Christ? (*I Corinthians 1.24*) - then for Christ's sake use it to bring down to the dust of your feet the assembled hosts of the hidden foes who will not let go until they are literally compelled to by Divine power operating thro' the members of Christ on earth – that is ourselves. The triumph is sure but eternity will reveal what part, if any, each of us has had in effecting Satan's defeat on this issue.

4719/2 / 26th November 1947 / From Seascale –

(*Concerning AEW starting to write up the testimony today, 15 years to the day from November 1932*) -

Is this surprising when we know God has a time for everything under the sun?

4720/1 / 27th November 1947 / From Seascale –

(*After Mrs Ware found herself on the steps of the Friends Meeting House in London, exactly 15 years, to the very day and hour, after they held their first 200-day warning meeting there in November 25th 1932*) -

Praise God for inadvertency – it is always thus He works.

(*Concerning Palestine*) - Britain has made the whole matter to stink in the nostrils of those who are to some degree honestly trying to get a solution for Palestine.

1948

4801/1 / 15th March 1948 / From a faithful supporter in Penzance –

Maybe He (*the Lord*) intends us to let go of everything that would hinder and find no joy, peace or satisfaction except in communion with Himself.

… Our confidence in the message remains unshaken … where we can't trace, we trust, and in spite of our shortcomings and failures we still wait for the Lord from Heaven. We remember you in our prayers and many a time I have felt the answer to your prayers.

4809/2 / 11th June 1948 / From Lanehead, Coniston, to an interested enquirer –

... Jesus – the Wonderful Numberer ...

This chronological structure, which is astronomically perfect in every detail and embraces no less than four chronologies, holds the vast edifice of Divine Truth together, just as the steel framework does the modern skyscraper.

Sacred history is transformed because each event is seen to take its appointed place according to a predetermined plan of time, the date of which from the Fall onwards has been fixed in terms of our own and the Bible's calendar. The Bible critic is thus to be silenced, and all the world is to behold evidence which affords such proof of the veracity of God's revelation as has never yet been allowed to appear before men, and this as a last demonstration of the long-suffering mercy of God towards a world on the brink of doom.

... the sham pretensions of religious Christendom and all its paraphernalia of iniquity will come crashing down before a revelation of the Holy Scriptures which for a time will silence rationalistic infidelity and assure the apostate of his doom.

4811/3 / 29th June 1948 / From Lanehead, Coniston, to the same recipient as in 4809 –

(*Concerning the Church, that it is not to go through the 70th Week of Daniel 9.27, the period that includes "the great tribulation"*) –

Once it is realised that this coming seven years is a period of retributive judgement upon the Jews nationally (i.e., the Seventieth Week) and the Gentiles governmentally (the Seven Times) for the rejection and killing of John the Baptist and Christ in the seven years, AD 26 to 33, and that it is in fact these very seven years re-lived, then it is easy to see that the

Church has no place in such a period, as it did not then exist.

Furthermore, a Christian is one who has partaken of the grace shown to mankind in the seven years (AD 26 to 33) when as Peter declares, Jesus "went in and out among us" (Acts 1.22).

4812/2 / 19th September 1948 / From one of the group currently in Essex, to AEW at Lanehead –

... one of the hardest things to bear is the waiting, but grace has been given for the patient waiting as light from heaven has shone upon the path each year, enabling faith to place its footsteps upon that which God has shewn, so that that Word has been made good to us which was spoken to Joshua by the Lord when he was being commissioned to bring Israel across the Jordan - "Every place that the sole of your foot shall tread upon that have I given you" (*Joshua 1.3*).

(*Concerning religious Christendom*) - they are "willingly ignorant" (*II Peter 3.5*). That is, they do not, I believe, want to know, because it would mean changing their course.

4813/1 / October 1948, exact date unknown / From London SW3, to those at Lanehead –

To us this is not a religious side issue but the supreme issue in our lives – we can well say the ruling issue. It is due to the faithful Bridegroom that some should so regard His coming.

4814/1 / 1st November 1948 / From London SW3, to those based at Lanehead –

(*Concerning AEW being in London rather than at Lanehead*) - Yet nevertheless it is well to have the change and to be compelled to rub shoulders with some of our fellow-mortals whose pathway is ever in "the madding crowd". If one had to abide in such a sphere one would need to cultivate an inward separateness such as marked our Master when He was moving amidst the hurly-burly of everyday life in the crowded towns and villages of Palestine. No wonder He often retired to the Mt of Olives or some other mountain rendezvous.

1949

4902/3 / 24th September 1949 / From Lanehead, to an enquirer –

(*A long extract is included here as a good example of AEW's understanding of the Scriptures on various points of debate, such as "the day of the Lord", the Rapture, the tribulation and the Second Advent, and of his thorough approach and robust style: he "knew his stuff", and would make short work of anyone disagreeing with him who appeared not to have a good scriptural case in their support. We see once again in this extract AEW's longing for the Church to accept the Testimony, given over the years through AEW and his colleagues by the Holy Spirit*) –

(*Concerning II Peter 3.10 and "the day of the Lord"*) - "But <u>the day of the Lord</u> will come as a thief in the night; in the which the heavens shall pass away with a great noise, and the elements shall melt with fervent heat, the earth also and the works that are therein shall be burned up".

Here we have given us the two limits of "the day of the Lord": its entrance as a thief, and its end when the present heavens and earth are destroyed by fire and the new heaven and new earth brought in as described in the end of the Revelation. This we learn was to be at the end of the thousand-year reign of Christ.

From these facts there emerges a most solemn situation. We have proved beyond any possibility of dispute that the 6000 years of man ended on June 12 1933. We have also learned that gentile governmental supremacy also ceased with the completion of the 2520 years from Jan 8th BC 588 when they began. The fact therefore stands out that "the day of the Lord" <u>opened at the moment that the six days of man ended</u> and, as foretold by Paul and Peter, it opened as "a thief in the night". Indeed no one on earth knows it but ourselves because no one knows the 6000 years of man then terminated.

... This in fact means that all the great events since 1933 have come about by direction of the Lord and in fulfilment of the prophecies. Hitler is the Assyrian of Isaiah X and God's predicted scourge to Israel outside the land. Mussolini is the seventh head of the Image referred to in Revelation XVII 10 ... Mussolini's Roman Empire lasted 7 years to the day and he fell 7 years and 77 days from its inception on May 9th 1936. The State of Israel rising on May 14th 1948 was the grandest and most positive fulfilment of prophecy since the Fall of Jerusalem in AD 70 and one of the greatest ever.

... There is not much to say about the tribulation theory (*that is, the belief that the Church is to pass through the tribulation period*) ... (*Its supporters*) have sought to bring utterly irrelevant Scriptures to bear upon their theory that the Church is to go through the fearful judgement era as defined in the revelation. They apply the Olivet Discourse to the Church and think the elect there spoken of are those of this dispensation, when they are the Jews who believe and who are referred to in Isaiah 65.9 ...

The tribulation theory is killed outright by the plain statements of Paul in I Thess. In chapter 1.10 ... we read – "to wait for His Son from heaven", but this is followed by those vital words, "Whom He raised from the dead, even Jesus who delivereth us out from (ek) the coming wrath". This is the literal translation of the Greek.

Then again in I Thess V, lest believers should take alarm, the Apostle confirms the above by saying (verse 9) "For God hath not appointed us to wrath but to obtain salvation by our Lord Jesus Christ, who died for us that whether we watch or sleep (i.e. die), we should live together with Him".

That should be enough for anyone. We shall be here when the day of the Lord opens, but at a given moment the Lord would appear to raise the dead and change the living members of His body and remove all from this sphere to heaven. Then a period spoken of as "the great and terrible day of the Lord" (see Joel II and Malachi IV and Acts II) will open – this period to be preceded by celestial phenomena and the appearing of Elijah. This "great and terrible day of the Lord" is the judgment era and lasts for seven years and is called Daniel's 70th Week (see Daniel IX 27), and it must not be confused with "the day of the Lord", of which it forms the judgment element. I have just looked through all references in the Old Testament given in Scofield Bible (Is(*aiah*) II) and I find all refer to "the great and terrible day of the Lord". Therefore the expression "day of the Lord" used by Paul and Peter forms a New Testament revelation given to the Church.

It is a staggering and solemn fact that the whole Church is in grievous error as touching the Lord's Day, the Lord's Supper, and the Lord's Coming. Now just at the end the Lord calls a few of us to come apart while He opens to us the Scriptures so that we, at His appointed time, may go forth in His Name and carry the light and truth to all His own, if and when they rise up and respond to the cry "Behold, the Bridegroom, come ye out to meet Him".

Thus there shall be light at eventide and all ignorance shall be dispelled, and the Church end its days in the enjoyment of all the light possessed at the beginning and so fulfil not only the prayer of John XVII but the command of the Apostle in Romans 15 that ye may with <u>one</u> mind and <u>one</u> mouth glorify God; and again in I Corinthians 1.7-10 when he writes "Now I beseech you, brethren, by the name of our Lord Jesus Christ, that ye all <u>speak the same</u> thing and that there be no divisions (schisms) among you, "but that ye be perfectly joined together in <u>the same mind</u> and in <u>the same judgment</u>.

When it pleases the Lord to allow the truth to go forth in all its purity, it will not be optional to believers to declare that which is palpably the Truth is not the Truth, for this would deprive the Lord of the joy of beholding His own speaking <u>the same thing</u> and of being <u>in the same mind</u> and <u>the same judgment</u>. Presently the Lord is going to make the nominal Christian world acknowledge those whom He owns as His (Rev III.9) but this could not be until all have bowed to the truth and are of one mind and one heart.

The sum of all I have endeavoured to set forth is this. The Second Advent of Christ is an event which takes place at a given point of time after "the day of the Lord" has opened. This being so the Apostle urges the Thessalonians not to sleep but to watch and be sober "so that that day did not overtake them as a thief. To know when "the day of the Lord" would open they must be fully instructed in "the times and the seasons".

... In plain language the Morning Star is Christ Himself revealed by the Spirit through perfect understanding of Chronology, the very portion of the Bible despised and turned from by the masses of deluded believers who have been taught that such matters are not for us and that to be engaged in them is a sure sign of a low spiritual state.

Well may we thank God for allowing us to have part with Christ in the recovery and setting forth of truth which will transform the Church before it is translated to Heaven.

CHAPTER 8
1950 - 1957

1950

5010/3 / 8th September 1950 / From London SW3, to those still at Lanehead –

(*Concerning the first major book AEW is starting to write about the work and the Testimony, a book later fully entitled* **World in Liquidation, The Coming Of Christ At Hand** *and published in May 1953*) –

In a sense we are declaring war on the whole of religious Christendom and must act in such a way as to gain the full support of God …

Never before have we written for the world and in the consciousness that it is actually going out to accomplish God's purpose. (*By these pages*) – which <u>by the facts they contain</u> will create horror in religious Christendom … its circulation will be enormous no doubt … but probably 250 to 300 pages …

5012/2 / 19th September 1950 / From London SW3 –

What has to be made clear - and that is the reason all this had to come first - is that God demands that people should see how manifestly it (*the Testimony*) comes through a channel which is utterly apart from religious Christendom. New light given over the heads of all to a few unknown who stood icily apart from everything in religious Christendom, and who now are the condemners of all.

So often many points are only a matter of opinion, and the rule should be: no change (*to what they have already agreed concerning the Testimony details*) unless obviously wrong or unless by a change the meaning becomes much more clear.

5017/2 / 16th October 1950 / From London SW3 –

For us all now our days should be worked with <u>sacrifice</u> and no ground given to a do-as-you-please life ... any effort to just live a normal life is to give ground to the adversary and to weaken the cause of Christ. How true that knowledge of the Bible is <u>not</u> communion, which is having common interest with Christ at each moment about everything.

5018/2 / 25th October 1950 / From London SW3 –

I am unquestionably tired but I seek to depend day by day for the needed help to bring this paper to conclusion in a right manner ... we could hardly expect so solemn a matter to be created in ease or comfort.

I trust we may all indulge in "our utmost for His highest" – if not we shall look foolish at the Judgment Seat of Christ, presently.

May the Lord see us through, but not only so, may He see us through as those led in triumph - in the train of a Conqueror, as Chambers puts it. Farewell and with greetings and love to all.

Yours in Him, AE Ware.

(*Now a series of brief extracts from 1st November 1950 to 10th December 1950, each written from London SW3 to those at Lanehead, with AEW pressing on with the writing while the old questions over targets and timings remain*) –

5020/3 ... shows we are in line with the Spirit's thought. So, I press on and am thankful for the strength to do so.

5022/2 (*Concerning a shortage of funds*) - We may be near some deliverance but it is a grand thing to know how to be abased.

5023/2 ... Am in grip of nasty cold but it all keeps one dependent.

5026/2 ... Keep up the prayer barrage ... I am touching the very heart of all that is in these pages.

5027/2 ... when things move we should all at times be South. This is a matter for prayer and seeking God's way. We really need clear light on the whole future.

5028/2 The great problem is, Are we now to act on the assumption the Lord is to appear next June?

(*There now follows a gap of several years in the correspondence.* **World in Liquidation** *was published in 1953, but despite there being so much of value within it, the book received bad reviews, these arising once again mainly over the "date-fixing" predictions which, also once again, turned out to be mistaken. For most of these years some group members remained based at Lanehead, though Mr and Mrs Ware were usually based at Willingdon in Sussex from early 1956 until mid-1957*).

1956

5610/1 / 20th February 1956 / From Willingdon in Sussex, to those still at Lanehead –

The Bible answers all its own queries ...

(*Concerning the gift of a menorah gift from Great Britain to Israel*) –

Israel will again be the only light in the world as formerly. The Church's candlestick has been removed (*since June 1933*) ...

5614/1 / 2nd March 1956 / From Willingdon, Sussex –

I hope ... that your seasons of prayer are effective and leave you with the sense of having been in the presence of God.

... it is up to everyone to keep to the proper and appointed time for meeting. It is an appointment with God and if anyone is lawfully detained they should send word so as not to hinder others, but nothing really should be allowed to interfere with the one occasion in which the concerns of Christ are given exclusive attention.

(*Concerning the first woman to join the prayer group which until then had been men-only*) –

I hear Mrs Xxxxx has commenced joining you. This puts a great responsibility on her to keep in that place of unobtrusiveness becoming to her sex and maintaining "a meek and quiet spirit, which in the sight of God is of great price" (*I Peter 3.4b*).

At a prayer meeting (*the content*) must be exclusively God-concerns. If a wrong element intrudes or anything not "in the Spirit", it creates self-consciousness and those most sensitive to the Spirit will be the first to feel the self-consciousness. Prayer made under such conditions will be artificial and from the mind. The Holy Spirit alone can indite prayers that avail before the Throne.

(*Concerning a young man also possibly joining the prayer group*) –

... it would be wholly out of place and out of proportion that one so inexperienced should join those who have been long on the road and able to view prayers as a conflict with the powers of darkness as in Ephesians VI. Xxxxx's sincerity and keenness no one doubts and it is good to have him in our midst, but he would be the first to see the unsuitability of putting a pupil of the Second Form suddenly into the "Sixth".

This weekly gathering should be a fixed appointment and not be left for the convenience of any to decide ... nothing is so sweet as Christian fellowship.

An absence of love will make such occasions boring ... I wonder if at heart we are really "tinkling cymbals" (*I Corinthians 13.1*) with a religious "get up".

5629/2 / 6th May 1956 / From Willingdon, Sussex –

May the Lord reward her (*a daughter of one of the group members*) and all these younger members for standing by us and upholding Divine principles.

5633/1 / 11th May 1956 / From Willingdon, Sussex, to a supporter with some questions –

Why are the myriads of prayers never answered? Surely because God's people know not the judgment of the Lord touching the present hour (Jeremiah VIII.7).

... I am convinced that no other way is possible now (*that is, than for Christian believers to meet in homes*), if we are to uphold the principles of the unity of the body of Christ.

(*Concerning II Thessalonians Chapter 2*) – who will say whether "the apostasy" is an event or a phase?

God gave Sir Edward Denny of the Brethren light on this subject over 100 years ago and I for one have long rejoiced in that light though his own group rejected it ... (*In essence, this was*) the knowledge that the 70th week was lived from AD 26 to 33 and then cancelled by God because of what happened, in order that it might be brought in again at the end of this age as a period of retributive judgment; (*this*) is the key to all Bible prophecy and Bible Chronology.

That God should give light to some at this end on this subject, (*that is, over the timing of the Rapture*) should surprise no-one, and that he should give it to those who have returned to the original ground established by the Holy Ghost at the beginning should not surprise you, as you have done so yourself.

... Why the Brethren never saw the difference between the Lord's Supper and the Breaking of Bread I cannot tell. We take the Lord's Supper (with the two emblems) – as the Jews the Passover – once a year in the evening of April 29th (*) which is the anniversary of "the night in which He was betrayed". We break bread together at midnight on May 2-3rd (*) because it is the anniversary of the Lord's resurrection as kept by Paul and the Church at Troas in AD 59. We break bread at Pentecost (June 21st) and at other times.

((*) *Strictly speaking these dates are one day out, and, according to the Company's own findings, should read April 28th and the midnight of May 1st-2nd. These dates just given are the exact anniversaries in our current Gregorian Calendar of the Last Supper that was held in the evening of Thursday 30th April AD 33 (Julian Calendar); and the Resurrection, which occurred at the midnight between Sunday May 3rd and Monday May 4th AD 33 (Julian Calendar).*

Because the Gregorian Calendar now mistakenly trails the Julian Calendar by 2 days, the correct dates in our present Gregorian Calendar for these two observances are therefore April 28th and May 1st-2nd.

However, presumably the need for exact precision, to the very day, over the dates in question is less important than the upholding of the underlying principles – namely the annual observance of the Lord's Supper being linked to the date of the Passover and Last Supper, and the thanksgiving for Christ's Resurrection at the midnight hour).

... In my book (**World in Liquidation**) I give the facts which no one can gainsay. Anyone among God's people who accept these facts, namely, that Christendom was then "cut off" and the Assembly rejected by our Lord Jesus as His witness in the earth, will be allowed of God to partake of all the light He has since given. To all such the Lord will be revealed as the Day Star (*II Peter 1.19*) and every such one will possess in his or her heart the bright shining of a good light that removes all uncertainty as to the time of His appearing. It is when all His own awaken from sleep that "the Spirit and the bride" will say "Come" because they see Him as the Morning Star (*Revelation 2.28 & 22.16-17*).

5636/1 / 25th May 1956 / From Willingdon, Sussex –

(*Concerning Billy Graham being supported by the Church of England, an article by a bishop*) – ... shows that C of E support for Billy Graham was his undoing as so many "converts" died in the dead atmosphere of dead churches and chapels. Underneath I have marked a statement by a well-known writer as to losing his faith at confirmation.

5645/1 / 22nd June 1956 / From Willingdon, Sussex, to Lanehead –

God's ways are passed finding out (*Romans 11.33*) and it is useless to make plans for Him ... all such experiences (*that is, their disappointment at there being no "sign" they were hoping for on a significant date*) are a part of the price we have to pay as watchmen.

To be without expectations is to cease to watch.

5647/1 / 6th July 1956 / From Ovingdean, Sussex, to Lanehead –

(*Concerning the years since 1933*) – whereas we have been shut up in prison and silent.

(*Concerning AEW possibly to come north to Lanehead soon*) –

I hope I may find Christ in control at Lanehead.

(*Lanehead was rented from a family based at the time in Syria*) –

... a <u>Syrian tent</u> given to us four leprous men as a token of God's purposes in the gathering of riches and food with which to meet the needs of the starving in Christendom (*see II Kings Chapter 7.3ff*).

Lanehead may be used for subsidiary purposes but if those dominate and the primary purpose is subordinated to these, then the Spirit is grieved or even quenched and there will be no power to carry on the work of God. I am not at all sure that we shall find <u>liberty</u> to do what we have to do. The work will be hard and exacting and will allow no time for holiday jaunts. But still if we four men are free in spirit we ought to be able to complete the work in a few weeks of concentrated effort.

(*The work referred to here was the writing of* **The Restored Vision** *by Mr Ware, carried out with the practical support and advice of his three colleagues. The book, 'exploring the time scale of Jesus' life as seen in the Bible', was published in 1957. See Part 4, 'To Take You Further'*).

5649/1 / 16th August 1956 / From Willingdon, Sussex, to Lanehead –

These are testing days and the powers of hell are not likely to leave us alone now that we have a sledge-hammer for the Word of God ready to wield, which will crush so much that is utterly false in Christendom.

5652/2 / 27th August 1956 / From Willingdon, Sussex, to Lanehead –

(*Concerning a planned visit to Rome by some of their supporters now not going ahead*) –

Rome is the home of the Harlot Church and the Testimony is the spearhead of the true Church and there may be a reason why we must not even visit the 7-hilled city ...

5664/2 / 29th October 1956 / From Willingdon, Sussex —

(*During the writing **of The Restored Vision***) –

... <u>Gentiles</u> of any description have so <u>little</u> capacity to appreciate the way the Jewish feasts were woven into the chronological fabric of the Lord's Pathway – though once it gets out that the actual <u>Truth</u> has been recovered, interest would flame up anywhere in the world.

5667/1 / 4th November 1956 / From Willingdon, Sussex, to Lanehead -

... we realized again that all we <u>know</u> is that we <u>don't know</u> the means God will adopt to launch the testimony, though we know that the moment is near.

... a powerless UNO (*United Nations Organisation*) is like a toothless old woman unable to respond to their poignant cries for help (*from the Hungarians after the Soviet crushing of an uprising in Budapest*).

What collapse and what need for a <u>strong</u> power to arise "having great iron teeth" (*Daniel 7.7*) to withstand Communism and its barbarity.

1957

(The letters reveal that this was a time of much trial and testing) -

5704/2 / 10th January 1957 / From Willingdon, Sussex, to Lanehead –

I count much on your prayers. I have seldom felt so hopeless about everything including myself.

5705/3 / 14th January 1957 / From Willingdon, Sussex, to Lanehead –

I regard the present as <u>most critical</u> and feel our whole position as a company is at stake. We cannot go on much longer living as we do and accomplishing <u>nothing.</u>

5709/8 / 16th January 1957 / From Willingdon, Sussex, to Lanehead –

(*To help increase the credibility of* **The Restored Vision**, *Mr Ware had approached a Jewish biblical scholar asking him to verify their findings and conclusions regarding biblical Chronology from his Jewish perspective. The reply from the said gentleman did not impress! - as AEW explains here to his colleagues at Lanehead)* –

You will note I wrote him (*in AEW's reply*) in a gracious manner in spite of the fact that he has not accepted a single fact we give and has opposed them with really childish excuses … here was an Israel rejection of the Written Word after 1924 years.

… Was it necessary that we should go first to this (*Jewish scholar*) who has a perfect knowledge of New Testament Scriptures and yet rejects the Lord as Messiah, and refuses to accept the light granted of God to us concerning His personal pathway? Was it not that he dare not acknowledge the accuracy of our statements as to dates because <u>they prove</u> Jesus was the Messiah? To acknowledge one would have been to acknowledge all, so he resisted the lot and uses his scholarship as a shield.

… really it is rubbish to say scholarship and the Bible agree and therefore "your calculations are somewhere at fault. This would involve an error on your part, not on the part of the Bible".

He totally evades the literal translation of the Greek "first (day) of the sabbaths" ... (*This plural word "sabbaths" is the literal meaning of the Greek that is used in all four Gospels regarding the actual day of the various visits to Jesus' tomb after His resurrection, Matthew 28.1 / Mark 16.2 / Luke 24.1 / John 20.1. This tiny but crucial difference between "sabbath" and "sabbaths" set the Watchmen on a path of discovery.*

The mistranslated word "sabbath" is widely used in subsequent Bible translations because, as the years passed since the earliest days of the Church, the original timings of these events were lost under the wrong assumption that the resurrection had occurred early on the Sunday morning. But the Watchmen found otherwise, and established not only the correct time of Jesus' resurrection, but also many other beautiful new truths about the divinely pre-planned, utterly precise timings surrounding Jesus' death and resurrection. Full details of this journey are given in AEW's 'The Restored Vision' and FLP's 'Miracle of Time'. See also Editor's comment regarding FLP's letter 8227, page 259, paragraph beginning "So, as soon as the apostolic era had passed" ...).

Now, back to AEW's letter ...) How does he (*the Jewish scholar*) get 'the day <u>after</u> the sabbath' which he uses in his translation? There is no Greek word for, or reason in, the text to interpolate 'after' – it is pure invention.

(*This extract is thus a good example of a supposedly academic dismissal of the work of Messrs Ware and Paine and their colleagues, but without any convincing reasons presented to justify that dismissal*).

5713/1 / 5th February 1957 / From Willingdon, Sussex, to Lanehead –

In going over the time measurements on the journey South I felt there is no loop-hole for anything further and we must face it.

(*One of the group thinks*) - that action by the Spirit of God throughout the Body is the only possible hope of bringing the members into line, (*that is, over the imminent coming of the Lord*), and that such an act would be a sign to the world which could not be resisted.

... We have the right to announce the Lord is coming this year and that action on His part is called for ... how long does God intend to allow between the Cry and the appearing?

(*Again we see in this extract their certainty over the date for the Lord's return, their sense of responsibility to make this date known beforehand, and their uncertainty as to the Lord's wishes over their methods and timings in making the date known*).

5729/2 / 14th May 1957 / From Willingdon, Sussex, to Lanehead –

The state of God's people is terrible and worst of all lethargy and lack of interest ... All books etc and workings on prophecy are in hopeless error, I got several when in London.

Do pray as to my own movements. We leave here 5 weeks on Friday and have nothing in view. I hope we may come North and have a rest from such places as this.

5750a/1 / 20th August 1957 / From London W6, to Lanehead –

What a fuss is made of the (*Dead Sea*) Scrolls, and what a far greater fuss will be made when it is found as we reveal, that the Bible itself contains proofs of everything as to time on the Lord's life.

5753/1 / 30th August 1957 / From London W6, to Lanehead –

(*Concerning the imminent publication of* **The Restored Vision**) –

The review letters all go out early next week and this calls for much prayer as so much depends on reviews. I have named about 30 papers and will send list for typing on week-end ...

5755/1 / 1st September 1957 / From London W6, to Lanehead –

(*Concerning the purpose of* **The Restored Vision** *and therefore the most suitable methods for promoting it*) –

What is God's object for the book? We must first remember and never forget that we believe God intends to raise up a testimony to Christ and of Christ in the world – a testimony that stands apart from everything else. How then does the new book fit into this purpose, and is it right to follow the accepted way of getting a book launched by sending out say 50 copies for review?

... We must remember also that the light in our book is not for people to take into their sects, but for people who come out of sects and take their places with Christ outside ('Come ye forth to meet Him' (*Matthew 25.1,6*)). The light in the book must be obeyed – it is light from God and sent by Him – but to obey will mean throwing over Dec 25th and Sunday as "the Lord's Day", as well as abandoning the Lord's Supper save as an annual event. To do these things would demand separation, that is, a coming out.

If so then the object of the book is to test God's people as well as enlighten them, and therefore the more it circulates the more it will work. Will God, therefore, prosper its sale by causing some at least to testify to the importance of what is revealed to the Christian cause?

... and that it is His will that all who are Christ's should separate and take their places outside the camp of Religious Christendom.

You and we will pray much that the books going out this week may find favour and not be relegated to bookshelves of unreviewed volumes. So much depends on the reviewer and his attitude to the Bible ... We are sending to The Listener and is there a hope the BBC will call for talks on these vital religious themes?

5756/1 / 6th September 1957 / From Eastbourne, to Lanehead –

... there is a need for the spoken word of testimony as well as the written word. A subject with so much detail has to be written to be absorbed, but when it comes to acting out the implications of what is written, the need is "the foolishness of preaching" (*based on I Corinthians 1.18*) or direct personal exhortation.

Are we to wait for invitation or can we go direct out to the world? We certainly are not to go to those who rejected our testimony 24 years ago, rather "let them return unto thee" (*Jeremiah 15.19*).

5757/2 / 14th September 1957 / From Eastbourne, to Lanehead –

One feels however that it will not be mere human efforts of the sort that will get the truth out, but some act of God moving with responsible people who will testify and say "It is truth". Then it will go worldwide.

5761/1 / 24th September 1957 / From Eastbourne, to Lanehead –

(*Concerning a supportive letter received from a Roman Catholic priest in Malta*) –

It is a remarkable letter and confirms my belief that he is a true child of God and a real lover of the Master. Does this not mean that God wishes us to know He has sheep in that very strange fold?

... I feel assured that once the book **(*The Restored Vision*)** gets a start it will go rapidly and spread. "He could not be hid" is a pertinent word (*Mark 7.24b*), and there exists a latent interest in millions towards Christ and something deeper in those who are His.

5762/1 / 27th September 1957 / From Eastbourne, to Lanehead –

... if God is with us He can fan a small flame into a scorching heat ...

5764/1 / 3rd October 1957 / From London, to Lanehead –

How happy we are now that we <u>know</u> our material cannot be assailed.

CHAPTER 9
1958-1978

1959

5904/1 / 16th September 1959 / From a supportive Indian lady, Mrs M.R. Xxxxx, on leave from India, and sent to AEW from Cheshire –

You have kept all the labour of yours away from people, or say the time has come for people to get ready. You all dear friends do not be disappointed. Your work in Christ is not wasted. Oh, no, you will see the result and may Good result soon. So cheer up please.

Good-bye till we meet again in this world or with Christ. Good-bye.

Yours in His love, Xxxxx.

1960

6001T/1 / 28th January 1960 / From East Dean, Sussex to Dr A.M. Xxxxx, a supportive friend in India -–

(*Recently*) - we had a very happy event here (*a family wedding*) ... We held the service in the house and about 34 friends were present.

It is important to note that "a church in a house" must function in all departments of the Christian economy.

6002T/1 / 16th February 1960 / From East Dean, Sussex, to Dr A.M. Xxxxx in India –

... we know that once a person has committed himself to an opposite view (*regarding their testimony*), it is only God Who can change him, as this requires a humble spirit.

Unless the subject of the Lord's Coming and prophecy in general have been studied in a humble and patient spirit, wrong views are certain to be held and held tenaciously ... It is God's prerogative to give understanding to whom, and at what time, He pleases.

(*Concerning some staff in evangelical training colleges in Britain*) –

... (*they*) throw over the Millennium (*the view known as "A-millenialism"*) and any national restoration of the Jews, and take their stand all out that OT prophecies are not to be interpreted literally but only in the light of the New Testament (*the view known as "Replacement Theology"*).

I have seldom read such nonsense, which is most solemn as it shows God is allowing darkness to descend upon those of His people who are presuming at this late date to suggest that the Holy Ghost has not yet given light to the Church on such matters. The views these men advance is that of the RC Church in the dark ages.

... Soon Israel must possess all Palestine up to the Jordan's West bank and this must include Jerusalem which will remain trodden down of the Gentiles, (the Arabs), until "the times of the Gentiles" actually end by the Lord's Second Appearing when "the fulness of the Gentiles" will be come in (*Luke 21.24 / Romans 11.25*).

(*We know with hindsight that in the 'Six Day War' of June 1967, Israel did capture the West Bank and the old city of Jerusalem – further steps in the gradual fulfilment of the end-time prophecies concerning the Jews*).

(*Concerning a Bible commentator in America*) –

He is a fearful mixture as he rejects inspiration and seeks a natural reason for all Bible phenomena, but nevertheless brings out many interesting facts. His books don't add anything to the Inspired Word.

No one can explain what God did in answer to Joshua's request concerning the Sun and Moon, or what He did to make the walls of Jericho "fall down flat" (*Joshua 10.12-14 / 6.20*). If we did know we, who are believers, would be no better off. The same principle would apply to all Bible miracles.

6008T/2 / 5th April 1960 / From East Dean, Sussex, to Dr A.M. Xxxxx in India -

... God will give the Church nothing else but the Chronology of His Word upon which to rest her faith.

Then those who denounce "date-fixers" will be ashamed into confessing that to disregard Bible times is a sin, when only thus can Christians be found "watching".

(*In signing off*) - You are in His bonds.

6009T/1 / 13th April 1960 / From Dr A.M. Xxxxx in India, to AEW –

<u>It does not matter</u> ... whether people scoff or not, let them laugh if they feel that way, but go giving them the main facts.

I don't feel myself inclined to emphasise the date too much, but to say, "soon, very soon" at any of the anniversary dates – to begin with, say of next year, March 30th, May 1st, May 4th – 12th June, 21st June. These are the great dates which have been recovered.

... (*Satan*) seems to be fighting in the last ditch and we can only <u>overcome</u> through the "power of the blood of Jesus".

6010 / 17th April 1960 / From Dr A.M. Xxxxx in India, to AEW –

... In dealing with this vast subject (*of Bible prophecy*) we are conscious that Christ's outlook is necessarily far greater than any single interpretation, and that this fact makes it necessary not to be dogmatic but suggestive. To write as if one were right and everyone else wrong would be the height of unwisdom ... The prophetic outlook "at hand" which you rightly emphasise will always hold good ... but there is always the possibility of the Church's failure to be <u>reckoned with</u>.

... What I wrote in my last letter was not to throw doubt on your conclusions but to show that I still hesitate to take the "chronological plunge", which I confess was new to me and still I find in many ways confusing. If more light is needed keep praying for my enlightenment.

All progress be with you as you con over all the points of your vision, there is more light yet to be had, and I would deeply like to go over 100 points with you and clarify my vision. You are still far ahead of me.

6011/2 / 27th April 1960 / From Dr A.M. Xxxxx in India, to AEW –

... already I realise (for myself and you) that Satan is not going to take this warning (*that is, concerning the expected imminent return of Christ*) lying down. He has never been inactive, and least so now.

6012/ff / 28th April 1960 / From East Dean, to Dr A.M. Xxxxx in India –

We note that you get no encouragement from the professionally religious circle. It is the same here and indeed all over the world.

(*Here is a further example of their sincere expectations of the return of the Lord in a particular year, based mainly on their interpretation of various biblical "types" and antitypes"*) –

(*We are*) put upon our faces before God as to whether it is His will that we should commit ourselves to 1961 as the year both of the Second Advent and the opening of the Apocalyptic era.

I must, however, reiterate the fact that we are morally convinced that God has now lifted the veil of secrecy from the time measurements of His Word in order to prove to us that the Lord is coming in 1961 (*that is, that they should therefore now raise the cry, once again, "Behold, the Bridegroom ..."*).

Surely it is for this purpose He called us and separated us and has kept us silent for 27 years, so that He might teach us every detail of the wonderful chronological structure into which He has built the eternal Truth we call the Holy Scriptures, before rendering testimony again.

The Ware-Paine Testimonies

6019T/1 / 4th July 1960 / From East Dean to Dr A.M. Xxxxx in India –

We became "four lepers" in 1943, when, remarkable to relate, we went to live in a house in the Lake District which belonged to people who lived in Aleppo, Syria. We remained in that Syrian house for 15 years and our last act in 1958 before leaving was to send a letter to the Archbishop, with a copy to the Queen.

(*We are assuming*) - it is God's intention that those in high places should investigate the facts and, having done so, be compelled to admit to Christendom that the conclusions we have drawn concerning 1961 are irrefutable.

... but I would not care to be on a platform with Dr Xxxxx whose avowed modernism shows that he has not got "the doctrine of Christ".

6021T/1 / 11th July 1960 / From Mrs M.R. Xxxxx in India, to AEW –

I am sorry to say our Pastors or leaders are wasting their time. They have no answer in their own life. People can't wait. Just the Holy Spirit is guiding them.

(*Concerning Almighty God*) - He is <u>great</u>. When we are willing to listen to Him He is always there to speak – (*this*) is my own experience. Just now I felt His Holy Spirit is with me though I am a big sinner ... I need your prayers <u>very</u> much.

You know, Mr Ware, Indians are very open and you can talk to them easily on any subject. They are not reserved like English people.

6026/2 / 3rd November 1960 / From Applethwaite, Keswick –

(*Concerning where the Lord will return to at the Rapture, written shortly before the US Presidential election in which the candidates were John Kennedy and Richard Nixon*) –

One thing is certain, that if USA elects an RC President the Lord will not visit that land as they will be blameworthy with all the light they have.

That England's intellectuals could go in the witness box to uphold the filthiest book ever written, (*that is, "Lady Chatterley's Lover", involved in a recent trial with its publishers over its possible censorship*) and one which spits at every law of God and morality, reveals that it is time for judgment to fall and sweep away those who defy God and His laws.

Daily fellowships for prayer are OK but liable to be just a sincere habit, whereas a period set apart for prayer with one objective is likely to be far more effective if <u>the will</u> is at the back of the prayers. One can pray just to fill in the time.

May God help us and save us from unreality. There is bound to be conflict here and there …

6030a/1 / 17th November 1960 / From Applethwaite, Keswick –

(*Oswald*) Chambers this A.M. was helpful as he refers to the way God can only make appeal to His nature that is in us after regeneration.

I had very good letters from India … They seem to have come out of a cloud and M. (*Mrs M.R. Xxxxx*) sent sweet apology for some remarks she made in previous letter. Both letters showed a sweet spirit.

6030bT/1 / 19th November 1960 / As from East Dean, Sussex, to the Archbishop of Canterbury regarding his impending visit to the Pope –

(*This was written by AEW in Applethwaite, and then typed up and posted by FLP in East Dean. It is another good example of their faith and courage in approaching people in positions of national leadership, and sets out clearly Britain's unique constitutional position regarding the Protestant Reformation, which remains the case today.*

Once again though we can see why their confident prediction of the Lord's expected return, in 1961, would be greeted with hesitation, especially as such predictions had been made previously and had turned out to be mistaken. Time and again these date predictions, subsequently seen to be mistaken, diverted attention away from the veracity of the Bible

Chronology figures which had been gradually made known to them over the years and which lay at the heart of their testimony, as they still do) –

Britain is the only great power that still officially honours the work of God's Holy Spirit at the Reformation four hundred years ago; and for this reason she has been appointed to fill a place of importance in God's end-time counsels.

Our Lord, when He comes a second time, as I expect next year, will come to this land because we thus honour the Reformation. He certainly could not visit any country that had rejected the light then granted.

… as a nation we have an established Protestant Succession and the national Church is bound by Parliament to the Reformation Prayer Book and the Thirty-nine Articles. These facts carry immense weight with Almighty God Who has been able to preserve us as a nation from many calamities thereby, and this in spite of the gross unfaithfulness of large numbers to Reformation principles.

6032/2 / 23rd November 1960 / From Applethwaite, Keswick –

(*Strong reactions to a brief acknowledgement from Lambeth Palace of AEW's letter having arrived there! We clearly see here AEW's anger and frustration, arising from his longing that someone, somewhere, would pay heed to what they were saying. He sticks to his sense of calling and duty, to remain faithful and to "get the job done"*) –

Like Goliath this vast octopus of iniquity (*the Professing Church*) holds the fort. Israel could do nothing until Goliath was killed … I must say I wonder if the Archbishop is not the Philistine's leader in this land. We must face it that the Lord intends to put that crowd in its true place and to exalt His own true followers as we get it in Rev III.

… the matter has to be presented, if I may say, in a scholarly way and not with religious talk. I mean this, that if we can get home, by virtue of the facts, that Christ must be really coming this June (*that is, June 1961*) we have accomplished the purpose given us to perform.

… So I believe my duty is to keep on the one line – the Chronology, and from it put people in a vice from which they cannot escape.

Fear comes from unbelief and unbelief comes from the devil and has to be trodden under foot when writing such as I have to now – burning bridges with every word.

I dare not guess how we can be ready by Dec 4th but this type of service can <u>never</u> be done casually. It is bound to be a rush job but if of God perfectly controlled. (*The "rush job" on this occasion was to get something written and published as soon as possible after 25th November which is 200 days before 12th June 1961 when the Lord's return was expected. This would thus serve as another 200-day warning, repeating their actions of November and December 1932*).

… but my last word is pray, pray, pray and remember there are powers against us but Christ must triumph and He has a great work in hand to complete the Church and restore His own.

6033/1 / 24th November 1960 / From Applethwaite, Keswick –

(*In prayer when troubled*) – I was conscious of being heard and feel a start has been made in getting out into full liberty.

6033a/1 / Late November 1960 / From Applethwaite, Keswick –

What about Dec 4th? I see this. We <u>must</u> hold a meeting in London of <u>all</u> our own crowd and there tell the truth for what it is worth. Being a natural coward I found I am continually looking to the Lord for courage to go through with what is before us …

6034T/1 / 23rd December 1960 / From East Dean, Sussex, to Dr A.M. Xxxxx –

(*AEW has learned a new movement is starting in India*) –

What impresses us most is that this movement … is accomplishing the very thing we have long desired to see, namely, groups of believers who have withdrawn from all association with sects and societies.

The commercialising of Christmas is a terrible thing and we totally ignore the day ...

1961

6105/1 / 27th March 1961 / From East Dean, Sussex, to Dr A.M. Xxxxx in India –

(*Concerning the newly-published New English Bible, New Testament*) –

We have made a brief examination of this New Version and it fills us with anger, for it clearly uninspires the very obviously inspired Authorized and Revised Versions.

The truth is it is not the Bible, but a human paraphrase which omits words which are absolutely vital to the context. It really seems to us that it is a production which proves the apostasy of British Protestantism by which it was produced and by which it is now being acclaimed and used in Churches and Chapels.

It furthermore proves that though the authors were accepted scholars in various respects, they were devoid of understanding the spiritual nature of the Word of God, and consequently frequently marred it by changing an exact translation for expressions more pleasing to the ear or the understanding of the unspiritual.

(*Concerning their continued desire to make their testimony known*) –

... for the Testimony to go out following some act or sign which will, we believe, at one stroke change the course of history.

6108 / 31st July 1961 / From Broughton, Lancashire, during a short break –

... as the days are very evil and it is no occasion to be time-killing ...

1962

6201/1 / 31ˢᵗ January 1962 / From East Dean, Sussex, to Dr A.M. Xxxxx in India -

(*A justification of the group's work over many years*) -

... but for ourselves we cling to the promise that at the end the Vision (*another term they used for their "testimony"*) will "speak and not lie", but faultlessly disclose the truth, because "the vision is for an appointed time" (*both quotations from Habakkuk 2.3*).

God wanted the whole Church to concern itself, like the prophets of old to which Peter refers, by searching in order to learn the time the Vision should be fulfilled. As the Church has ignored, or positively rejected, Bible Chronology, God called a few of us together to give ourselves up to His service in this matter, as it was impossible that no one in the Church should know God's purpose – as if it were so, there would be no one to sound that "cry" which is destined to awaken the whole of Christendom to the fact that the Bridegroom is immediately to appear.

We therefore cannot agree with those who say that the time of the Second Advent is not to be known, since we are confident God called us for this purpose and has unfailingly over the years lifted the veil of secrecy, a year or two at a time, so that representatively there were those in the Body of Christ kept ceaselessly on the watch on behalf of all the members.

(*Concerning a renowned Swiss theologian of the time*) –

(*He has*) - I suppose, helped in some measure to check the onrush of Liberal Theology, but where does he himself stand? Is he not tainted with some Biblical criticism? All the current talk about uniting the various denominations is completely without reality, since the whole lot have been rejected and can only be viewed by God as empty shells, the leaders, one and all, being completely out of touch with the mind of Christ – if, indeed, they were ever truly converted.

6203/3 / 5th August 1962 / From East Dean, Sussex -

I confess to being much weighted down about the whole position. It seems impossible to be silent much longer.

... I count on your prayers and the supply of the Spirit of Jesus the Christ for guidance.

6204/2 / 12th August 1962 / From East Dean, Sussex -

We live from day to day as (*an elderly relative*) lingers, and accept her exodus will be at God's time and not our convenience ... We can only ask for mercy to be shown to this aged one in her departing hour.

(*In a letter Mrs M.R. Xxxxx in India*) - was very depressed. She wrote openly about things over here (*in Britain*) and was clearly stumbled by what she saw and heard. This is a cause for humbling and prayer. In reply yesterday I referred to the strain of circumstances but even that savours of defeat ...

(*A colleague*) has visibly grown of late and is I believe truly submissive but too strong and confident in his judgments and too family minded. This is not criticism but a call for prayer. We all have our failings which are obvious to others and not, perhaps ourselves. This also is defeat.

(*Quoting words written recently by Dr A.M. Xxxxx to AEW*) –

"You have something there which I find nowhere else. Hang on to it until it becomes clear what the will of God is". How good and gracious that he should so speak.

(*Quoting some words from one of the leaders in the Plymouth Brethren movement*) –

"The Word without the Spirit leads to rationalism; the Spirit without the

Word leads to fanaticism".

1964

(*We now see a marked decline in the number of letters sent and received. AEW was now nearly 80 years old and the Bible Chronology figures had been established and published long before, (notably in Part Four of **World in Liquidation**, in 1953). The letters tend now to be written to and from various people in public office, in which AEW keeps them updated over his latest understanding of where events had reached in God's time plans*) -

6401/1 / 24th January 1964 / From East Dean, Sussex, to the Queen's Private Secretary –

(*Here is a helpful example of AEW's handling of why past errors have occurred*) -

(*I am altering what I originally told you*) - due to the fact that the unveiling of Bible times was constituted so as to form a progressive study in order to induce watchfulness on the part of the Christian Church.

1969

6910b / 17th December 1969 / From a Christian leader in Surrey, to AEW, now living near Godalming –

(*This extract is included as being as good an example as any of a courteous yet robust rejection of AEW's actions in these years. Some reacted in similar fashion, while others, such as the Private Secretary to the Queen Mother, remained patient and non-committal throughout AEW's correspondence with them*) –

The Second Advent is surely one and the same thing as the Lord's appearing in glory (Titus 2.11-13). I do not accept that the Lord's Second

Advent is something for which the date may be known. (*By the phrase "the Second Advent" AEW always means "the Rapture", with the Lord's later "appearing in glory", as referred to by the above correspondent, as therefore being the Lord's <u>Third</u> Advent*).

My own conviction is that the very fact that anybody gives a date for the Lord's Return is enough for me to believe that this date, whatever it is, will NOT be the time when He comes. However, I write to give my judgment on this matter – and I think, as one whose life-long ministry has given one a certain determination not to accept any theories that appear to conflict with Holy Scripture, however godly may be the men who affirm their views.

Please understand that I cannot enter into further correspondence over the matter. I am more than busy and write now only to send a reply to your letter ... I only hope that you do not get caught up in a heap of controversy because of the views you now put forth again. I know of nothing so soul-withering as religious controversy.

(*We can imagine AEW's reaction in receiving a letter such as this, and his determination to "carry on regardless", which he duly did*).

1970

7004/2 / 20th May 1970 / From A.N.D in Jerusalem, (a new correspondent), to AEW –

(*Here is a most interesting description of the differing understanding and priorities of a Jewish and a Gentile believer in Jesus as Messiah. A.N.D and AEW went on to have a long and close friendship by correspondence, with mutual respect surviving their occasional disagreements*) -

I study the WORD as a completed Jew and son of Abraham, Isaac and Jacob. You study it as a "Christian", as a mystical, "added", Seed of Abraham, Abraham the believer prior to his circumcision. Hence our understanding of the PROPHETIC and LEGALISTIC parts of the WORD cannot be unanimous.

Your position places the ECCLESIA (*that is, the Christian Church*) in the centre, and Israel in the background. My position has ISRAEL as focal, and the ECCLESIA, as a TEMPORARY AFFAIR, within the Jewish people and not outside or apart of it.

(*We can see that A.N.D is mistaken over AEW's views on this issue. AEW and his colleagues, surely more than anyone, were strongly conscious that since June 1933 the "Church Age" and the "Times of the Gentiles" had now passed, so the "ecclesia" was, and is, indeed "a temporary affair", sandwiched between God's dealings with Israel, just as A.N.D wrote in his letter*).

You will not understand and endorse my position just as I do not understand and endorse yours. Unity is IN the Messiah, and NOT in prophetic, and eschatologic, and dogmatic positions. If you are IN HIM, and prove it by ACTIVE love, then am I your brother.

1971

7101a / 18th January 1971 / From another Christian leader in Surrey, to AEW –

I am afraid I must confess that I find it impossible to follow the lines of your teaching.

This is probably because of your basic premises that the interpretation of the prophecies of the Scripture depends on numerological factors which are not evident to the ordinary reader.

7113 / 26th April 1971 / From MBM in Jerusalem, another new correspondent, to AEW –

However my youngest daughter is not well, and is hospitalised, due to mental strain and ignoring her Creator.

7116 / 3rd August 1971 / From A.N.D in Jerusalem, to AEW –

(*Concerning some good progress*) - It is the Creator's work indeed, and the groups of radicals opposing us are fighting a losing battle. Pray for us and the work here.

Your Brother in the faith, A.N.D.

1972

7202/1 / 1st February 1972 / From AEW near Godalming, to a supporter in Northern Ireland –

(*A defence of AEW's mistaken predictions for the Lord's expected return in 1970 and 1971, followed by an insight into the spiritual realities in Northern Ireland, which was then into the third year of "the troubles"*) –

You like many others will have thought that because the Lord did not come in 1970 or in 1971, that I and those with me had made a blunder, but this was not so by any means, but evidence that the Lord had some really on the watch.

... the Lord Jesus has made the position of Ulster very clear to us; and I believe Ulster is the only sphere in the Commonwealth that still stands up for the truth of the Reformation against the gathering forces of darkness which have their centre in the Vatican; that will forgive murder and violence if it can bring God's true people under its heel which it never will do.

7226T/1 / 23rd May 1972 / From AEW to A.N.D in Jerusalem –

The Church is our Lord's heavenly Bride, but when He takes her from the earth, He becomes betrothed to a Jewish Bride the Remnant.

7227/1 / 4th June 1972 – From MBM in Jerusalem, to AEW near

Godalming –

(*Tough times in Jerusalem, a situation AEW knew all about from his own experience in England*) –

I stand all alone, am a member of no church, group or society. If I were I would have had fewer money problems. I am not a fanatic, but I cannot compromise and dance to the music of others who think they know better. I was a missionary for some 15 years, and had to compromise all along.

... The word "lukewarm" is rendered in the Hebrew with POSHER, which means COMPROMISE. Since then I went "outside the camp" and stand alone WITH HIM.

In Hebrew the name for our Lord is pointed to read YESHUA and not YAHSHUA! please note.

7234/1 / 29th August 1972 / From a Christian leader in Hampshire, to AEW near Godalming –

The confusion that reigns in the Church on the subject of the second Advent is most dishonouring and lies at our door, and certainly not that of either the Holy Spirit or the Holy Scriptures.

7239/1 / 21st September 1972 / From AEW to supporters –

(*AEW corrects a predicted date, as being no longer 18th September but now known to be 18th October*) –

Here then is another patent instance of how God refuses to give a ray of further light on Chronology until the appointed date has been kept ...

Having been called, as we have, to be recipients of this most solemn light; it would be out of place to think of one's bruises, or to bewail, as did Jeremiah when he cried: O LORD Thou hast deceived me" (XX,7). With thanks to God for your fellowship in "watching", AND EVER REMEMBERING that the Amos sign (*Amos 8.13-15*) will herald the almost immediate return of Christ for His Church.

1973

7331/1 / 24th October 1973 / From A.N.D in Jerusalem, to AEW –

(*Concerning the Yom Kippur War*) –

There are eight nations against Israel, but the Almighty is more powerful than this combination of human strength, and Israel will be the final victor in the end. This war could lead us into the fulfilment of Ezekiel's prophecy for the ending time in chapter 38.

… We are sure living in the very last days of this wicked Gentile age, which is similar to the time of Noah before the flood when the earth was filled with violence (*Genesis 6.11*).

The end is near, and we must all be spending much time in prayer for help from above. We all need more of the Holy Spirit in our lives to fill us with overcoming power and victory over the flesh, and fill us with zeal and enthusiasm, also joy in the service of the Master, for He is soon coming.

We must be found profitable servants in His work. Matt. 25; 30.

1975

7531/1 / Exact date not known / From AEW near Godalming to a young Christian leader and enquirer in Sussex –

(*Concerning* **World in Liquidation**, *published in 1953*) –

… which book was never allowed to prosper because of the Lord's ban in Revelation III.3.

1976

7601/1 / 8th January 1976 / From MBM in Jerusalem, to AEW near Godalming –

I appreciate all the data you have been sending me but find it difficult to follow, and this is one of the reasons I keep my mouth shut. I hate to express agreement or disagreement on matters I cannot fully grasp. A minister in America, a Dr Xxxxx, ... stated that the rapture of the Church was to be on Yom Kippur in 1975. That day has come and gone and proved him a false prophet.

... Personally I believe that Daniel 9.27 has been fulfilled by the Messiah Himself. He is the One Who confirmed the Sinai Covenant as evidence by the Sermon on the Mount. He was cut off in the middle of the week so that he did not carry out all He should have. The other half of the week will come into focus when He returns in power and great glory.

... The "Beast" has nothing to do with Israel. He is to be the scourge of apostate Christendom.

1977

7704/1 / 4th February 1977 / From AEW near Godalming, to a correspondent whose letter had recently appeared in The Times –

... as for years I had realised, as you have, that the Christian Church came into being many years after the death and resurrection of our Lord; and that in speaking of "my Church" in St Matthew XVI He obviously could not have been referring to it.

... The truth is the New Testament has two Gospels and two Churches. The Gospel of the Kingdom, as preached by the Baptist, our Lord, and the Twelve Apostles, was exclusively Jewish. The Jewish Kingdom Church came into being on the Day of Pentecost; and remained the only Church until AD 59 when St Paul with a company of Gentile converts received its blessing, as stated in Acts XXI verses 18 to 20.

This Church (*that is, "the Jewish Kingdom Church"*) is never again referred to in the New Testament, but all attention is given to the Christian Church which mystically was born, as the body of Christ, on this occasion.

St Paul preached the Gospel of the Grace of God, which united believing Jews of the Dispersion and believing Gentiles into One Body – the Mystical Body of Christ, as described in Ephesians II and III.

The prototype of this Church was the Ephesus Assembly: and when St Paul was released from prison in AD 64 he visited the assemblies of Asia and Europe, and then went to the Far West and fulfilled the reason he gives at the end of II Timothy IV verse 17.

If these facts were understood, a vast amount of confusion would be eliminated. Perhaps you will graciously let me have your comments.

7709/1 / 28th April 1977 / From MBM in Jerusalem, to AEW near Godalming –

I do not have such deep insight in chronological matters. My speciality is in other Bible themes. We learn from one another and complete one another's knowledge.

… thank you. May you live to see the King in His beauty without being called to pass the shadow of the valley.

1978

7802/1 / 22nd February 1978 / From a longstanding supporter in Buckinghamshire, to AEW near Godalming, and to WS, the one colleague from the Company still living with Mr and Mrs Ware –

Dear Ones in Christ Jesus our Lord,

Greetings in Him whose Love is everlasting …We do rejoice with you as to the quickening and strengthening you receive from the Lord even at such an advanced age. We note the close dates when your combined "times" will be 181 years! (*that is, the ages of AEW and WS added together*).

***

Arthur E Ware died peacefully at his home near Godalming on 13th May 1978

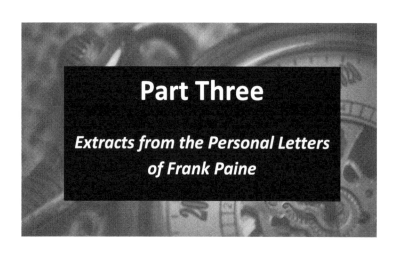

INTRODUCTION

For the first time we are able to publish in these pages extracts from the personal letters of the late Mr Frank Paine (FLP), by kind permission of his daughter Grace.

These letters span the years 1969 – 1983, a time of great spiritual excitement and expectation with the "the charismatic movement" at its height.

They emphasise FLP's desire to see the work of his companions and himself, these faithful Bible Watchmen, made more widely known for the Jews and Israel, for the Christian churches, and for the wider world.

These letters frequently refer back to the years of the Watchmen's work from 1927 onwards, giving us fascinating insights into how their studies gradually progressed.

They also demonstrate Frank's special gift in identifying the date-significance of current events of his own times, in particular with regard to the Second World War, the founding of the State of Israel and the various Moon landings of the Apollo space programme, (themes he covers in his book **Miracle of Time**).

The letters contain many gems of Christian instruction, guidance and encouragement, forged on the anvil of Frank's rugged experience and of great benefit to Christ's disciples today.

A brief word is appropriate here about the differences in character and gifting between AEW and FLP, and the differences in the nature and timing of the letters which each man sent and received.

The hundreds of letters written by AEW as the leader of "the Company", cover a 48-year timespan from 1930 to 1978. These letters were mostly written "in the heat of the battle" as it were, as their Bible Chronology work, with all the setbacks and progress this work involved, slowly moved forward under the Holy Spirit.

By the mid-1960s the Company as such no longer existed: two men of the original six had moved away in 1943 for various reasons, and a third had died at Lanehead in the 1950s. This left AEW, FLP and WS, a single man without close dependents who served in effect as AEW's personal secretary and continued to live with Mr and Mrs Ware until AEW's death in 1978.

The Bible Chronology figures had been finalised and publicised, and AEW's two main books, **World in Liquidation** and **The Restored Vision**, written with the agreement and practical help of his remaining colleagues, had been published in 1953 and 1957.

The Wares, with WS, and the Paines, left Lanehead near Coniston in 1958 to live in rented accommodation in the south of England, the former being based in Sussex and then Surrey, and the latter mainly in Somerset.

This sets the scene for the FLP letter-extracts now included in these pages.

The letters written by FLP cover a 14-year timespan from 1969 to 1983, (there thus being far fewer FLP letters, written over a much shorter time period, than those written by AEW). The Company's main Bible Chronology work had been completed long ago and the "charismatic movement" was now in full flow – much to FLP's joy and wonder.

As with the letters of AEW, we can detect several common themes running through FLP's letters, which give us an interesting contrast with those of AEW. The main FLP themes which it is helpful to be aware of include:

1. **Frequent descriptions of the years of "the Company" and their work together** from many years ago. These extracts also include explanations and justifications for what they did and why, and give a different "take" on the work from that gained from the AEW letters, helped at times by

the benefit of hindsight on FLP's part after the passing of the years.

2. As with AEW, **FLP is 100% certain of the veracity of the Testimony**, and that, if only it could be properly publicised, its effects upon Israel, the Jews, the believing Church, Christendom and the nations, would be truly massive.

3. FLP and his wife spent a very significant year **in Florida in 1971-1972**. During this time they received a prophecy, specifically addressed to them, to make the Bible Chronology more widely known.

They made many friends and developed many contacts in this time, including with a lady who had personally encountered the Lord Jesus Christ in a remarkable way for a period of three months in 1950 (an experience which FLP subsequently established was highly significant in terms of Bible Chronology).

Other contacts were with local Christians, as well as with some famous Christian individuals with US-wide and worldwide Gospel missions. Not surprisingly FLP longed to have his work accepted and publicised by such influential people and organisations, but first he had to convince them that it was sound and that it was worth their taking him seriously. Sometimes they did this, and sometimes they said they would do this, and sometimes they didn't do this!

4. **FLP's writing of different books and articles**, (which culminated in **Miracle of Time**) as part of his constant desire to "get these truths out" to his own generation.

5. **His love for Israel and the Jews**, and his longing that "the Testimony" would be available to them and received by them.

6. **The old, longstanding questions** faced so often by the Company members over the years: How exactly could their results be made known most effectively? To whom should they address their Testimony? – to Israel, to the Church, to Christendom, to the nations? How should this be done, and when? When was it right to "wait on the Lord" for specific

leading, and when was it right to step out in faith, believing their actions would indeed be blessed by the Lord even though they might lack a sense of specific and timely divine guidance?

7. **FLP avoided bold predictions as to the date of the Rapture**, even though he was as keenly expectant for this event as AEW. We know that it was the many such predictions made mainly by AEW over the years which aroused so much criticism of the men and their Chronology work.

Perhaps FLP had always been wary of such firm predictions in himself, or had come to see later on that the great controversy that these predictions caused actually distracted attention from the real "meat" of their main Bible Chronology Testimony.

8. **The refusal of FLP's local Christian fellowship to receive the Testimony**, to the point of telling FLP not to speak of these matters.

This of course puzzled and grieved him, but he carried on elsewhere with courtesy and persistence, always eager to explain the Testimony where opportunity arose. FLP loved to expound the Scriptures in the light of the crucial underlying Time-framework which he and his companions had been shown by the Holy Spirit over all their years of research.

These recurring themes explain the context of many of the letter-extracts which now follow, as well as the wide range of correspondents with whom FLP kept in regular contact. Besides those in Britain, these correspondents were located in the USA, Canada, Sweden, Israel, Sudan and India.

We see clearly, quite apart from his focus on his Bible Chronology work, how faithful a friend and correspondent was Frank Paine, and how much he was loved and respected by the many who knew him.

As with the letters-extracts of AEW, we include these extracts here in chronological order, leaving them "to tell their own story" as much as possible, with some editorial explanation or comment, written in italics, included when appropriate. To keep these extracts as close as possible to the original letters we have retained at times occasional oddities of spelling, grammar and abbreviation as used by FLP.

For each entry we show the catalogue number of the original letter, the date of writing, the author and his or her location, the recipient's initials, and the recipient's location if appropriate. As with the Ware extracts, to preserve confidentiality we sometimes replace actual names with "Xxxxx" or similar.

The FLP letters-extracts vary in date, length, subject and recipient. As with the letter-extracts of Mr Ware, some can be read through quite quickly, others will repay slow reading and careful reflection with the help of an open Bible and a thorough Concordance.

Because these extracts were written at a different period and by a different character from AEW, and yet both sets of extracts cover the same issues, we gain from these FLP letters-extracts an extra and fascinating angle in our understanding of all the work that went on.

To achieve all that this small group of Bible Chronologers did achieve, each member of the group was necessary, and none more so, humanly speaking, than Arthur Ware and Frank Paine. At times these two Christian warriors got on each other's nerves, and at times they had strong disagreements. But throughout their fifty-plus years of acquaintance, each recognised in his own way that Arthur Ware needed Frank Paine, and Frank Paine needed Arthur Ware. They thus provide us with a classic example of I Corinthians 12.14-21.

It is appropriate to repeat at this point that our purpose throughout the writing of this book is simply to honour these godly men, to make their work and findings known afresh in these turbulent times, and to display more clearly the glory of Almighty God.

CHAPTER 1
1969 -1975

1969

6901 / 3rd January 1969 / From FLP in Chard, Somerset, to RB –

... that "watchmen" must do their duty, whatever the outcome.

1970

7001 / 23rd January 1970 / From FLP near Axminster, to P –

We who were engaged in this research had, more or less, to unlearn everything as we were led on, because God's thoughts were not our thoughts, and we had to learn His ways of measuring time – and we found they were absolutely marvellous, glory to His Holy Name!!

7007 / 11th April 1970 / From FLP near Axminster, to EP –

Without true timing, the detail of history would get in a meaningless muddle. Prophecy is merely history written beforehand, and to preserve it God has now allowed the time program, hidden in His Word, to come to light.

1971

7109 / 5th April 1971 / From FLP in Jacksonville, Florida, to JF –

(*Concerning a book in draft form written by FLP, which he is keen for others to examine and accept its trustworthiness*) -

The facts in the book I have been told (and know this personally myself) are not open to question, as God has designed that modern history should abundantly confirm the exact dating of the Bible's Chronology and in this way set a seal on the truth to do with the Lord's life, as well as the whole pattern of His dealings with Israel from Abram to the present day.

But the real question is what to do with this revelation which, because of its note of authority, is not likely to be popular with the scholastic or religious world!

7112 / 8th April 1971 / From FLP in Jacksonville, Florida, to B –

The Appendix *(of FLP's book referred to in 7109)* gives "all the Scriptures by which the Chronology can be checked".

The great question is, how God intends to use this revelation, and whether it is first to appear in the form of a book. He is certainly not going to give away the priceless secrets of time except as His people are willing to "search the scriptures" and "measure the pattern" (Ezekiel 43.10) and few seem in the mood to do this to-day!

Our plans are quite uncertain (as they should be!) …

7116 / 7th May 1971 / From FLP in Jacksonville, Florida, to Dr HM –

… when the truth concerning TIME … is released … it will have the effect of setting in order every vital doctrine and performing all that which is outlined in the rest of the psalm! (Ps 19).

7118 / 25th May 1971 / From FLP in Jacksonville, Florida, to AK in USA –

We have found prejudice against the study of this side of the Word of God to be of satanic origin in England – fear and suspicion being at the root of this prejudice.

It was this, however, that enabled research to continue unimpeded, as, no doubt, the purpose of God was to keep this truth from becoming known in a public way until His appointed time.

7124 / 28th June 1971 / From FLP in Jacksonville, Florida, to OR –

(*Explaining about his book which gives so many details of the Watchmen's "Testimony"*) –

… what I'm speaking of is scientific facts – knowledge which anyone from teen-age years upwards is capable of checking.

… Could any subject be more worthy of serious investigation than this?

I explain in the book that just as the BONES, all perfectly IN JOINT, are necessary to the true structure of our bodies, so are the time MEASUREMENTS of the Bible, all perfectly coherent – like bones in a joint – necessary to our right understanding of the Scriptures, and this is the HEALING to which I refer.

7134 / 8th August 1971 / From FLP in Jacksonville, Florida, to B and C –

(*News from Sweden*) - confirming that the revelation we have had to do with time has been accepted … This brother (AW) now writes: "Yes – now at last I think I am convinced!"

(*AW is not AEW, but a Salvation Army officer in Sweden with a great concern for the salvation of the Jews. He became one of FLP's most regular correspondents, being interested in, and supportive of, Frank's Chronology work*).

7136 / 12th August 1971 / From FLP in Jacksonville, Florida, to WW –

(*Concerning the Apollo Moon landings*) –

God is going to prove to this unbelieving world that their very highest achievements in the realm of science only serve to prove that His Word is true 'from the beginning' – and we know, of course, that one of the objects of these Moon missions is to try and ascertain how old our part of the universe is!

7137 / 12th August 1971 / From FLP in Florida, to EF in Florida –

We know that the <u>time</u> elements are all-important in the fulfilment of prophecy and I believe are to constitute 'many infallible proofs' (*Acts 1.3*) for this present generation …

7143 / 30th August 1971 / From FLP in Florida, to Brother D –

(*Concerning a recently-received negative critique of FLP's first book*) -

In my judgment he has failed to show one place where he has any real understanding of the ways of God in time-measurement in the Bible … The detail in the book, however, which your reviewer does not attempt to touch, amply proves the Bible's figures to be true. … (AW) only saw what was <u>untrue</u> by discovering what was <u>true.</u>

Obviously, we have had to receive light from God on this side of the divine revelation - just as much as people who enjoy the Baptism in the Holy Spirit have had to receive a revelation of what was beyond the reach of their minds – and we all know how modern scholarship resists any kind of revelation!

May I ask why a "Full Gospel" publishing firm should go to a modernist and rely on "scholarship" for understanding of a matter like this? Do we not all see where modern scholarship has landed Christendom at the end of its days? What IS modern scholarship but man's effort by his limited intelligence to do without revelation and explain the things of God, when God Himself has said that this is impossible (I Cor 2 11-14)?

Your reviewer refers to 'scholars' pointing out that genealogies are incomplete, and cites Matthew 1.8 where 'three successive kings' are omitted from the genealogical record. This had no bearing on my book, but as a result of his raising the matter I rejoice to say clear light was given from Scripture as to WHY these three kings were omitted from our Lord's genealogy; and it is always important to know 'the reason of a thing'! (*Ecclesiastes 7.25*).

I shall look forward to seeing what your second reviewer has to say, but if he cites the usual seminary teaching, instead of actually dealing with the facts presented in the book, we shall know what to expect!

I write the above in love, because increasing numbers of Spirit-filled children of God are now conscious that 'the end' is very close and are crying out to know the truth.

7151 / 21st September 1971 / From FLP in Florida, to WW –

I have a strong impression that the Lord is really on the verge of quickening the whole body. He must do this before there can be any large-scale gathering of the unsaved.

7155 / 3rd October 1971 / From FLP in Jacksonville, Florida, to JF –

(*At this moment*) - ... exactly at the right moment when God wants the Church as a whole to face this vital question of whether we are to remain in subservience to a man-made religious set-up (call it what you will) or not.

It is a matter of 'LET MY PEOPLE GO THAT THEY MAY SERVE ME', and I feel that as we pass the turn of these 2,000 years from the time of our Lord's death and resurrection in AD 33, God will begin to move in a mighty way to set His people free ...

(*There are some encouragements*) - 'but there are many adversaries' (especially in the scholastic world) and we must continue to pray and use the name of Jesus.

7166 / 3rd November 1971 / From FLP in Jacksonville, Florida, to PB –

... one can see there is simply no limit to what God can do, once individuals begin to wake up to the immensity of what He has uncovered from His Word.

7167 / 3rd November 1971 / From FLP in Florida, to Mrs VL in USA –

(*This is the lady who had had personal, visible, regular visits from the Lord Jesus Christ in a remarkable way for a period of three months in 1950. FLP later established the chronological significance of these events at that particular time*) -

We found that with God there were no such things as 'loose ends' in the timing of history – it was always exact to the day, and this was because He requires His people now at the end to know the truth to do with the earthly pathway of the Lord Jesus, and He also requires Israel to know it.

The Bible, indeed, is a most amazing book when the true dating of its history is known, and God has used TIME always for the glory of His Son (Psalm 19).

1972

7213 / 3rd February 1972 / From FLP in South Chard, Somerset, to EF in Florida –

But all knew without a doubt that we had acted for God in 1933 and again in 1937, and that the truth concerning Time had come to light.

We had a deep regard for R.H. (*that is Rees Howells, a greatly-blessed leader in the Welsh Revival, who subsequently had a remarkable ministry of intercession and prophecy*), but no one outside our immediate circle and families knew what God was purposing as the work developed.

In 1939 Watchman Nee said to Mr Ware, "Be patient, brother", but none of us dreamt how much patience we would need, or that the 'yet forty days' warning of 1933 would turn out to be 'each day for a year'!

I wish we could keep names completely out of it, my own obviously included. We were essentially like those 'leprous men' in II Kings 7 – thoroughly out of court with the rest of our fellow Christians because of our 1933 testimony. They still think and say, if they ever refer to the matter, that we all went up to the top of the hill to wait for the Lord to come!

7224 / 8th March 1972 / From FLP in South Chard, to DW in Florida –

(*About an acquaintance now going to live in Jerusalem again*) - utterly independent of all sects ... to live in a flat where all can come to her, i.e. to make known the oneness of the Body and the reality of the church 'in the house' because no place on earth has been so 'put off' (as Israel) in regard to denominational Christianity!

7225 / 15th March 1972 / From FLP in South Chard, to EF in Florida –

Do you not agree that prophecy is really written so that when it is fulfilled it may be seen that God foreknew it?

7238 / 3rd August 1972 / From FLP in Combe St Nicholas, Somerset, to B and F –

(*After 12 June 1933 we*) later found from Scripture that that day was the end of the 6,000 years and were able to measure back to every part of the Bible perfectly as a result. (It was only by this means that we knew October 29th 1 BC was the actual date of the Lord's birth).

7245 / 28th September 1972 / From FLP in Combe St Nicholas to EF in Florida –

A morass of figures will get no-one moving, so all must be simplified.

I feel the devil wants to keep this whole revelation under the carpet as long as he can - but God, as we know, has 'a time for every purpose' (*Ecclesiastes 3.17*) ...

We, as a company, have been kept silent for almost forty years – apart from official action and individual testimony from time to time. We have been gathering up, but the time for giving out must come soon. The question is, what is the way of the Spirit?

7247 / September 1972 / From FLP in Combe St Nicholas, to EuF –

(*Concerning the Watchmen's first meeting in London on 2nd May 1933: for 2 hours people listened in total silence then*) –

…the first person to jump up on to the platform to congratulate the speaker afterwards was the Jewish Chronicle Reporter …This address was printed and the Christians in England were considerably stirred, but the purpose of God was to warn the nations as a whole …

7252 / 20th November 1972 / From FLP in Combe St Nicholas, to EF in Florida –

(*FLP first quotes something he has heard from a friend in America*) –

"believers in the US have been warned against the subject (*of Bible Chronology*), (because of) fears it will 'divide' God's children".

(*He then reacts!*) - Well, of course it will divide them! Didn't Jesus divide the Jews when He came? Praise God, if the Truth concerning Himself divides at first, it will ultimately unite all, as we know, just as He united His disciples after His resurrection.

… with forty years' experience of 'watching' for Him, I know He will not fail to bring all of His people into a state of real awakening before he actually does descend.

Practically all who are going on with God are experiencing a deep work of refining at the present hour, and this is no doubt to equip them to enter into His mind and thoughts more perfectly as we come to the time of the Translation (*also known as 'the Rapture', see for example I Thessalonians 4.13-18 and I Corinthians 15.51-52*).

… what we have found as a sure guiding principle in 'watching' was to hold fast to the data the Word provides until God gave more light, and this He never failed to do.

I wrote (*an earlier book*) … to compel the attention of any serious student of Bible history, so that a proper instigation of the facts could be instigated.

It needs a few believers brought together by the Spirit, who would be willing to do what you suggest – sit down together for a couple of weeks or more with determination to grasp divine principles of time measurement and gain full assurance that this revelation is of God and the actual unfolding of the Scriptures in relation to Time.

1973

7307 / 15th January 1973 / From FLP in Combe St Nicholas, to B and F –

... the seventh and last Apollo Moon landing, like all previous successful Missions, was perfectly patterned so as to confirm the perfect accuracy of the Bible's Chronology. If ever we have seen "the handiwork" of God in the "firmament" it has been in these lunar signs!

7318 / 9th March 1973 / From FLP in Combe St Nicholas, to D and P in Florida –

(*Regarding Daniel Chapter 9*) – I always get blessed by reading Daniel's prayer – read it till you weep, David.

7322 / 11th April 1973 / From FLP in Combe St Nicholas, to EF in USA –

God will never use anyone who thinks he can do the job.

(*Mention of Dr AMcL, a correspondent in India interested in the Testimony*) - "He read, and re-read **The Restored Vision** (by AEW) 'umpteen times' and wrote another book afterwards to correct things he had taught, as a result of seeing this fuller light".

1974

7402 / 2nd January 1974 / From FLP in Combe St Nicholas, to DW in Florida –

Won't it be good to see some of our slightly suspicious intellectual friends wake up to the fact that the Word of God is like granate (*sic*), a foundation absolutely sure and safe to build upon and He wants us to <u>prove</u> it.

7412 / 24th February 1974 / From FLP in Combe St Nicholas, to PB in USA –

(*Concerning the Custodian of the Garden Tomb in Jerusalem, who had brought a direct warning of judgment to, and concerning, Britain, from the Church in Jerusalem, during his various preaching engagements in Britain*) -

Now his consistent testimony is that no one bats an eyelid and though he is forthright in delivering the message, everywhere he is politely ignored. ... He said today from the pulpit that he is "horrified at the blindness of the leaders of the body of Christ in this country".

On 11th June 1966 the Queen had to be present at a Fellowship of the Faiths of the Commonwealth in London, where Christ and the Bible were put on exactly the same level as Mohammed and the Koran, and the Hindu and Buddhist faiths. Do we wonder at the blindness of Britain?

1975

7516 / 25th June 1975 / From DW in Florida, to FLP in Somerset –

I rejoice in your quality, Frank, that has come from dwelling with Him. I thank God for the complete inability I have had to minister life through the Chronology. I thank Him for His wisdom in keeping it hidden until I've grown up more and can bear it or the church has grown up and can receive it. Know this my brother, that I love you and appreciate you. In the Lamb, David.

7521 / 28th July 1975 / From FLP in Combe St Nicholas, to PC –

...nothing with God is haphazard, for 'as for God, His way is <u>perfect ...</u>'

(*Psalm 18.30*).

... but in this matter we have got to have 'unleavened bread' or nothing!

(*The German higher critics and Darwin*) - got going, and have ruined the faith of multitudes and millions in the fact that the Bible is the verbally-inspired Word of the Living God. After all, it is exact measurement which is used in every science to prove or disprove a matter. How much we need the Holy Spirit, Who is 'the Spirit of truth' (*John 14.17 / 15.26 / 16.13*) all the time, to deliver us from our own thoughts!

... Do write again when you get time ... Soon we shall 'see Jesus' and, praise God, 'be like Him, for we shall see Him as He is' (*I John 3.2*).

7524 / 13th September 1975 / From FLP in Combe St Nicholas, to BE in Khartoum –

I feel it will not be long before liberty is given to publish the findings of these past years for the benefit of the Israelis, for they are the people who are in desperate need of knowing what God has revealed.

7529 / 15th November 1975 / From FLP in Combe St Nicholas, to BE in Khartoum –

Brother, the great need to-day is to pray and to keep on praying until Heaven moves.

CHAPTER 2
1976 -1983

1976

7602 / 2nd January 1976 / From FLP in Combe St Nicholas, to AW in Stockholm –

... but all the time I am thinking of the great outside world – the scientific world, astronomers and so on - and I know that if once THE PLAN could be published, it would be a challenge which would be too great for the world to meet.

You yourself know how Ivan Panin's research into the numerics of the Scriptures cannot be challenged, but we have seen God, the Almighty, bring the same perfection of measurement and design into the Bible's Chronology, which has always been too great a problem for students to expect to be able to master.

7606 / ?? January 1976 / From FLP in Combe St Nicholas, to AW in Stockholm –

... Ivan Panin's most amazing discoveries to do with the SEPTENARY DESIGN hidden behind the Hebrew and Greek texts of the whole Bible – designs which can be found nowhere else in any other writings in the world.

... When Panin discovered this gigantic proof that the original text of both Hebrew and Greek Testaments was 'sealed' with these perfect numerical designs ...

The proof that they (*the Jews*) have, indeed, 'the living God' and 'the God of Israel, Who only doeth wondrous things' (*Psalm 72.18*), is amazingly demonstrated mathematically in their own Masoretic Hebrew Text from

Genesis to Malachi. It has been there all the time!

And once Israeli scholars have woken up to this fact, they can then be challenged with the Septenary design of the new testament Greek! What further proof will they need that JESUS CHRIST OF NAZARETH was and is truly their MESSIAH?

7612 / 22nd April 1976 / From FLP in Combe St Nicholas, to AW in Stockholm –

(*FLP explains how he felt his arms being physically forced back down during one of his prayers for help, with these firm, loving words spoken to him by the Lord*) -

Do not ask Me for what you already have!

7617 / 14th June 1976 / From FLP in Combe St Nicholas, to AW in Stockholm –

More wonderful time patterns of '153' have come to light – but no one is interested until the whole story can be told.

1977

7701 / 4th February 1977 / From FLP in Combe St Nicholas, to AW in Stockholm –

(*Concerning the deep divisions over "the Lord's Supper"*) –

How the devil has tried to mix everything up, as he always does, and how he has succeeded in dividing Catholics and Protestants and so many sects over this which should be the time when our unity ought to be displayed to the world.

7705 / 30th May 1977 / From FLP in Combe St Nicholas, to AW and his wife in Stockholm –

I feel so much alone, holding so great a revelation as we do about the whole course of TIME which has been kept secret for so long.

7708 / 24th October 1977 / From FLP in Combe St Nicholas, to AW in Stockholm –

The difficulty has been to get <u>somebody</u> (like yourself) to look into our writings sufficiently to realize that God HAS opened our understanding in regard to the Bible's Chronology. It is like trying to get the 'bride' to wake up, in the Song of Solomon!

7709 / 2nd November 1977 / From FLP in Combe St Nicholas, to AW in Stockholm –

This day is the sixtieth anniversary of the Balfour Declaration, when AEW, now 93, "received his call of God to 'watch' with the Scriptures this end-time restoration of the Land to the people of Israel, and then of the Jews to their land.

1978

7803 / 10th February 1978 / From FLP in Combe St Nicholas, to TF –

(*Concerning 12th June 1933*) –

Not a single measurement can be made into the past accurately, unless 12th June 1933 is seen to have been the end of the 6,000 years – and, of course, the opening of the 'consummation of the age'.

And this of course means that the knowledge of the Lord's life has been sealed up until the Chronology as a whole has been investigated and accepted.

7809 / 5th April 1978 / From FLP in Combe St N, to AW in Stockholm –

(*A critical review has arrived*) –

After a cursory glance I can say that I have never in my life seen a more hopeless mixture of the Bible's Chronology with the muddle the archaeologists and scholars are in, and I feel nothing can do more damage to the actual truth of God than these efforts of man to obtain with his puny mind what the Holy Spirit alone can reveal, and I believe, has already revealed!

… To see a believer messing about with figures as Xxxxx does, WITHOUT ANY KNOWLEDGE AT ALL OF THE PERFECT OUTLINE OF THE CHRONOLOGY, is pitiable, indeed, but how many follow this course!

(*Concerning Velikovsky's book 'Ages In Chaos'*) – If you want a really careful gathering up of what the El Amarna Letters, the Karnak bas-reliefs, etc, reveal, this book is absolutely invaluable, and shows the Bible's account is true, while the scholars and higher critics have really 'fallen into the pit which they have digged'! (*Psalm 7.15*). Yet the world has believed <u>them</u> and derided the inspiration of the Holy Scriptures.

7811 / 7th May 1978 / From FLP in Combe St Nicholas, to AW in Stockholm –

I can't do more than give the facts as I know them, and leave it to the Spirit of God to bring conviction about the truth through the exactitude of the figures.

1979

7903 / 1ˢᵗ May 1979, Zif 4,5739 / From AW in Stockholm, to FLP in Somerset –

The secrets have to be revealed, not reasoned out by men.

7904 / 24th May 1979 / From FLP in Combe St N, to AW in Stockholm –

It is easy for the Enemy to try and persuade you that the whole thing is 'too deep' or too 'involved', but you will find more and more that the Holy

Spirit will bring assurance as you 'take the kingdom by force'! (*Matthew 11.12*)

7908 / 9th June 1979 / From FLP in Combe St Nicholas, to H and GP in Jerusalem –

God is really stretching His hands out to meet our needs in every department of our lives in these last days. And why should He not give the <u>full</u> knowledge and understanding of His Word also?

7911 / 20th June 1979 / From FLP in Combe St Nicholas, to AW in Stockholm –

I am sure you will never regret being bold in your witness, but for myself, I know God has reserved a mighty weapon to use against the 'scoffers', and that is, Fulfilled Prophecy.

Israel's perfectly timed restoration to their land will be used to awaken the 'sleeping virgins' (*Matthew 25.5*) ... but only God can do this when He is completely ready.

"Though it tarry, wait for it!" (*Habakkuk 2.3*) is the wisdom of God when He is about to move.

7915 / 2nd August 1979 / From FLP in Combe St Nicholas, to BE in Khartoum –

... by no means whatsoever could anyone discover the true course or end of the 6,000 years, by human intelligence ... Jesus Himself is 'THE TRUTH', and Truth is always the gift of God – it has to be received ...

His Word is 'true from the beginning' (*Psalm 119.160*), but no man can prove it by his own wit or wisdom. God had to keep on answering prayer and keep on adding to our vision, or we would have made no progress whatsoever.

7919 / 6th November 1979 / From FLP in Combe St Nicholas, to Mrs NP in London –

This research had to be conducted more or less in secret, because of the prevailing prejudice against the subject by Christians in this country, though not, I am glad to say, in America where part of the writing was done.

1980

8005 / 19th June 1980 / From FLP in Combe St Nicholas, to H –

… it was only after June 12th, 1933, had been revealed by God beforehand and then confirmed by history, that we were given the end-point from which we could measure back accurately to Genesis 1. No amount of searching would have availed apart from this God-given revelation.

8009 / 22nd August 1980 / From FLP in Combe St Nicholas, to RB –

No wonder the devil insists on keeping the saints in cliques, big or small, and even house groups must have a 'leader'.

1981

8115 / 4th May 1981 / From FLP in Combe St Nicholas, to RB –

(*Concerning why the Lord's Supper should be only held annually*) –

(*RB's letter to FLP is the first time FLP has ever heard from someone else*) - the true reason why the Lord's Supper must be an annual reminder of the date of the mighty foundation of our faith, that is, for the instruction of succeeding generations. It is so clear in Exodus, and yet it has always been missed. Praise God!

8118 / 1ˢᵗ June 1981 / From FLP in Combe St Nicholas, to the Rev JD in Sussex –

(*God gave Sir Edward Denny*) ... the key which would unlock the whole of the Bible's Chronology and this was to see that the Scriptures contain two entirely separate chains of time, and you can't mix them!

God's principles of measurement are moral. We were shown that God cannot reckon time to man, except on the basis of cycles of '70 times 7 years' of forgiveness, and when the period from Adam to the Cross was measured in this way, it was found to contain exactly 80 Jubilees (80 times 50 years) which are 4,000 years – the great 'FOUR DAYS' which the Lamb of God had to be kept waiting to die from the Fall of Adam (see Exodus 12.3-6) to when He laid down His life for us.

God has had to show that in every respect the Chronology is exact to the day, and that it should perfectly reveal the Plan of Redemption.

All this is only possible by revelation - 'the date that fogged many was the 2520 years from 598 BC when Jehoiachin was over thrown.

That came to Sept 1923 when the Palestine Mandate became operative, though it had been given to Britain a year or two before.

Then we found that the 2520 years from the Siege of Jerusalem in 588 BC (see Ezekiel 24) was the one which God took account of.

1982

8205 / 25ᵗʰ January 1982 / From FLP in Combe St Nicholas, to RT –

All the light we have, of course, stems from the revelation that God did 'cut off the Gentiles' at the end of the 6,000 years and at the end of the 1960 x 354 d(*ays*) from AD 33, just Forty Jubilees from when Stephen was martyred, but the stages of the 'seven times' and the war years have fully confirmed the whole position, that is to anyone who accepts the

Chronology – but it all needs to be taught.

Well, we can't go off half-cocked against the modern Goliath, and our armour must be the whole truth (which I believe we have, and have had for many years). I feel secretly, or privately, there has to be an investigation by unprejudiced young people (young, because not tainted with the prejudice of the older set).

8211 / 15th April 1982 / From FLP in Combe St Nicholas, to RB –

(*Concerning the apparent discrepancy between the 480 years and the 450 years of I Kings 6.1 and Acts 13.20*) -

<u>I then realized that we stand completely alone in this wide world</u>. Unless we have the most absolute proof that our Chronology is truly of God, we don't stand a chance. ...

And unless people know what was revealed to Sir Edward Denney (*sic*) about the two chronologies, there is no reason for anyone to accept the 450 years as coming 'after' the division of the land when it is so flatly contradicted by the 480 in I Kgs 6.1.

8217a / 12th May 1982 / From FLP in Combe St Nicholas, to R and J T –

(*Concerning Jeremiah 22.30*) - It requires a spiritual mind to appreciate how different God's thoughts are from our normal thinking. The results never cease to prove abundantly that we have the truth, but how to bring others in unless they have real faith in what the Lord has revealed to us right from 1933 onwards, is a puzzle.

I was turned back to that great sky-picture of the Crucifixion that many hundreds witnessed over the sea at Ipswich in the clear evening of <u>April 27th</u> in 1944 and which they all wrote to the Daily Express about ... Not a soul knew the significance of that sign, 40 days before D-DAY and just one year before Himmler sued for unconditional surrender in 1945.

8227 / 18th June 1982 / From FLP in Combe St Nicholas, to B and C –

(*The Company's work*) … has been a complete revelation beginning from the starting-point of TIME in Genesis 1.

And God had to reveal miraculously the actual close of the 6,000 solar years, confirming it so positively that we knew, unlike all other Chronologers, that we had a DATE (day and year) from which we could measure back the whole course of time.

Then we had to see that the LUNAR CALENDAR (astronomic) perfectly fitted this course of time in the Bible, and with the mean of 354d 8h 48m 33.6 secs anyone could check.

(*For example, in* **Miracle of Time** *FLP shows how the Apollo Missions 'perfectly confirmed both the end of the 6,000 years and various aspects of the Lord's life'*).

Next, we were shown the amazing design of what we had to call 'The Chronology of Redemption', which proved that Jesus died on Friday, May 1st, AD 33, the last day of FOUR THOUSAND YEARS ('four days') as Exodus 12.6 requires) from the day of Adam's Fall in 4075 BC.

We were shown the exact time between His death and Resurrection was TWO DAYS AND NINE HOURS (the TENTH HOUR being the MIDNIGHT HOUR of the Bible's many types, and the pattern God has used throughout history to express resurrection. …

Then we were shown that 2,000 LUNAR YEARS (to the day and hour) would run from the Passion Week (April 27th AD 33 – May 4th) to end with the YOM KIPPUR WAR (Oct 6th 2pm 1973 – Oct 13th) after which Israel went on to cut off the Egyptian 8th Army on the other side of the Canal.

Oct 6th, of course, was the important date, and NINE years have run on to this year, when we may expect the MIDNIGHT HOUR ((the 10th year) to begin.

Arthur Ware gave the BBC warning on October 3rd 1973, that in THREE

DAYS "the sun would go down over Israel" (*Jeremiah 15.9 / Amos 8.9*). As the sun goes down at the end of a day, so this warning implied that TWO DAYS OF A THOUSAND YEARS would come to their end on the Jews' Day of Atonement in 1973. So, in this aspect, a 'third day' came 'as a thief' (and the Arab's Oil Embargo or their 'oil weapon', has certainly stolen wealth the western world has sadly needed in these days of Inflation, etc).

It is infinitely too big a subject to deal with in a scrappy way like this, but I'm doing it to show how far removed from the natural effort of man the revelation of God has been.

And, of course, with God there is no confusion and He has shown, I believe, how the two holy convocations of Unleavened Bread and Tabernacles were fulfilled in the Lord's own calendar after He arose from the dead.

Wherever one looks, the plan and patterning of God in time shows perfection, and once that has been seen, no one will want to look at the imperfect any more.

Just as an instance, in 1935 we learnt from the perfect Chronology of the Scriptures, that the Nativity was at 'Tabernacles' in 1 BC, but now 47 years afterwards, the Rev. DP has seen, apart from the complete plan of the ages, and not knowing the actual solar date, that, if there is one thing more than another that is an 'abomination' to God, it is 'Christmas' – and he feels sure the Lord was really born at the Feast of Tabernacles! ...

The simple fact Mr R has got to learn is that the New Testament shows there are TWO Passovers. The first, the 'Lord's Passover' on the Thursday night He kept with His disciples. The second was 'the Jews' Passover' when He was crucified. (With God, of course, this day, Friday, was the fifteenth of Nisan, when the sacrifices of Numbers 28.17-23 were offered).

... So, as soon as the apostolic era had passed, and the true dating of the Passion week and all to do with the Lord's perfect Sacrifice had been forgotten in the mists and darkness of the second century, the day of His resurrection was mistranslated as 'the first day of the week'. But the Greek was clear: it was 'the first (day) of the sabbaths' – that is the seven sabbaths to Pentecost. It certainly was not a Sunday! (*See also Editor's comment regarding AEW's letter 5709, on page 209*).

For God had declared that He literally hated the 'new moons and sabbaths and appointed feasts' of the Jews (Isaiah 1.13-15, Amos 5.21 and 8.10).

… So He allowed those two days (our Saturday and Sunday) to pass, with the moon 'turned into blood' to signify the character of the next two thousand years which they typified.

So we see, as we near the end of the long 'Christian Dispensation', or Diaspora (as it has been for the Jews) that it is really the magnification of the time of Christ's death and at the end of it we are going to experience a season of awakening 'at MIDNIGHT', just as Matt 25, Acts 16, Acts 27.27, Ruth 3.8 and other 'Midnight' types indicate.

8235 / 21st September 1982 / From FLP in Combe St Nicholas, to AW in Sweden –

I think he (*a mutual acquaintance*) will see that no one can get at the truth right through the Bible's history without God revealing the beginning, or ending, dates miraculously, as He did with us, otherwise one would build up a structure on a false foundation.

1983

8303 / 20th August 1983 / From FLP in Combe St Nicholas, to DH in California –

(*FLP expects*) - 'an all-out show-down is close ahead'. But I see that this last wave of drug-sodden anti-christianism has come like a flood in the

The Ware-Paine Testimonies

past two years, and we have to be prepared to meet it with dynamic truth concerning Jesus, especially as the Messiah of Israel.

8307 / Unknown date / Handwritten notes "taken from a tape of poor quality" by FLP –

(*Concerning John 21, the 153 great fishes*) –

(*The net*) is the Lord's own ministry – His testimony, and His testimony is going to inclose the whole Church in these final days of this age.

People don't want tradition, they don't want what is 1/2 truth or error. They want the Truth, concerning God's Son and they are going to get it. Praise God! God is the God of Truth.

So what we see is - that God has in view the complete Church. And Jesus prayed that they all would be one. This vast company is the result of His resurrection.

***

Frank Paine died peacefully and suddenly at his home in Somerset at 11 am on 11th November 1983, this time and date being 65 solar years to the hour and day since the Armistice marking the end of the First World War.

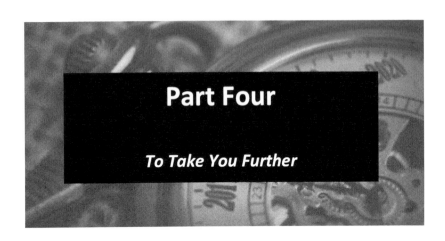

TO TAKE YOU FURTHER

In the light of all that has been told of the "Ware-Paine Testimonies" in this book, this final Part can help with further study of Bible Chronology for those who so wish.

Listed below are various books and articles related to the "Ware-Paine Testimonies".

1) AN INTRODUCTION TO BIBLICAL CHRONOLOGY

By Roger Price

Roger Price was a highly respected Bible teacher ministering in churches, fellowships and conferences in Britain and Europe until his death in 1987.

These four audio talks, each approximately 80 minutes long, are recorded consecutively over 5 CDs and are accompanied by nine exploratory charts.

They give an excellent introduction to the main principles of Bible Chronology as established by Sir Edward Denny, Grattan Guinness, Arthur Ware, Frank Paine and their colleagues, and provides a clear stepping-stone into the later books and charts.

Visit www.ccftapes.co.uk/ Specific Topic Studies / STS 28-48 / STS 41-45 Chronology Set

***

2) Some copies of THE CHRONOLOGY OF THE WORLD AND THE CHRONOLOGY OF REDEMPTION, **the Bible Watchmen's original 24" x 42" chart,** are still available, with explanatory notes.

Please note that these charts, though new, are 70 years old and show signs of their age. They also include a predicted date of 1958 for the start of the millennial reign of Christ which clearly turned out to be premature, this being one example, among others that have been mentioned in this book, of the Watchmen sometimes reading too much into the biblical types they had been studying. Abridged versions of this original chart are shown in **World in Liquidation** and **The Restored Vision**.

Please email the author at info@fsmins.org, with 'Original Chart' in the Subject line, to ask for details.

***

3) MIRACLE OF TIME

By Frank Paine (written in the 1970s and 1980s, and published in 1993, some years after his death)

MIRACLE OF TIME gives an overview of the whole project, and of the whole Bible. It ranges from Genesis, making the point that the Creation Week of Genesis 1 is key to God's entire subsequent management of Time in the Scriptures and in the world.

It then covers later events in the Bible, before addressing significant events since 1933 in this our own generation, through WWII, the founding of the State of Israel, the Six Day War, the Yom Kippur War, and the moon landings of the 1970s.

Its message is clear: God is still using Time.

The Chapter Headings of MIRACLE OF TIME - Frank Paine

1. The Importance of Understanding God's Time Measurements

2. Time Limited to God's Fore-ordained Plan

3. Events leading up to "the World's Second Tower of Babel"

4. The Nations Forget God

5. The Consequences of Forgetting God; Consummation of the Age

6. Some Keys to the Understanding of God's Calendar

7. The Week of Creation Patterns All Time

8. The Beginnings in Genesis

9. The True Passover

10. Daniel's Seventieth Week

11. The "Parousia" and the Rapture of the Church

12. The Birth of Jesus

13. God's Hidden Day of Atonement

14. The Death and Resurrection of Jesus

15. The Eightieth Jubilee; Yom Kippur 1973

16. Jesus Keeps the Feasts of the First and Seventh Months

17. The Meanings of the Feasts for the Church Dispensation

18. The Sign Miracle of John 21

19. Biblical Signs in the Heavens

20. The Pattern of Events 1933 - 1948

21. Biblical Signposts which Signify the Divine Establishment of the Modern State of Israel

22. The Chronological Significance of the Apollo Missions to the Moon

Appendices

Explanatory Notes

Charts 1 - 11

Afterword

Scripture References

Index to Time Periods

General Index

Visit www.ccftapes.co.uk/BooksShiloah

***

4) Printed Booklet, THE FOURTH PAPER from WORLD IN LIQUIDATION

As mentioned in Part 1, Chapter 3, in this Fourth Paper, now available as a printed booklet, the whole 6,000-year history of Time, from Creation to June 1933, is recorded in meticulous detail across nine Divisions of Time.

It serves as an invaluable and handy source of reference and could be kept with your Bible.

Visit www.ccftapes.co.uk/BooksShiloah

***

5) THE RESTORED VISION

By Arthur Ware (first published in 1957)

This book is the culmination of 25 years of Bible Chronology studies by Arthur Ware, Frank Paine and their colleagues.

It concentrates on the "earthly pathway" of our Lord Jesus Christ as recorded for us in the Gospels - His life, ministry, death, resurrection and ascension. The numerous precise dates that are given have been worked out to the day and hour from the Scriptures, and have been scrupulously checked for their "astronomical accuracy" according to the phases of the moon. We are not in the realm here of fairy tales or make-believe.

For the first time for nearly two thousand years we are shown wonderful new light concerning the true, deep spiritual significance of what was going on beneath the surface in the life and ministry of the Lord Jesus Christ. In particular we gain a much fuller understanding of Jesus' relationship with His Father, and of how and why the Jewish Feasts played such a major role throughout Jesus' "earthly pathway".

The Chapter Headings of THE RESTORED VISION - Arthur Ware

1. The Time and Manner of the Incarnation and Birth of Jesus of Nazareth the Eternal Son of God

2. When He is "Twelve Years Old" the Dark Shadow of Calvary Crosses Our Lord's Path

3. "The Beginning of the Gospel of Jesus Christ, the Son of God"

4. The Course of Time Between the Baptism of Our Lord and His First Sign-Miracle at the Wedding at Cana of Galilee

5. Our Lord's Public Testimony Opens in Jerusalem at the Passover - 4th May AD 30

6. Our Lord Commences His Ministry in Galilee, Autumn of AD 30

7. Our Lord's Third Sign-Miracle at the Unnamed Feast of John V

8. The Second Year of Our Lord's Ministry in Galilee, including the Murder of John the Baptist by Execution

9. The Last Phase of Our Lord's Earthly Pathway Opens

10. The Discourse at the Feast of Dedication - 14th January AD 33 - Our Lord Reveals Himself as the True Shepherd of Israel

11. The Transfiguration of Our Lord Jesus Christ and its Prelude - the Last Forty Days Open on 23rd March AD 33

12. The Final Departure from Galilee - the Raising of Lazarus as the Seventh Sign-Miracle of John's Gospel

13. The Last Week Opens with Our Lord's Visit to Jericho on the Sabbath - 25th April AD 33

> Chart showing the Five Calendars in Current Operation during the Time of the Death and Resurrection of Our Lord Jesus Christ

14. The Pathway on Earth of Our Lord and Saviour Jesus Christ Draws to its Close

15. A Brief Review of Events on Friday 1st May AD 33, in the Divine Calendar, the Sabbath - 15th of Nisan - the Day Our Lord Jesus Christ Accomplished His Exodus out of this World

16. The Revelation of Holy Scripture Concerning the Resurrection of Our Lord Jesus Christ on Monday 4th May AD 33 - the Manifestations of the Risen Lord during Forty Days

17. The Ascension of Our Lord Jesus Christ into Heaven on the Sabbath 13th June AD 33

18. The Pathway in Time of the Mystical Body of Christ - the Church

Appendices & Index

Visit www.ccftapes.co.uk/BooksShiloah

***

6) UNLOCKING THE SIGN MIRACLES OF JOHN IN THE CONSUMMATION OF THE AGE

By Jonathan R Hill, first published in 2015

In the context of Bible Chronology this book unveils the wonderful use of gematria and other numbers within the Holy Bible with particular reference to the Gospel of John.

The author writes - "This book is intended to help people understand what the Bible says concerning end time events, including the Rapture of the Christian Church and the Tribulation for Israel ... that God has self-authenticated His authorship of the Bible is just a starting point. Realising the presence of coded patterns and types which unfold the consummation of events in these last years is where it gets really interesting".

Drawing on the crucial work of Bible Chronologers such as Denny, Guinness, Ware and Paine, Jonathan Hill then uses his own skills in numerology, gematria and computing to reveal the extraordinary patterns found within the Hebrew and Greek texts of the Bible and the many insights they provide with special reference to the eight "sign miracles" of John's Gospel affecting us all in these times.

The Chapter Headings of UNLOCKING THE SIGN MIRACLES OF JOHN IN THE CONSUMMATION OF THE AGE – Jonathan Hill

Figures

Preface

Acknowledgements

Introduction

Sign 1 Water changed to wine (John 2.2-12)

Sign 2 The nobleman's son revived (John 4.46-54)

Sign 3 The infirm man raised (John 5.1-15)

Sign 4 Feeding the five thousand (John 6.1-14)

Sign 5 Walking on the sea (John 6.15-21)

Sign 6 The man born blind (John 9.1-41)

Sign 7 Lazarus raised (John 11.1-44)

Sign 8 One hundred and fifty-three fish (John 21)

Mathematical Framework of the Consummation of the Age

Chart – Timeline Types from AD 33 to Millennial Kingdom

Chart – Consummation of the Age in Numerical Type

Appendices

Bibliography

Scripture Index

UNLOCKING THE SIGN MIRACLES OF JOHN IN THE CONSUMMATION OF THE AGE by Jonathan Hill – (printed paperback copy, 268 pages), currently priced on Amazon at £10.99.

***

7) "UNLOCKING THE BIBLICAL WATCH"

By Jonathan R Hill, first published in 2019

The author writes – "The transition of world power away from the Gentile nations in favour of Israel has been in play for over a century. The nation of Israel will shortly be established in global authority under Messiah's rulership, after an intense period of judgement and the short reign of anti-Christ. The 'biblical watch' connects the 'waypoints' of this transition with extraordinary detail and based on scriptural principles".

The Chapter Headings of UNLOCKING THE BIBLICAL WATCH – Jonathan Hill

Figures

Preface

Acknowledgements

Introduction

The Midnight Resurrection

The Jubilee

The Heavenly (Spiritual) Realms are 'inside' Time

Numbers, Triangles and Pyramids in Scripture

The 'High' Numbers of Scripture

The Call to Watch

The Issue of imminency

Tools of the Watch

The Watch

Appendices

Bibliography

Scripture Index

UNLOCKING THE BIBLICAL WATCH by Jonathan Hill – (printed paperback copy, 403 pages), currently priced on Amazon at £12.99.

***

AFTERWORD

In whatever way we may react to the various strands of **The Ware-Paine Testimonies**, it is clear that the work of Arthur Ware, Frank Paine and their colleagues remains worthy of serious attention today.

Those Christians who are supportive of these men and their work can be greatly encouraged by their findings. For the many truths revealed from the Scriptures to these Bible Chronologers over their years of study demonstrate beyond doubt that God deals with His creation within a complex and beautiful framework of Time. We can be sure therefore that He is still doing this - linking significant events with particular dates and significant dates with particular events - and will continue to do so until all His promises and plans have come to pass.

In our response we do well to worship, watch and witness!

> *"Praise God from whom all blessings flow,*
> *Praise Him all creatures here below;*
> *Praise Him above, ye heavenly host,*
> *Praise Father, Son and Holy Ghost".*

***

May the Lord use this book as He sees fit, as He continues to "feed the people with knowledge and understanding" (Jeremiah 3.15).

SELECTIVE INDEX

Please note:

1) Because references to the divine Names of Almighty God, Father, Son, and Holy Spirit, occur so often throughout this book, only a few selected examples of these references have been listed in this Index.

2) Entries starting with **a figure** are listed together under the **Figures** heading.

A

Abdication, 110, 111
Abishag, 86, 189
Abraham, 96, 225
Academic Bible scholars, 74
Agag, 122
Ages, 29, 102, 107, 157, 174, 214, 232, 259
'Ages In Chaos', 253
'aion', 157
Aldrin, Buzz, 60
Antichrist, 30, 47
Antitype, 31, 32
Apocalypse, 87, 187
Apollo Moon landings, 59, 60, 61, 234, 241, 247, 258, 265
Archbishop of Canterbury, 106, 139, 156, 218
Ark, 124, 130, 131, 137
Armistice, 261
Ascension, 41, 46, 59, 65, 266
Assembly, 130, 131, 170, 181, 205

B

Balfour Declaration, 13, 14, 43, 51, 191, 252
Baptism, 56, 115, 138
BBC, 211, 258

Beast, The, 91, 230
Birth of Abraham, 42
Blood, 83, 114, 132
Body of Christ, 80, 188, 189, 204, 231, 248
Book of Revelation, 172
Bread of God, 32
Bread of the first-fruits, 33
Breaking of bread, 57, 138
Brethren, (Plymouth), 11, 204
Bridegroom, 53, 65, 102, 120, 142, 151, 161, 169, 195, 198, 216, 222
Buddhist, 248
Bullinger, E W, 16

C

Calendar, 6, 27, 28, 37, 38, 67, 76, 148, 194, 259, 268
Calendar of Israel, 41
Calendar of Jehovah, 41
Calvary, 108, 267
Chambers, Oswald, 85, 96, 109, 171, 172, 178, 201, 218
Charismatic Movement, 234, 235
Christ the Bridegroom, 52, 63
Christ's Kingdom, 28, 31
Christ's Reign, 172
Christendom, 43, 51, 52, 53, 54, 57, 63, 90, 103, 118, 120, 130, 131, 144,

145, 150, 151, 157, 158, 159, 160, 161, 162, 163, 164, 173, 184, 185, 187, 189, 190, 191, 192, 194, 195, 200, 205, 206, 207, 211, 217, 222, 230, 235, 236, 242
Christian Church, 31, 166, 224, 226, 230, 231, 269
Christian Denominations, 51, 56, 121
Christian Dispensation, 32, 33, 56, 62, 162, 172, 260
Christmas, 67, 111, 221, 259
Chronology, The, 16, 28, 30, 86, 96, 112, 154, 155, 172, 181, 187, 215, 220, 240, 248, 252, 256
Chronology of Man, 40
Chronology of Redemption, 28, 30, 39, 258, 263
Chronology of the World, 23, 58
Church, The, 2, 4, 6, 17, 22, 29, 30, 32, 33, 36, 44, 47, 49, 55, 56, 57, 58, 67, 68, 75, 76, 86, 98, 102, 103, 104, 105, 107, 108, 119, 121, 123, 124, 134, 135, 136, 154, 155, 156, 157, 158, 159, 160, 161, 162, 163, 165, 166, 168, 169, 171, 172, 173, 174, 175, 181, 182, 187, 189, 191, 194, 195, 196, 197, 198, 199, 202, 204, 205, 209, 214, 215, 220, 222, 227, 228, 230, 236, 243, 247, 265, 268
Church Age, 30, 56, 226
'Clearing the clutter', 69
Coming of the Lord, 51, 55, 140, 209
Commandment to restore, 42
Common purse, 99
Consummation of the Age, 40, 46, 47, 48, 58, 63, 69, 264, 160, 173, 270
Cornelius, 43
Creation, 6, 23, 29, 42, 44, 45, 60, 121, 157, 264, 265, 266
Cross, The, of Jesus, 86, 88, 104, 113, 171, 172, 177, 255

D

Daniel 2 / 13, 29, 30
Daniel 4 / 21, 29, 35, 48, 51, 93
Daniel 7 / 30, 207
Daniel 9 / 11, 30, 43, 47, 48, 58, 192, 194, 230
Daniel 9.24-27 / 11, 153, 162, 198
Darwin, 248
Date predictions, 3, 7, 21, 48, 75, 77, 218
Date-fixer(s), 2, 17, 50, 158, 215
Date-Fixing Fallacies, 152
Day of Atonement, 33, 41, 258, 265
Day of Consummation, 46
Day of Jehovah, 182
Day of the Lord, 39, 52, 112, 196, 197, 199
Devil, The, 106, 111, 124, 130, 142, 143, 148, 151, 154, 185, 191, 220, 245, 251, 255
Dedication of the Temple, 42, 45
Denny, Sir Edward, 11, 12, 14, 28, 30, 92, 204, 255, 263, 269
Denominational assumptions, 55
Dispensation(s), 29, 181, 265
Divine time keeping, 125
Dunkirk, 23, 155, 156

E

Ecclesia, 124, 226
'Ecclesiastics', 127
Egypt, 42, 61, 156
El Alamein, 156
El Amarna Letters, 253
Elijah, 198
Enemy, The, (Satan), 109, 120, 121, 122, 137, 163, 190, 253
Enoch, 159
Ephesus, 127, 231
Esther, 109, 189

Exodus, 32, 37, 38, 42, 45, 102, 110, 112, 113, 127, 128, 143, 150, 191, 255, 256, 258, 268

F

Fall of Man, The, 28, 32, 39, 42, 194, 197, 255
Fall of Masada, 43
Feast of Ingathering, 33
Feast of Tabernacles, 33, 259
Feast of Unleavened Bread, 32
Feasts of Jehovah, 32, 38
==========
FIGURES
10th Day of the 7th Month, 33
10th Day of the First Month, 32
14th Day of the First Month, 32
153, 16, 17, 35, 135, 251, 260
1917 AD, 43
200 cubits, 16, 35
200-day warning, 16, 17, 36, 141, 176, 193, 220
2520 years, 12, 17, 35, 48, 59, 93, 196, 256
37 / 33, 51, 60
40-day warning, 17
50-cubit gallows, 109
70th week, 90, 162, 172, 194, 265
==========
Final Judgment, 47
First Corinthians 15 / 17, 31, 47, 58, 65, 89, 246
First Corinthians 15.51-52 / 17, 47, 58, 65, 246
First Thessalonians 4.13-18 / 17, 47, 58, 65, 246
First World War, 261
Flood, The, 29, 42, 45, 112, 113, 229, 260
Four lepers, 217
Four main Testimonies strands, 77

Friends' Meeting House, 16
Fulness, The, of the Gentiles, 62, 214

G

Gematria, 35, 59, 268, 269
Gentile Bride, 181, 182
Gentile world dominion, 17
Geological Museum, 20
Germany, 118, 132, 166, 186
God's Sabbath, 38
Grattan Guinness, Henry, 12, 16, 21, 30, 48, 51, 263
Great Tribulation, 30, 47, 194

H

Habakkuk 2.2 / 101, 144
Harlot Church, 207
'Haughty clerics', 131
Heaven, 85, 90, 98, 104, 124, 129, 139, 140, 144, 173, 193, 199, 249, 268
Heavenly diary, The, 65
Higher critics, 248, 253
Hill, Jonathan, 35, 62, 269, 270, 271
Hindu, 248
Hitler, 13, 139, 166, 197
Holy Scripture, 79, 142, 157, 159, 160, 162, 167, 225, 268
'Hour of Translation, The', 81, 137
Howells, Rees, 244

I

India, 213, 215, 216, 217, 218, 220, 221, 222, 223, 237, 247
Israel, 13, 38, 41, 46, 58, 59, 61, 62, 64, 65, 121, 123, 124, 128, 131, 132, 135, 143, 153, 162, 175, 182, 189, 195, 197, 202, 208, 214, 219, 226, 229, 230, 234, 235, 236, 237, 239,

244, 250, 252, 254, 258, 260, 264, 265, 267, 269, 270

J

Jacob, 31, 47, 144, 153, 225
'Jacob's trouble', 31
Jehoiachin, 256
Jerusalem, 12, 30, 42, 43, 45, 46, 51, 58, 153, 197, 214, 225, 226, 227, 228, 229, 230, 231, 244, 247, 253, 256, 267
Jewish Bride, 227
Jewish Chronicle, 245
Jews, 8, 12, 13, 30, 31, 32, 33, 38, 39, 46, 47, 51, 58, 61, 64, 76, 119, 127, 147, 153, 162, 194, 197, 204, 214, 231, 234, 235, 236, 241, 246, 250, 252, 258, 259, 260
John 21 / 16, 17, 35, 260, 265, 269
John Kennedy, 217
Jonah, 158, 166, 179, 184
Jordan, 129, 130, 131, 169, 177, 195, 214
Joseph, 153
Jubilee Cycle(s), 12, 27
Judaism, 171
Julian Calendar, 41
Julius Caesar, 27, 41
June 12th 1933, 54, 75, 91, 116, 130, 154, 158, 159, 162, 173, 181, 196
June 1933, 6, 16, 19, 20, 22, 23, 39, 40, 43, 44, 45, 46, 48, 49, 50, 51, 52, 53, 54, 58, 75, 82, 86, 87, 90, 129, 144, 173, 202, 226, 245, 252, 266

K

Karnak bas-reliefs, 253
King George V, 20, 49, 106

L

'Lady Chatterley's Lover, 218
Lamb of God, 31, 32, 255
Laodicea, 135, 158, 168
Laodiceanism, 188
Letter of explanation, (Rapture) 66
Levites, 84, 129, 137, 170
Leviticus 23 / 32, 33
Leviticus 25 / 12, 28
Liberation of Palestine, 43
'Life of Faith', 115
'Light for the Last Days', 12
Lord's Day, 198, 211
Lord's Supper, 56, 57, 138, 180, 198, 204, 205, 211, 251, 255
Lot, 96
'Love feast', 57
Lukewarmness, 188
Lunar Calendar, 257
Lunar Years, 27
Lunations, 60

M

Manna, 128
Masada, 43
Masoretic Hebrew Text, 250
May 1948, 46, 58, 59
Meet in homes, 55
Messiah, 12, 30, 41, 43, 47, 53, 56, 208, 225, 226, 230, 260, 270
Messianic Calendar, 41
Middle East, 61, 65
Midnight Hour, 258
Millennial Kingdom, 59
Millennial reign of Christ, 17, 264
Millennium, 172, 214
'Miracle of Time', 8, 24, 32, 35, 42, 57, 59, 209, 234, 236, 258
Mohammed, 248
'Mood of the age', 69

Morning Star, 199, 205
Moses, 38, 102, 150
Mother Ivey Bay, 91
Mount of Olives, 195
Mussolini, 118, 197

N

Naish, R T, 16, 60
Name of the Lord, 115, 127, 183
Nativity, The, 259
Nazarite(s), 84, 119, 135
Nazi-ism, 166
New Heavens and a New Earth, 47
New Moon, 37, 38, 60
Nicolaitans, 127
Nine Divisions of Time, 45
Noah, 229
November 1932, 16, 17, 18, 19, 36, 48, 49, 50, 51, 75, 118, 120, 141, 193
November 25th, 121, 126, 160, 166, 167, 193

O

Oil Embargo, 258
Olivet Discourse, 31, 197
'Outside the camp', 98, 127, 131, 150, 211, 228

P

Palestine, 13, 51, 153, 193, 195, 214, 256
Palestine/ian Mandate, 13, 43, 51, 256
Panin, Ivan, 250
Passover, 31, 32, 33, 38, 40, 56, 204, 205, 259, 265, 267
Paul, 57, 62, 65, 130, 157, 168, 190, 191, 196, 197, 198, 204, 230, 231
Pergamos, 127
Peter, 52, 136, 173, 179, 195, 196, 198, 203, 205, 222
'Phasis', 38
Philadelphia, 127
Philip Mountbatten, 191
Plan of Redemption, 12, 256
Possessions, 20, 56, 65, 66, 161, 164
Powers of darkness, 105, 178, 184, 203
Prayer Book, 191, 219
Prayer meetings, 80
Princess Elizabeth, 191
Professing Christianity, 171

Q

Queen, The, 21, 217, 224, 248
Queen's Hall, 17, 19, 21

R

Rapture, The, 17, 31, 47, 48, 54, 58, 65, 66, 90, 125, 196, 204, 217, 225, 230, 236, 246, 265, 268
Redemption Chronology, 12, 59
Redemption Stop-watch, 58
Redemption Years, 28
Reformation, The, 111, 219, 227
Remnant, 155, 227
Replacement Theology, 214
Resurrection, 34, 35, 115, 162, 205, 258, 265, 268, 271
'Restored Vision, The', 8, 24, 28, 34, 35, 37, 41, 57, 59, 174, 206, 207, 208, 209, 210, 212, 235, 247, 264, 266, 267
Return, 45, 47, 115, 225
Richard Nixon, 217
Roger Price, 263
Roman Empire, 104, 153, 197
Romans 11.22 / 157
Romans 11.25 / 62, 214
Rome, 29, 136, 207

Rommel, 156
Russia, 166

S

Sabbath, 33, 38, 40, 46, 119, 268
Satan, 21, 47, 48, 75, 80, 82, 83, 86, 88, 94, 97, 101, 105, 106, 108, 109, 114, 117, 118, 122, 124, 127, 128, 132, 136, 137, 138, 145, 146, 148, 179, 184, 193, 215, 216
Satan's synagogue, 127
Second Advent, 158, 196, 199, 216, 222, 224
Second World War, 140, 234
Secular Chronology, 39
Septenary Design, 250
Sermon on the Mount, 230
Set-apart leadership, 55
'Seven Times', 12, 17, 21, 29, 35, 48, 50, 59, 90, 93, 107, 116, 147, 178, 194, 256
Seven Weeks of Harvest, The, 33
Seven years of tribulation, 31, 58, 66
Seventieth Week, 90, 162, 172, 194, 265
'Seventy times seven', 12
Seventy Weeks, 11
Sheaf of the first-fruits, 33
Sheep and goat nations, 47
Shunammite, 163
Sinai Covenant, 230
Six Day War, 59, 214, 264
Sleeping in Christ, 33
Smyrna, 127
Son of God, 59, 68, 69, 79, 124, 143, 267
Son of Man, 60
State of Israel, 197
Stephen, 43, 256
Sun and Moon, 183, 214
Sunday, 18, 19, 80, 89, 120, 121, 175, 205, 209, 211, 259
Sweden, 237, 241, 260
Sword of the Spirit, 82
Syria, 59, 61, 206, 217

T

Tabernacles, Feast of, 40, 259
Temple of evidence, 100
Testimony, The, 6, 7, 8, 54, 55, 63, 64, 67, 68, 69, 74, 75, 77, 86, 87, 89, 98, 99, 102, 105, 106, 110, 117, 118, 124, 126, 129, 131, 133, 134, 136, 137, 138, 139, 140, 142, 143, 146, 147, 150, 151, 154, 156, 162, 166, 167, 170, 172, 174, 184, 185, 191, 193, 196, 200, 207, 221, 235, 236, 237, 240, 247, 267
'Them that are without', 68, 119
'Thief in the night', 52, 54, 196
Times of the Gentiles, The, 30, 50, 51, 52, 90, 153, 162, 214, 226
Thirty-nine Articles, 219
Thousand-Year Reign, 47
Tower of Babel, 19, 49, 264
'Tribulation theory', 197
Two Churches, 230
Two Gospels, 230
Type(s), 7, 31, 32, 33, 34, 41, 48, 75, 125, 140, 142, 153, 159, 160, 162, 169, 184, 187, 191, 216, 220, 258, 260, 264, 269

U

'Understanding the Sign Miracles of John', 35, 62
United Nations Organisation, 185, 207
Unleavened Bread, 259
Unreckoned years,

V

Vatican, 227
Velikovsky, 253

W

Watchman Nee, 170, 171, 244
Watchmen, The, 166, 206, 239
Witnessing, 1, 5, 67, 68, 69, 70
'Wonderful Numberer', 87, 194
World Conference / WMEC, 13, 18, 19, 20, 21, 22, 43, 46, 49, 51, 52, 129, 157
'World in Liquidation', 6, 8, 43, 44, 45, 46, 53, 56, 200, 202, 205, 224, 229, 235, 264, 266
World War II, 59
Worship, 55, 57, 64, 65, 68, 175, 272
WS, 231, 232, 234, 235

Y

Years of Redemption, 40, 54
Years of the Messiah, 40
Yeshua, 228
Yom Kippur War, 229, 258, 264

***

THE WARE-PAINE TESTIMONIES

*The Story of Arthur Ware and Frank Paine
Bible Chronologers*

Oliver Bayley

ISBN 9781076884213

Published by Faithful Sheep Ministries
info@fsmins.org

Printed in Great Britain
by Amazon